COME SUNDOWN

THE LIFE AND LETTERS
OF A FRONTIER WOMAN

Olyve Hallmark Abbott

**Roots &
Branches**

Denton, Texas

Roots & Branches
An imprint of AWOC.COM Publishing
P.O. Box 2819
Denton, TX 76202

Manufactured in the United States of America.

ISBN: 978-1-62016-067-1 Paperback
ISBN: 978-1-62016-103-6 Ebook

10 9 8 7 6 5 4 3 2

DEDICATION

To my great-grandmother Permelia Nickell Hawkins for saving this treasure trove of letters. My grandmother, Anna Kate, fell heir to them, and then my great-aunt Louisa. And special thanks to my mother, Survella Shults Hallmark, who continued to save family letters, and who cherished the correspondence as much as I do.

TABLE OF CONTENTS

INTRODUCTION

COME SUNDOWN is compiled of correspondence saved by Permelia Hawkins, with continuity by the author, clarifying the letters and the history of the times. Text is edited in some places for clearness and spelling, with the letter writers' original usage preserved. This is one of many accounts of the westward journeys which permits the reader to learn the hardships and joys our ancestors encountered over a hundred years ago.

Kentuckians divided their loyalties, both before and during the Civil War. Although the Commonwealth of Kentucky declared itself neutral, the Union violated this neutrality by arming troops in the state. Friends, neighbors, and members of the same family lifted weapons against each other. Old grievances and bitterness carried over after the war. To make matters worse, flooding and drought impeded much of the state's rebuilding, with perhaps Northeastern Kentucky suffering the most.

Andrew Hawkins and Permelia Nickell married two years before the war began. While they tried to maintain their small farm, poor economic times hindered them from making much headway. Any cotton sold brought seventy-five cents a pound, but the Hawkins family had none to sell. Nor did the following years bring them much in material wealth.

By the late 1870s, Permelia's brother Jeremiah and his wife, Belle Atchison, moved to George's Creek, Somervell County, Texas. Jeremiah wrote home that cotton and crops grew fine, and people were the concerned variety. "You'd be smart to bring yourselves to Texas."

The idea of going to a new place brought a message of hope to Andrew and Permelia. Their eldest son Daniel had just married and stayed in Kentucky. Permelia's father, sister, and four brothers also remained. In July 1880, Andrew and Permelia with their six children left Kentucky.

From Morehead, the group of travelers crossed up to the Ohio River and with their worldly goods, boarded a steamboat, which later took them to the Mississippi. Anna, the eldest daughter, helped with the younger girls. She had never seen a steamboat before and thought floating bales of cotton were passing by until she saw smokestacks standing above the bales.

They took shore in their first destination of Memphis. The men put the wagons back together and they again set on their way. They planned to cross through Arkansas, and then to Texas. Jerry and Belle made it to Texas, and they followed the trail as well as the sun. All the children joined their parents in nightly prayers for a continued safe journey.

Trees and more trees appeared, some they had never seen, all "twisted-like." Later, they learned they were mesquites. As they approached George's Creek, the family did not see hills and valleys like they had back home.

The Hawkinses stayed with Jerry and Belle Nickell while making a decision about the house Jerry had found for them. It turned out they had only one choice. They moved into the house with its thirty acres, not far from a winding creek adjoining the Brazos River. The name of the community was "George's Creek," named after its founder, George Barnard, who arrived in the Republic of Texas in 1838.

From interviews with her great-aunt Louisa, Permelia's youngest daughter, the author obtained much information concerning the Hawkinses' journey to

Texas, as well as details throughout the book. According to Louisa, a child at the time, this was a story told her many times by her older siblings.

Andrew tilled the soil and plunged into sowing their Texas crops. They didn't have enough money for hired hands, so the children helped in the fields. Cotton, corn, barley . . . their faith in the Lord . . . and the weather.

As Louisa said, "Mama and Papa didn't take anything for granted. What's deserved was worked for. Come sundown, Papa finally came in from the fields and we ate a tasty supper."

THE FAMILY

Permelia Nickell Hawkins
Born July 4, 1843

Andrew Jackson Hawkins
Born February 2, 1829

THEIR CHILDREN

Daniel Boone, John Robert, Willie, Anna Kate, Eva Cora, Lizzie Frances, Louisa Ellen

PERMELIA'S SIBLINGS

Robert Isaac, James, Jeremiah Marr, Greenup Benjamin, Newton K., Elizabeth Mary

ANDREW'S SIBLINGS

James A., Lucyanne, William Morton, Margaret Jane, Jo Anne

~~~

Millicent Amelia Gilkison, wife of Daniel Boone Hawkins

O'Banion, Walter, and Amos Russell – Children of Millicent and Daniel

Addie Lame – Daughter of Lucyanne Hawkins Lame, Andrew's sister

Ella, Thomas Clark, and Anna – Children of Elizabeth Nickell and John H. Page

E. W. Cassity — Second husband of Elizabeth Mary Nickell Page

Ella Goodnow – Daughter of James Joshua Nickell, twin of Permelia's father, William C. Nickell

Survella Irene – Daughter of Anna Kate and Jim Shults

Golda – Daughter of Eva Cora and George Shults

PROLOGUE

Fort Worth, Texas
July 4, 2014

To my daughters, Devon and Taryn,

While working in the garden this early morning, I noticed the maidenhair fern seemed especially cheerful. I think this must be the fern your great-great-grandmother Permelia enjoyed so much in Somervell County. She was right, you know, streams and gardens do provide a place of solace. I guess I'm reminiscing a little since this is the day of her birth—over one hundred and seventy years ago.

Andrew and Permelia came to Texas, hoping to find a better place to raise their children.

Permelia's beloved Kentucky didn't offer much of a solution, with the political Tolliver-Martin Feud just getting its start.

For many years, Permelia saved letters from family and friends. The letters were handed down through generations, to Grandmother Anna Kate, Great-Aunt Louisa, to my mother, Survella, then to me—when they easily could have been neglected or tossed aside.

I would have enjoyed knowing Permelia Hawkins and her family, but then it seems I do know her, through her correspondence. You might like to know her that way, also.

Her letters are in her lovely mahogany box--the one with the inlay of roses. The key has long since been lost...

CHAPTER 1

Brother Jim Nickell stabbed – Martin-Tolliver Feud begins – Feuds in Texas, too – Jails everywhere – Daniel and Millicent come to Texas – Permelia's sadness

~~~

From Permelia:

George's Creek
Somervell County, Texas
October 4, 1882

Dear Robert Isaac,

We are all well as I write to you this lovely fall day. As I study about my brothers and sister, I wonder if ever I will see them again. I can't see us coming to Kentucky to visit any time in the near future.

Since we have been here I often think of the encouragement that brother Jerry gave to us about coming to Texas. Everything he said was true tho' he couldn't cover it all. I feel comfortable here but seem to wait for something better to happen. I think that it will.

Sometimes I sit by the narrow stream off the big creek, to help sort thoughts on my mind.

Of a still morning, the stream pebbles just sit there same as me and watch the water while a lacy fern grows on the lime banks. Why this little fern stays mostly green in winter too, is strange I think. I have tried growing it in pots and it isn't happy there. I expect that means there is a place for everything—and for people too.

You can see by the photographs how the children have grown. They exchange them with their chums. My letters are great enjoyment. If they don't come often, I read them again like they just arrived. You know how anxious I am about my correspondence.

Brother Greenup does not write often, so I will depend on you to keep me informed of his well-being. It is growing late and I must go to bed now.

With our wishes for God to keep watch over you.

Your sister,
Permelia

~~~

Until men made mail deliveries to rural communities, newspapers listed names of those who had mail held for them in Cleburne, Texas. Citizens often coupled this fifteen-mile buying trip to Cleburne with collecting their mail. Neighbors gladly took turns picking it up.

Percy Blackwell and Hugh O'Neal served as the first mail carriers from George's Creek to Fort Spunky, along a rough and often muddy road. They delivered mail twice a week on horseback.[1] Another man, Mr. Daves, reportedly delivered mail in a mule-drawn hack, riding from Glen Rose to Rainbow, Nemo, and George's Creek. This trip called for the mules to be fed and watered, as well as the driver. As a rule, they stopped at the Bandy house, and then returned to their place of origin.

James H. Chambers served as postmaster in 1876, and Usher F. (Linder) Barker in 1881.[2]

Mr. Barker operated the post office in connection with his general store.[3]

~~~

From Robert Isaac, Permelia's brother:

Morehead, Ky.

November 2, 1882

Dear Sister Permelia,

I have delayed writing too long and this letter will cast a mark upon this November day.

I take up my pen and explain.

The distressful details that led up to brother Jim's near death are lengthy, but Jefferson Bolling and him got into some kind of argument. Bolling slashed him with a knife and killing was certain in his mind.[4] Dr. Henry Logan attended Jim in good time, barring complications. Now charges have been filed against Bolling and Jim asked me to tell you all is well.[5]

I don't fault Jim for being involved, since it is not a single thing to fault. There is no help for it now. As we all know, we are in troublesome times here. I am purely staying away from it as far as possible and so is Pap. Pap has fully recovered from his illness, with God's help.[6] But I have serious concern for what is yet to come in Morehead. The town is building, but it's a general chafing in the attitude of many folks in this place.

Now don't suffer yourself about Jim. His Sally will see to him. Tell brother Jerry we think of him and those twin boys and tell him I will write. I hope ever in this life we can see them and Belle, as well as you. God bless and pray God will keep us all well. Isabel sends her love as I do to you all.

Your brother

R. I. Nickell

~~~

The *Ashland Independent*, newspaper of Ashland, Kentucky, reported on October 5, 1882: "Last Wednesday while James W. Nickell was driving his team near the depot at Morehead, he was suddenly

attacked by Jefferson Bolling, who Nickell was supposed
to have insulted. Bolling used a knife on Nickell,
stabbing him a number of times. It is hoped he will
recover."

The Hawkins family hoped to leave turmoil behind
them, but total peace was not in Texas either. Shortly
before Permelia's brother Jerry and his wife Belle came
to Texas just prior to 1880, a lynching occurred next
door in Hood County. Certainly most citizens opposed
it, some sheriffs included. It appeared if the law took the
side of a mob, there was often another grave dug and
less justice prevailed. Once people stood together on the
same subject, their decision often became the right one,
even if wrong.

The lynching came about because of troubles
between the Truitt and Mitchell families.

They had a personal disagreement over land titles,
and Mr. Mitchell was hanged for killing two of the
Truitts. This occurred long after they started out as
friends.[7]

No two feuds were exactly alike but they all had their
similarities, many beginning with political disagree-
ments or family disputes. They led to shootings,
hangings, burnings, stabbings and almost always,
deaths. Most people thought it was not necessarily a
disgrace to run away from a feud.[8]

Old Nelson Mitchell, known as "Cooney," was a
loner-type, with long black hair and a white beard. With
shooting back and forth between the Truitts and
Mitchells, Cooney wound up at the end of a rope. His
young son was killed trying to sneak poison to him in
his cell, not wanting his papa to be executed.[9]

With so much land and cattle in Texas, and people
wanting more, motives for trouble easily developed.

~~~

From Permelia:

George's Creek
Somervell County, Tex.
January 6, 1883

My dear son Daniel,

We all hope you are in good health as we are. I am writing to tell you that your father and I want you to come to Texas. You will have to know we love you and will accept Millicent in our family. Perhaps I did not say that right as I did not mean it to be critical.

As much as we want to see you we yearn to see our grandsons. Your brothers and sisters would like to have shared Christmas with you. Louisa has grown already so much and John Robert is almost as tall as you were three years ago.

Andrew is working hard at his farming. He plows most of our land with help from the boys. Texas is cold in a different way than at home. You haven't had hot summers like we have. I will endeavor to make Millicent feel welcome. Let us know your decision as you never write, and I could not bear it if you no longer have caring for us.

God bless you all,
Your loving Mother

~~~

From Daniel:

Poplar Plains, Ky.
February 12, 1883

Dear Mother,

I am asking your forgiveness for me not writing to you. I always looked forward to your letters even though I didn't answer them. Just know we are in good health and hope you are the same.

It's true I wanted to go with you and Pa to Texas but we couldn't under the circumstances.

I wasn't sure you wanted us to and you know Millicent wanted to stay here. Since your letter I have about convinced her to come to Texas. Times are not so good here and maybe they are better there. God knows you want to see our boys. Millicent thinks you may still feel the same for her as you always did. But I would like you to give her another chance. I've told her many times that you understand the circuit preacher couldn't always come by whenever someone wants to be married. At least I hope you understand. We were living out so far that he didn't come by even when we left word for him. Then maybe he never got the message either.

But my prayer is you will let bygones be bygones. As long as I know you feel right about it then I want to come when we can. Millicent is pretty headstrong and thinks you don't want to share your son with her on top of all the other. But Mama I know this isn't so as I know you want me to be happy, as you have always said. I try to work hard and get her what she wants and I find her hard to get along with at times too, but I love her.

I would like to start right in farming whenever I do come to Texas. If I have enough money I could rent some good acreage—not much—but enough to get a start on. Elseways, could you and Pa use some extra help? I sure would love to see you all because God knows how much I have missed you.

Maybe I was waiting on you to ask. Please tell my feelings to my brothers and sisters so they will know.

> Your loving son,
> Daniel

~~~

Daniel's choice for a wife had not pleased Permelia, and he was aware of this. Millicent's parents told her she couldn't be sure about Texas. They should stay in Kentucky, a land they knew.

Most distressing to Permelia was Millicent had a child at the age of fourteen. She said she had married a man named Baily. The baby died and Baily died soon after.[10] During the intervening years, Permelia had time to think over her estrangement with her son Daniel, and wrote the earlier January 6th letter to him.

~~~

From Robert Isaac:

Morehead, Kentucky
Rowan County
March 19, 1883

Dear Permelia and all,

It pleases me to write to you this day and we hope you are well. We are having a cold March with very cold nights. There is no lack of wood so comfort is ours.

Jack, I saw your sister Margaret Powers a few days past and they seemed fine. Clay Powers is planning to build an opera house.[11]

Now Permelia, your letter showed too much worry. I told you Jim is going to be all right. Bolling's trial is drawing out and on. The grand jury laid down two hundred and fifty dollars against him. William Scott Moody is on the jury, so is Jack Johnson. Jim was right lucky we have to admit. He could have died easy as not. If they don't get on with the trial, Bolling is like to get out of it as I would expect a trick from him. He is saying it was self-defense. We hear he says he has a witness, but I question that.

Isabel is feeling well today but has not for a week or so. Pap and I have a lot to do this spring. This is about all there is today for this time. Let God be with you and my nieces and nephews. Oh how we would like to see you.

Your brother,
Robert Isaac

~~~

From Permelia:

George's Creek
Somervell County, Texas
June 24, 1884

Dear Robert Isaac,

Andrew and I hope you are all well. The weather here is beautiful and it looks like our crops are at last showing success.

Daniel and Millicent arrived in George's Creek about December. Little Ban and Walter are as dear as can be—such good boys they are. I promised I'd do my part to make Daniel's wife welcome. Truth is she made that long trip on a train and being four months with a child. She was sick by the time they got here and went to bed all through Christmas and into Spring. The doctor said she could get up from there when she had a mind to.

They stayed with us two weeks and she never left the bed. Daniel found a place in Nemo right after Christmas but continued to wait on her hand and foot. Well, I won't say more about it and I didn't feel like talking to anyone here and want to get it off my chest. I will keep you informed and like I said I will do my part to make things right.

But now let me tell you about our new grandchild. His name is Amos Russell, born in May. He is a right precious little thing. The other boys are good to have around. Ban is tall for his age I think.

We hope our brother Jim and Sally make up their minds to come this way. There's good land for anyone who can work it. And if a man didn't know anything about cotton before he would certainly learn in Texas. We are all well. Our love to you and Isabel and to little Della.

Your loving sister,
Permelia

~~~

From Robert Isaac:

Morehead, Ky.
September 1, 1884

Dear Permelia and all,

With pleasure I write to you in answer to your most welcome letter. I am glad to hear you are all well.

My oh my what a few weeks we have had here. We had elections in August and such a time was had. I was in town and saw a good bit on election day. Oh everybody nearly imbibed and the whole town was in an uproar. It was not the place to be as everyone seemed a target whether involved or not.

I tell you things will get worse as politics can be a terrible and dangerous business. You remember Solomon Bradley. He was shot dead. They say John Martin and Floyd Tolliver were responsible. Nothing has been done about Jeff Bolling yet, and I'll call it he will get himself out of this trouble. How do I know? Well the law finds it hard to be lawful. It stands to reason

Bolling and the Tollivers would organize on their own. That is all the wisdom I can offer on the law at this time.

Tell Jack I see Ap Perry ever so often but have not seen his Emma in some time. Her sister Addie has probably grown up by now. I will keep you informed as this town is apt to break wide open. Now I hope everything works out with Daniel and his family. Isabel sends her love and will write soon. God bless us all. Our love to everyone.

R. I. Nickell

~ ~ ~

Jim Nickell and Sally considered coming to Texas with the Hawkinses, but they were settled with their family and told Permelia they thought it best to stay where they were. Had they decided to join them at that time, Jim could have avoided near tragedy. Permelia worried constantly over her brother's wellbeing.

In those times families needed all the right reasons to leave their homes. Jim and Sally's right reason for leaving would be the lawlessness of Rowan County. Jim hoped to sell his farm first, since he needed the money before making such a move.

Permelia thought the day might come when her confident and independent brother would review his decision and join them in Texas. One thing she knew was Robert Isaac would never leave his Kentucky.

~ ~ ~

From Permelia's brother, Jim Nickell:

Morehead, Ky.
November 12, 1884

Dear Sister Permelia, Jerry and families,
    This letter is to tell you that Sally and we are coming to Texas. Brother Bob's going to work on selling my land and I would be obliged if you could locate a place for us. I will pay money if it is good land. If not I would rather rent some fit acreage until after I come and see for myself.

It's time we left out of here and would rather it be in Texas than Missouri or Illinois. It is certain it will not get better here for a long time to come. I thought of Linn County with Uncle Daniel, but if what Jerry says is right we could do better there with you all than any other place.[12] They charged Jeff Bolling and let him out on $250 bail. More than likely this will go on and maybe without an end. The trial is set for next term in February, but then it's already been put off. P. G. Day will testify for me as he seen the whole thing. Jeff started it and then my foot was already in place before I could shut my mouth. He drew on me in a hurry. You and Jack would not believe the county unless you could see for yourself.

Look for another letter as soon as we can set a time for coming. I have a lot of ends to tie.

If not next spring, we'll have to see.

We send best wishes to you all, and God keep you well. Tell brother Jerry to write as I won't write him this time. Tell the girls their Uncle Dim said hello.

Your brother
Jim

~~~

</div>

From Edmond W. Cassity, 2nd husband of Permelia's sister Elizabeth:

<div style="text-align:right">

Olive Hill, Ky
December 16, 1884

</div>

Dear Permelia and family,

I take the present time of writing you, hoping you are all in good health. Your sister Elizabeth Mary has not been feeling well, but is somewhat better since morning. She is helping Ella cut a dress for herself and Ella learns fast and is a great help to her mama.

I expect your brother Bob told you of the happenings in
Morehead. Some say it's a real feud. Bob said further that
Jeff Bolling was called up to Circuit Court. Floyd Tolliver and
John Martin got into it the first of the month and it's a
wonder they didn't kill each other on the spot, but just Floyd
died.

Then they jailed Martin over in Winchester County
waiting for his examining trial. That didn't work out since
Tolliver's cousin finagled Martin's release with intent to kill
him, which was his fate. We hear all kinds of stories and
guess we won't ever know all the details. Fact is, they're
both dead now, John and Floyd.[13]

What do you hear from your brother Jim and Sally? If
they write to you then you know more than we do for now
and when more news comes we will write it to you.

Your nieces and nephews are well. Clark helps a lot and
so does Ella. Anna keeps us moving all the time. It grieves me
when Elizabeth is not fit, as she is one of the dearest women
on this earth. We wish you could come here or we could
come there. Every year I get the fever to see the Texas
country.

Until then let my wishes for your continued health and
that of your family be so. May God watch over us, one and
all.

> From your brother and sister.
> Edmond W. Cassity and Elizabeth Mary Cassity

~~~

The jails in Morehead and surrounding towns were
small but accommodating. However, as soon as anyone
mentioned "necktie party," the law frequently moved a
prisoner from one jail to the other for safekeeping. The
citizens of Morehead elected Permelia's Uncle Andrew
Nickell as jailer, a position he held for several years.

More jails over the country cannot have been adequate, but in 1887, a resident of Santa Fe, New Mexico, showed her Chicago guests around town, choosing to take them on a tour of the local penitentiary. They arrived at mealtime and viewed convicts marching from their cells. "They kept their arms folded until all were seated, and the signal given to commence eating. The prison was well-lighted, warmed and ventilated, so the poor wretches were well cared for."[14]

At least one Texas jail sounded much like an upscale hotel, according to the following 1885 article in *The Glen Rose Citizen*, the town's newspaper:

How They Are Treated

There has been a vague whispering that Charlie Miller, Somervell's deputy sheriff and jailer, was not so kind to prisoners as he ought to be, with the talk reaching the inner chambers of that split-wall edifice.

J. S. Burk, one of the inmates repelled the accusation and now writes the following note to *The Citizen*:

"To the Citizen: Having heard some talk that the officers of Somervell County are freezing and starving the prisoners in jail, I beg you to deny the charge, and to say that I never was better treated anywhere. I have not suffered from the cold a minute and my fare has been excellent and abundant. The prisoners in the Glen Rose jail have no just cause to complain of the officers in charge.

J. S. Burk"

~~~

From Robert Isaac:

Morehead, Kentucky
February 1, 1885

Dear Permelia and Jack,

We hope you are enjoying good health by the time this reaches you. Just a short letter to tell you that the Commonwealth of Kentucky has filed an indictment on Jeff Bolling on Feb. 34th. P. G. Day and E. H. Hamilton, and Z. Young are witnesses for the court. Zach Phelps is foreman. Bolling said his witness is Lloyd Waddell. Says he can prove it was self-defense. We can believe it or no but personally I say no. At any rate it is put off again until next circuit court.[15]

We are having the coldest February I can remember. We are as good as common except for my fourth finger. I nearly cut it off chopping wood. Now how long have I been chopping wood with never a scratch but this time I nearly got it good. I wrapped it tight before I bled to death. I poured whiskey in it back at the house and finally sewed it up myself.

The Doc later said I did a pretty good bit of sewing and wondered how I'd be at quilting.

Take care of yourselves and God bless.

Your brother,
R. I. Nickell

~~~

Weeks often passed without a letter in Permelia's mail. Then two or three would come close together. Sometimes her own letter would be returned with one of a recipient's. She had looked forward to the prospects of a telephone, although no one knew how much the charge would be to call across the country. They just hoped they would be able to afford one in the first place.

Telephones got their start in Somervell County in the 1880s, and people made much "t'do" over the new-fangled instrument. June of 1885 saw the completion of lines to Walnut Springs. The current opened and sound could be transmitted, but the town didn't have an experienced person to adjust the phone. No intelligible message made it through for some time.

Excited residents waited for all sorts of greetings to sing through the wires, but "the thing refused to talk."[16]

September 1885

The following letter came to Permelia from Edmond W. Cassity. Louisa said that after reading the letter, "Mama sat staring at a lock of yellow hair. I asked her what was wrong but she didn't give me an answer. We had what Mama called the Hawkins Bible and then there was the Nickell one."

After studying the letter for a time, Permelia placed the lock of hair in her Nickell Bible.

When Andrew came in from the fields, she told him of the awful troubles in the place they used to call home. She picked up the letter once more and read it to her husband. Louisa said, "Papa put his arm around mama."

Louisa observed her mother's sadness, but was afraid to ask more questions. She watched the entire episode in silence. She remembered her mother saying, "It is difficult to weep over what cannot be helped. That still doesn't stop me from grieving." Louisa got up from her chair and went outside and sat on the steps.

From Edmond W. Cassity:

Olive Hill, Ky.
September 14, 1885

Dear Permelia and family,
I take this opportunity of writing you a few lines hoping they will find you in a good state of health. I would like to

see you and I will if God permits me to live. Permelia, I am ashamed for not writing to you sooner, but I hope you will forgive me.

God knows the trouble we have seen this summer. Your dear sister Elizabeth took sick the ninth of February and we did everything that was in our power to do. We had four doctors with her, but alas, we had to give her up. She departed this life the ninth of August and we took her to Morehead to bury her there. Thanks be to God she went happy. She left us an example to live by, and by the help of God I am determined to follow in her footsteps. I know I will meet her beyond where parting is no more.

Two of your brother Greenup's children, Aquilla and Jessie, have been with us since last November. Ella has them to wait on and wash for all this time. Greenup seemed a loss as to what to do with them after his Laura died. Nonetheless, it is a big responsibility for Ella. She is one of the best girls you ever saw, and turned out more like your dear sister than you would believe. She goes right ahead and manages her work and does her own cutting and ironing.

Sister, I am trying to sell the children's land and as soon as we can sell it, we are coming to Texas. They want to come there and I can't leave them. We have always got along so well together. If they come then I will come with them for I told their dear mother that I would never throw them away.[17] I am better satisfied with them than I would be to go back to my own people.

Permelia, I trust you will forgive me for not writing sooner and by answering this as soon as you get it, so no more at present. Your sister picked on a girl by the name of Rose Ann Jones to comb her hair. She said for her to have a lock for herself, and for you to have a lock and she did so.

I remain,
E. W. Cassity

~~~

E. W. Cassity and Elizabeth were married for only four years. His letters proved his devotion to Elizabeth and her children by her first husband, John H. Page, who died August 1880 and was buried in Lee Cemetery, Morehead, Kentucky.

The lock of hair still remains in Permelia's Bible, just where she placed it over a hundred and twenty years ago. Permelia mourned Elizabeth for many months, finally wearing something other than black. Knowing her sister was gone brought emptiness, but Permelia had remarked that mourning was nothing to be ashamed of.

Louisa said, "Mama always let her memories be her strength."

CHAPTER 2

Jim and Sally to Texas – Andrew's sister leaves Morehead for safety – Nineteenth-Century schools – Permelia's surprise birthday – Mob shoots a boy – In 100 years, "Politicians will not corrupt."

~~~

Jim and Sally Nickell have moved to Texas, even though Robert Isaac had not yet sold Jim's farm. He planned to return to Morehead for the fifth rescheduled trial of Jeff Bolling and hoped his land would be sold by then.

~~~

From Robert Isaac:

Morehead, Ky.
September 20, 1885

Dear Sister Permelia,

We hope all are well. Jack, I don't see your sister Joanne much but Lewis was in town two weeks ago. He says they are all well though Joanne could be better. There was a lot of sickness in the county this winter.

Permelia, do not suffer yourself with not being here with Elizabeth. There was nothing you could do. I saw Edmond Cassity Sunday last and though he is taking it hard he is a formidable man. You need no hand to worry for the children. For that matter Edmond can take care of the situation as he loves them like they were his own. Thomas Clark is getting on as a young man and where some men practice shooting, he practices hitting a nail with a hammer as he wants to be a carpenter.

We have been up to Mt. Sterling off and on, as this Tolliver-Martin Feud offers too much violence here. It can be a beez nest if you go out on the wrong side of the road, if you understand what I mean. I mean anyone on the other faction might take offense to the way you're walking.

Just recognize that you and yours are in a safe place.

Love to all. Isabel is well and sends her love. She says she will write soon.

> Your brother,
> R. I. Nickell

~~~

From Robert Isaac:

> Morehead, Ky.
> October 26, 1885

Dear Permelia, Jack, nieces and nephews,

Here I will gladly write you and hope your days are not filled with news like ours are filled with here. Jack, you would not recognize what you see in Morehead these last days and months. Oh my, there are murders, shootings, some cowardly some not but most not called for. The sides won't be satisfied until all the Tollivers and all the Martins are gone and by that time the sides won't care maybe. Rayburn got killed this summer. Bolling and James Oxley were two arrested for it.[1] Did I not tell you Bolling was not through yet?

Uncle Andrew left as Morehead jailer. Does he write to you sister? Cousin Joe Myers was nominated for deputy. Knowing the law the way he does he would hold it up well. Bolling is being held over till the next term. They postponed it all summer. If Jim is not back from Texas for the trial,

Bolling may get off as it would not help matters. Bolling has more troubles to concern himself with anyway.

Jack, Clay Powers and your sister Margaret left town. Clay says it is temporary and they need to go for the safety of him and family. I am not sure what will become of his hotel and the opera house.

Isabel sends her love and Della is as busy as can be. Signs show a change in the weather as it has been hot weather and hot tempers for too long. There is nothing more to write at this time. You write soon. Are the children in school?

Your brother
R. I. Nickell

~~~

The children started their school right away upon coming to Texas. Anna Kate liked music the best. Her parents promised her if they could ever afford it, they would get her a piano, or maybe a small house organ. Anna practiced her flourishes and whorls from a penmanship book given to her by Alfred Elliott, her teacher.[2] The well-liked Preacher Elliott also owned a photographic studio.[3]

Land was set aside for schools in the George's Creek area years before the Hawkinses arrived. In small areas, pupils paid a dollar a year to attend a subscription school. When the settlers first came, they had no school until the community could afford to hire a teacher. From statistics, Texas seemed to take education more seriously than Northeastern Kentucky did.

In Live Oak County, Texas, the late 1880s had makeshift schools. Long stout tree limbs anchored into the ground formed an arbor-like structure. Crossed limbs attached on top created a basis for many cut branches. Propped branches closed the two ends, while the sides stayed open. This protected children from the sun as well as the rain.[4]

Louisa described her school as a dirt-floored log structure with a stone fireplace.[5] Earlier, George's Creek held classes under shade trees and children sat on split logs, weather permitting.[6]

People sometimes had to wait three years for enough growth in the area to warrant building a schoolhouse. If the school stayed small, the teacher was "very common."[7] They made shutters by nailing boards or rawhide to a doorframe and hung them on rawhide hinges.[8] Children sometimes rode horses to school, but most of the time they walked.

Not everyone in the family had a horse—many families had only one. County taxation records showed how many cattle or horses a man was taxed, which indicated a family's wealth.

Andrew's grandpa, Alexander Hawes, had a long-ago experience with his son and his animal. One evening in 1828, in Flemingsburg, Kentucky, Alexander's son sold a sick horse for eighteen dollars to a drunken man. The next morning the man had sobered and the horse was sicker. The beset man called the law on young Arthur Hawes.

Several men stood by during the transaction and knew the situation. They each received a subpoena the following day, and amidst laughter they told the story. The law ordered Arthur to return the money. He had to take care of his horse himself. Of course, eighteen dollars was a lot of money to pay for a horse in those years. The young man must have learned his lesson.[9]

~~~

From Robert Isaac:

Morehead, Ky
March 27, 1886

Dear Permelia, Jack, and all,

How good it would be to bring these lines to you myself. I could put stamps on a box and climb in but I am not ready for a pine box yet and would not care for anybody to make a mistake with it on the way to Texas. Tell me more about my nieces. I'm wondering if Anna Kate has any beaus? Maybe two or three? You remember sister, you were just about her age when you and Jack got married. Come now Katie you can tell your Uncle Bob.

I must tell you this. I was coming home on Saturday and George Kellog's son got thrown by his horse. You don't know them as they just came down to visit family and see the area. Anyhow he wasn't a half mile away when I came up on Vince alaying there. He fell on a ridge and the horse landed on top of him. Snapped that leg with just his boot holding things together. Wasn't any way he could help himself in his pain.

The only thing to do was go get his pa and a wagon. I was afraid to carry him on my horse for fear his leg might come clean off. His pa was gone with his wagon and I had to ride home to get mine. Mrs. Kellog sent her girl for the doctor. The boy was suffering but I finally got him home. That horse had come right on back to the barn but I never did hear what scared him enough to throw Vince. Last I heard was his leg was saved but it won't ever be the same.

Tell the boys and Cora, Lizzie and Lou I said hello and their Uncle Bob and Aunt Isabel love them. How will your crops be this year? Write as soon as you can.

Your brother,
Robert I. Nickell

~~~

According to *The Glen Rose Citizen*, residents of George's Creek could worry just a little about their crops. The gin and gristmill erected in George's Creek some years ago by Judge Chambers, was sold by his widow to Robert Norton and H. H. Wells. The gentlemen made the decision to move it to the farm of Mr. Jim Norton. Most of the citizens considered this quite a drawback in getting their cotton ginned.[10]

Permelia's birthday of July 4, 1886 lent a happier note. Still a young girl at this time, Louisa relied on much of what her sisters told her. However, she remembered this day very well.

Different noises awakened Permelia earlier than usual. Dressing quickly, she went to the kitchen where she found eggs and bacon, buttered biscuits, and steaming coffee on the table. The sisters carried out their surprise birthday breakfast without a hitch.

Willie and John hurried out after they ate, telling their mother to slow down now that she had aged. This particular summer, one of Texas' hottest and driest, caused everyone to slow down. Louisa recalled hanging wet bed sheets across the foot of the iron bed in an effort to stay cool, at least until the sheets dried. The boys slept on the porch, hoping for a breeze.

An unexpected birthday present was yet to come. While Willie rode his horse Tony over to Buck Creek, it reared, almost throwing him. He found the source of the squealing noise that scared Tony. He dismounted and gathered up four kittens from the base of a tree. He somehow managed to bring the long-tailed rascals home. They apparently hadn't seen their mama in sometime since they looked starved and had weak meows. Permelia's son wished her a happy birthday and with a big grin, dumped the kittens into her apron.

With persistence from the children, Permelia agreed to keep them. The girls immediately fed the hungry little things, then named them Spunky, George, Cat Creek and Fossil. Anna Kate claimed Fossil as her own and put a "ribbon bow" around her neck.

Andrew then brought in a package he had hidden safely away. Permelia never suspected a thing. He had ordered the lovely blue dress with lace collar and cuffs all the way from St. Louis. Permelia gave him a good thank-you hug. She later told Anna Kate how much she liked the dress, but felt they couldn't afford such a nice store-bought one.

Permelia had purchased a new Singer sewing machine in 1884 from the Singer Company in Cleburne. It had "handsomely carved" fixing drawers. On October 15th they paid thirty dollars and ten percent interest. They paid it off free and clear in one year.[11] Andrew teased her about being so small, but showed pride that she could make herself a dress with so little goods.

That evening, even though it was her birthday, as soon as she got the butter and eggs together, she baked a large cream cake to celebrate.[12] The children sometimes requested special gifts for birthdays and Christmas. Whenever possible, they received them, but Permelia first took care of their necessities.

Louisa had asked for only one thing for Christmas. Considered past the "doll stage," she still wanted a store-bought doll. She didn't expect it, but on Christmas morning she opened a box containing the prettiest China doll in the world, about fifteen inches long, with a brown and red silk skirt and weskit, embroidered underclothes and a dainty chemise. Permelia marked the doll with the date, "1886."

~~~

From Permelia's niece, Ella Page:

Blair Mills
Morgan Co. Ky.
April 4, 1887

Dear Aunt Permelia and family,

I am pleased for the opportunity to write you and hope you are all well. Do you know I am nineteen now? We are enjoying ourselves and this beautiful springtime. Pa Cassity is awful good to us and asks if we ever need anything.

Clark is always with him and helps with his work. Clark is only seventeen but can be a big help and wants to learn and he will be a good carpenter when he grows up, just like Pa Cassity.

You asked about Anna. She will be all right but is hard to get along with at times. She makes good marks in school, and is a fine speller like me. Ha! There is always something to do around here, but I don't mind really. We haven't had cousins Aquilla and Jessie for some time now. Chores have to be done and Anna does help with the churning and cleaning. I sew my clothes, and for Anna. We miss mama so much. Sometimes I just sit and study about her for the longest. But she's not really gone as I can still remember her. Please write.

I send my love, your niece,
Ella Page

~~~

From Robert Isaac:

Morehead, Ky.
October 10, 1887

Dear Permelia, Jack, and family,

My pleasure is to write you these lines today. My prayers are that you are all well. How is Dan making it out there? Tell him I asked about him and his boys.

Morehead's a might quiet than we've seen in many a day. I feel by now the feud is about done. Some call it the Rowan County War and I guess that's so. It's supposed to be a peaceful country from now on. That is not to say things can't pop up again.

Permelia, Fleming County's *True Blue Democrat* wrote about the Tolliver boys and family. I will send the paper along to you. It contains the truth for certain. Jim said him and Sally wouldn't be at peace until they got to Texas for good. Well now guess I've talked enough.

Your brother,
R. I. Nickell

~~~

Fleming True Blue Democrat

"This place is enjoying peace in the main at present. Occasionally we are disturbed by the noise of drunken men, who get merry or mad from the effects of the ingredients kept at the Tolliver bar room. Many of the citizens express indignation at the authorities for allowing Craig Tolliver's widow to reopen her bar room. If we were rid of it there would be less danger of internal wrangling. On Tuesday, the 13th inst., a gang of the Tollivers went to Farmer's near this place, and there received guns, reports say from Z. T. Young. A man asked them what they intended doing when they replied, 'We are going to clean up

Morehead'. The man got word to Morehead in advance of them; to receive their expected visitors. But instead of coming through town, they turned off one mile below and went up Dry Creek. After going up the creek a short distance they fired their guns a number of rounds to see how far they could be depended upon; they then proceeded on their way to their homes in Elliott and Morgan Counties.

"Friday night about eight o'clock our citizens were greatly excited over some heavy shooting in the upper part of town. It was generally supposed that the Tollivers had returned to fulfill their statement made at Farmers. There was considerable hurrying around to give the supposed intruders a cordial reception. The firing soon ceased, and the conclusion was reached that the excitement was caused by three drunken men who had left the bar room a short time before the shooting.

"George Walters, a boy who was shot, is still alive; he is part of the time conscious, but seems to be in great misery. Dr. Steel, of Olive Hill, says there is no hope for the boy. George is his father's pride, and great pains were taken to make a man of him. The father is greatly worked up over the shooting.

"The belief is that the boy was shot on purpose, because his father had taken an active part in having Hiram Pigman cleared. Craig's two boys and Pete Dillon's boy each had pistols. There will be some investigations made. The two Tolliver boys are aged respectively ten and twelve and Dillon fifteen years."

Another reporter comments in this paper, "We ought to have a state reformatory for such criminals as the Tolliver youths of Rowan. When a boy begins his murderous career at twelve, he is liable to get in a great deal of bloody work by the time he reaches his majority, unless a friendly bullet should rid society of him sooner."[13]

~~~

From the sound of the newspaper article, the Tollivers hadn't skipped a beat in their activities. A "friendly bullet," the paper reported. There couldn't have been too many of those around. It would seem when the young ones' feet matched up with the footsteps they tried to follow, more damage would be done.

Several articles concerning shootings, court cases, and similar happenings appeared on the front page of the above newspaper. It seemed to be the major order of the day. The following appeared in another newspaper in Louisa's possession:

"The Constitution of the United States was a hundred years old last Saturday. It has withstood a deal of straining and had many hard knocks in that time, and has several dents in it. What will happen to the old instruments in the next hundred years, might be an interesting subject for contemplation. But we shall not be around then to think or write about it. It shall be a country where politicians do not corrupt, nor boodlers break through and steal."

~~~

From Robert Isaac:

Morehead, Ky.
February 28, 1888

Dear Permelia,
I am hoping my letter finds you all well. We are in good health and pap sends you his best thoughts. He is also feeling well except for his leg and that bothers him some.

The news is that Uncle Jesse Atchison died Christmas. Jesse owned good Bath County land as far as you could see, and he was buried on it on the road to Wyoming in the Atchison Cemetery. In his own will he asked that a thousand dollars be spent for a monument and if that wasn't enough to make it right, then add more.[14] He wanted it done with decency, so Joe Myers told me. Cousin Joe was executor.

I'm not sure if more money was added, but it will for certain be an impressive monument. It was his money to be done with what he pleased and he surely had enough left for Charlotte. Our Aunt Charlotte is not in the best of health herself, but one thing sure is she gives help where help is needed if she doesn't let people take advantage.

Della and Isabel have gone visiting for the afternoon, but I know they send their love to you, Jack, and their cousins. Let us hear a letter from you soon.

Your brother
R. I. Nickell

~~~

Aunt Charlotte was a Pearce before she married Jesse Atchison. Her estate showed her to be as generous as her husband had been. Thousands of dollars in outstanding loans were due before her will could be probated.[15] If anyone needed anything, Aunt Charlotte offered it.

Permelia had taken their older children out to the Atchison place, where they marveled at the guinea hens. The fowls could squeal like a snake was after them, and Uncle Jesse would go out there with his rifle and find none in sight. The next morning they would find signs a snake had been there, and Jesse would be minus a hen or two. The Hawkins family now owned guineas on their Texas farm.

The farms in the Somervell area moved along at a steady pace, although the decline in cattle prices ended some of the big cattle drives to Kansas in the mid-1880s. This affected businesses over Texas and the Southwest, although stores still continued to advertise almost as if nothing had happened to the economy.[16]

With the railroad coming through Morehead in the early 1880s, the county seat of Rowan County became a growth center.[17] The Rowan County War dragged the town down again in the middle of the decade, but as the feud diminished, Morehead began mending. Permelia and Andrew could relax a bit more about the family they left behind.

~~~

From Clark Page, Permelia's nephew:

> Blair Mills,
> Morgan Co, Ky.
> July 1, 1888

To John Robert Hawkins
Dear cousin John,

I seat myself to drop you a few lines to let you know I am well and hope these words reach you in the same good health. This is the first I have written to you for a long time.

I want you to tell me if you are married yet and if you are not, do you have any fun with the girls out there? I got it put to me last Sunday at the Lick Fork School House seven miles this side of Morehead. John, Get some pretty girl out there who will write to me and send me her address. And don't forget it as the girls have all gone back on me.

Tell me how you are and what you are doing. I am going to work on a house for William Green Blair tomorrow. I get two dollars for building the house. Tell Willie to write to me. How is he getting along? So I will close for this time. Write

soon. Sister Ella reminded me that it was your birthday Aunt
Permelia, so a happy birthday to you.

Direct your letters to me at Blair Mills, Morgan Co. KY.
Clark Page in care of E. W. Cassity

~~~

Nearing Permelia's birthday in 1888, Anna Kate still had Miss Fossil as a reminder of Willie's present to their mother nearly two years earlier. One of the kittens died the first week, a coyote got another one and just two weeks later, Louisa ran to tell her mother of a stray dog with foam at its mouth, racing around the yard. She thought he might have bitten little Cat Creek, but Creek and Fossil had run under the house.

Permelia first looked through the screen door and then reached for her rifle. She thought the dog as truly mad. She stepped outside, took aim and ended his misery. Louisa stood at the door, covering her face with her hands. The dog had an old bullet wound in his flank. What a shame for an animal to have lived through one bullet only to die from another. At least the last one was from kindness.

CHAPTER 3

Daniel and Millicent leave Texas – A family tragedy –
High water – An anonymous gift – Science fiction –
Millicent writes – Anna Page in California – What
grandson to give away? – A snakebite

~~~

Daniel and Millicent with their three young sons lived in Nemo, a community a long buggy ride from Andrew and Permelia. They often brought their sons to their grandparents to stay for a few days. The girls enjoyed them, and did not feel put out by being crowded.

"The air was still a little thick between Mama and Millicent," Louisa said.

Daniel provided for his family, but he had hoped for more productive crops. He worked hard just like his papa. After the first two or three years in Texas, Daniel seemed contented, but Millicent determined to return to Kentucky. She made up her mind they would leave and arranged for traveling to the depot in Fort Worth.

Permelia and Andrew did not know of Daniel's illness until he and Millicent were almost ready to leave. When Permelia learned he had chills and fever, she begged him not to go until he recovered. He said it was too late to change their plans.

By the time they got to Denison, Texas, Daniel became too ill to go on. Millicent got word to Permelia that she called for two doctors and they took him off the train. Permelia sent a wire back saying since they were so set on leaving Texas, to either stay in Denison, or wait until Daniel was well, then go on to Kentucky. She later regretted her words.

Daniel died soon after being removed from the train on August 22, 1888. No one knew the exact cause, although the family presumed pneumonia. He was laid to rest in Denison, apparently without a permanent marker. Among Permelia's memorabilia, is an 1889 receipt for three dollars and sixty-five cents for a base and two-foot marble stone. It could have been for Daniel's grave, but the site is unfound. No cemetery was ever mentioned.

At the time of her son's death, Permelia could not bring herself to travel the distance. Louisa said she had never seen her mother in such a state. Permelia then directed her concern toward her only grandchildren and their mother. She grieved over their sadness, as they continued the lonely journey to Kentucky.

~~~

From Robert Isaac:

Morehead, Ky
September 12, 1888

Dear Permelia and Jack,

It is with grief that these words leave me. The pain you and your family bear over Daniel's parting may be lessened in knowing that it is God's will. It is my feeling in the long way, not to ask questions about what we do not understand. Just accept God's will as a Christian people do. If there is anything I could do to help your sorrow I would gladly do it all.

There is not much here at this time. The weather is mild although some sickness is in the town and that is not unusual. Isabel is well and is making supper for us and her brother Jesse B.

Jesse may be young yet but already he has bent his mind on coming to Texas one day.

This is a short letter but Isabel and I want you to know our feelings are of you all and your sorrow. We wish we could see you.

                                   R. I. Nickell

~~~

From E. W. Cassity:

                                   Blair Mills
                                   Morgan Co Ky.
                                   October the 4th, 1888

Dear Brother and Sister Permelia and family,

I take the present opportunity of writing to let you know we are all well, hoping you are enjoying the same like blessing.

Sister, your kind letter of September 22nd came to hand the 28th and found us in good health. We were glad to hear from you but the words you sent were far too sad. I cannot say how sorry we were to hear of Daniel but he is at peace and you must hold that thought in your heart.

Clark and I have been working our carpenter trade all summer. He has a contract of building a house for one Mr. Blair. Clark is getting to be a fine workman and has to holler out ever once in a while and ask me how to do something. He is mighty good about taking advice on his work.

We are glad to hear you have had such good crops this year. We did not raise any ourselves other than of our own need. Clark and I are busy enough with our carpenter trade and have plenty to do. However, crops were good here for other people.

I am also glad to hear about your church professions. We had one of the best meetings here last Friday and Saturday.

We had Brother William Downing from Missouri to preach for us. It had been thirty-one year since he left this neighborhood and you don't know how it filled my heart to stand before an audience to introduce worship for him. I could look back over the past and consider the number that had sat with me and listened to his preaching, and to see the few of them who were left to hear him again.

Permelia, Ella is not married yet and I do not think there is anybody good enough for her.

She gets more and more like your dear sister every day she lives. She is kind to everybody and tries to do everything she can for them.

Anyway Brother Jack, do not forget Harrison and Morton. Give our love and respects to everyone and their families.

I will now come to a close. May God bless us all and bring us safely home to heaven is my prayer. I hope you have found your church choice. I have not asked you before.

> E. W. Cassity, Ella and Clark Page
> To P. F. Hawkins and family
> Direct to Yocum, Morgan Co. Ky.

~~~

The only church in George's Creek when the Hawkins arrived in Texas was the Cumberland Presbyterian, organized in 1875.[1] Its location was right next to the graveyard.

The Methodist Church in George's Creek reportedly came about in 1883.[2] Later preachers of other denominations held baptismal services in Berry Falls at the creek. They used no baptismal robes. Men wore their Sunday-go-to-meeting clothes, as did the women. The preacher kept on his full suit and tie while wading into the water.

Permelia subscribed to *The Firm Foundation*, which arrived regularly. If bad weather kept her from church, she relied on this church newspaper. She never failed to read *The Cleburne Enterprise*, noticing the special news of surrounding communities.[3]

During this time, Andrew received a letter telling of the death of Isaac Phelps, his sister Lucyanne's husband. His family buried him in Siloam Cemetery at Farmers, Kentucky. Isaac served as Grand Master of the first Masonic Lodge in Rowan County.[4] His family gave all the land for the cemetery. A winding road leads to the beautiful area, shaded by overhanging tree branches. Andrew's parents, William R. Hawkins and Judah Hawes were buried in Siloam in the "Hawkins Corner," just above a green valley. While the last gravestone for the Hawkins family had a nineteenth-century date, a nearby stone bench is probably as aged.

~~~

From Permelia to John and Willie:

George's Creek, Texas
March 19, 1889

My dear children,

Mr. Hix just came over from Granbury and told us John was ailing. We are so sorry to hear that. I am uneasy about you. Be sure to write often so we won't have to worry.

We enjoyed the visit so much and we got home all right, even though it had been raining hard. I thought it would let up and stop but it had already been pouring. We crossed at Rock Crossing. We met a man that said the water would run over the wagon bed at the Marline Crossing and indeed it did. I was not scared at all and we got home before night. Later when I thought on it, the water was a bit fierce.

When I came home Rosa Atchison and her baby Annie Ester were sick and I had to go there. The babe is only five months old and real sweet. Then Mrs. Hodges sent for me and I was up with her all night. She had a big boy weighing thirteen pounds and they are both well.

I got a letter from Ella Story and got the nicest present Sunday evening. And yesterday a brown flowered dress came in the mail. We can't think where it came from. I am going up to Uncle Wright's and cut out and make a pair of pants for him.

Now I hope all the sick there is better—do you need me to come back? We are all well. I fear you will not have enough money. Do you? Be sure to let me know.

From mama to her children
P. F. Hawkins

<div style="text-align:center">~~~</div>

John Robert and Willie had accepted work over at Mrs. Scarbro's, not that their father did not need their help, but perhaps Mrs. Scarbro needed it more, at least for the time being. Mr. Scarbro had passed away and his widow found the physical "man's work" too difficult. Permelia and Andrew decided to ride over to see what they could do to help the Scarbro family, especially with moral support.

Permelia's friends all around knew they could call on her in any time of need. They often sent her gifts in return for what she did for them. While Permelia was not a nurse, she knew many remedies for various illnesses.

When a neighbor became sick the nearest woman went to her aid, many times quite a distance from her home. Permelia was often the "nearest" woman. In early days, to pass the time, a woman might even knit stockings as she walked to help a friend, provided she had no fear of Indians or animals.[5]

Nineteenth-century women lived close to the seasons and knew what they meant to the family's health. The responsibility of providing remedies usually fell upon the women's shoulders. They often applied mud to bites and stings. Sunflower seed soaked in spirits provided an unfailing cure for rheumatism. And of course, chopped onion was an approved treatment for what they called tonsillia.[6]

~~~

From John Robert:

Hood County, Texas
March 28, 1889

Dear folks at home,

Your letter just came to us and we are glad you didn't have real trouble in getting back. I am feeling well now and have been eating all the time to make up for what I missed when I was sick. It's hard to know when I have had enough.

Now sit down since this is going to be a long story if I can get it told like it was told to me. There was these two physicians that had been wanting to do some kind of experiment with hung criminals to see if they could bring them back to life. Well, they made arrangements to get this man sent over to the hotel after he was hung. So after the hanging, a boy came over to the doctor's office to fetch them to this hotel.

They went right to the room where the clerk sent them and sure enough there he was laying out still as could be. One doctor put a piece of metal in the man's hands. This metal was on wires on some kind a battery and then they turned on the switch. Well that man jumped out of bed and screamed and hollered so much they thought they'd brought him back to life. The clerk told them they hadn't brought him back to life at all. That man had sent for them to lance a boil.

So you know ma the doctors went to the wrong room. I tell you ma that man grabbed his gun and chased those doctors until he couldn't run any more. Can you just see it happening? You probably think I'm joking you for an April fool's joke ma but that's what was told to me.

It's been a real wet muddy week though, more than usual so it's go on and get it done. It was real good to see you Pa. I like to see you all so well and it won't be too long before I'm done. I suspect you could use my help. Take good care of yourselves and write when you can.

Your sons,
John and Willie

~~~

In the days when people listened for a heartbeat or held a mirror to a person's nose to see if he breathed, it was the best way to know if the patient was alive. A man fell off the house he helped construct many years ago in Comanche County. His friend tried to awaken him, but he showed no signs of life. They pronounced him dead. When the dirt was being shoveled upon his coffin, he awoke and pounded on the pine box. The few men who had not been scared enough to run into the woods, pried open the box, rescuing the poor man. The victim had simply been unconscious for two days.[7]

~~~

From Permelia:

George's Creek
Somervell County, Texas
April 10, 1889

Dear Millicent,

Andrew and I are writing to you in the hope that you and the boys are in good health. I am sure they have grown a great deal the last year.

My thoughts go back to when you left Texas and if Daniel had stayed here with a doctor looking after him, perhaps you would still have a husband and your boys would have a father. Daniel just needed to be in good health before you left Texas.

Are you taking on any kind of work at this time and do you live with your folks? I vow they are taking care of the children quite well. We would be glad to have the children stay with us for a visit if it would help you out. Perhaps little Russ is too young, but think on such an idea.

The girls are real little ladies and even Louisa has grown a bushel. Of course I still worry for Willie's health. Please take care of yourself so your sons will always have a mother.

From Permelia F. Hawkins

~~~

</div>

From Andrew's niece, Addie Lame:

<div align="right">

Morehead, Ky.
July 2, 1889

</div>

Dear Aunt, Uncle, and Cousins,

Good morning to you and I am happy to write to you this fine day.

Sister Emma and her husband Ap Perry visited us. He was up front with the Rowan County Feud. You know that Martin-Tolliver thing that's supposed to be over? Emma used to be scared enough for Ap, afraid that he would get killed and I think she still is scared.[8] Pa tells us all that takes place over there and I mean there are things to listen to. Emma told me some about what those Tolliver boys do but I didn't think of questions to ask until it was too late. You know me, I want to know everything and all. I hear the feud is actually over but that doesn't keep one from being on the lookout though.

Mama's not feeling too well. She has good days and bad days but she's not really over the la grippe yet.[9]

Do you like school? Are you all going? You may be so smart that you don't have to go anymore. There isn't much to say. Do you have any pictures? If you do I would like very well to have one of all of you. Aunt Permelia, can you send me one of you and Uncle Andy? I meant to ask you what kind of flowers do you grow in Texas? I must go now and help Mama with supper.

Your loving niece,
Addie Lame

~~~

As their children were growing, Permelia felt she belonged in Texas more every day. Louisa said her mother often commented that even with letters from family and friends, she considered Texas their final home. Comparing it with Morehead made it even more so.

Between August 1884 and late June 1887, violent deaths occurred at the rate of six per year.[10] The "Martin-Tolliver-Logan Feud" (sometimes Logan was included in the title) or the "Rowan County War" lasted four years. After twice sending troops to Morehead, solving nothing, the governor of Kentucky refused to send them a third time.

Under the leadership of Daniel B. Logan, citizen of Morehead, a posse of two hundred men armed themselves with Winchester rifles. They gathered in the nearby town of Olive Hill, and moving in on Morehead, shot the "last vestige of the Martin-Tolliver Feud into eternity."[11]

After the war, Permelia thought she could put that part of her life behind her. The Hawkins family still had personal and emotional battles to concern them in Texas.

~~~

From Millicent Hawkins:

> Poplar Plains
> Fleming Co Ky.
> July 21, 1889

Mrs. Hawkins and family,

After quite a delay I will answer your letter I received some months ago. I was so sorry to hear Willie was sick. I hope he is well and all the rest too. Ban has been sick and Walter but little Russ is fat and sweet as ever.

I have been back to my folks' home today but I am going away again soon. At my work I get one dollar a week and can take Russ with me. I can get a home any place I want to stay. My people never have got the children anything since they've been here, so they have little more than when we came.

I am sending your letter back to you. You said in it that if I had stayed there Daniel would have lived. I don't know what you mean by saying that. If you mean when we went on the railroad why didn't you tell Daniel to come back there instead of sending us word not to come back? You and Mr. Hawkins both didn't care for us and as the people here say, you have proved it. If you did you would do something for the children. Everybody says that if Pa feeds them you ought to help out, if you had any principle.

If you really wanted the children to come back there I would like for you to tell me how I would send them by themselves and without money. And more than that don't you know I would not let the children go there without me going with them? The time is drawing near when we all have to leave this world, but I hope you will think of the way you have done and don't blame me for Daniel's death. If he had never gone to Texas in the first place he might have been living today. He never had chills or sore eyes here either.[12]

If God spares my life and your life until I get money which I think I will have some day, I intend to get one of the doctors who was with him when he died, to talk to you and see what you will say then. If it was too much for you to stand why didn't you go up there after and talk to the doctor? I would go as far again to hear of one of my children's death if I thought like you, that he wasn't treated right. I would pay your expenses myself if I had the money, but all I have I work for and make it honest. If I don't have but two dresses thank God I came by it honestly. If nothing happens it won't be long until we have a home of our own and there will be no more trouble. You know I always treated Dan as well as he did me.

I hope how well you all may be and am glad you wrote. Have you had good crops this year? Everything is good here. Write again soon. Ban and Walt say they would love to see you all.

Goodbye to all.
Millicent Hawkins

~~~

Anna Kate, being the eldest sister possibly had a different viewpoint of Millicent than her sisters had. She would tell Louisa, "Never you mind . . . we'll see."

Louisa wasn't sure what she meant, but she sensed her mother was perplexed for the first time since Daniel's death. Anna Kate said their mother knew answers lay somewhere, but she would have to wait and find them.

On one occasion when Daniel was ill, Mr. Scarbro told Andrew he asked Millicent if she wanted to send for the doctor, but they didn't send for one. If Daniel didn't know how sick he was, perhaps Millicent didn't either.

~~~

From Andrew's nephew, John Morton Phelps:

> September 19, 1889
> Freestone, Ky.

Mr. Jackson Hawkins
Somervell Co, Texas
Dear Uncle,

I will write you a few lines this rainy morning. We are in just tolerable good health, and I hope this will find you all well. I saw Uncle Robert Nickell and his wife a few days past. They are well and were at a church meeting.

Well we have had several deaths in this neighborhood recently. Aunt Jane Phelps and Etna and Mollie Moss to name a few. Tell us how you are getting along and what you are doing.

I am wondering about the crops in Texas. Are they good for you there? Crops are no more than half here as times are hard. It has been some time since we heard from you. Mother sends her best wishes to all. Tell the girls we send them our best wishes too.

> Write soon. Your nephew,
> John Morton Phelps

~~~

John Morton was the son of Andrew's sister, Jo Anne. If crops were "half" in Kentucky, as he said, the Hawkinses experienced better times in Texas. Andrew had pastured and "clean-lined" his land. Rather than raise cattle, he stayed more to what he knew: farming corn, wheat, oats and cotton. He didn't have funds for raising cattle and couldn't give the stock the tending it needed. To him, the crops were more dependable.

They hoped to build a better and larger house. All the sisters wished for tall pillars and a winding flower-bordered path to the front door, but they would have to wait. If Andrew and Permelia waited until they could afford it, the children would be all married and they wouldn't need a larger house. Tall pillars were probably not on a high priority list for John Robert and Willie, at least not as high as repairing fence posts.

~~~

From Permelia's niece, Anna Page:

Capay, California
October 22, 1889

Dearest Aunt Permelia, Uncle Jack and Cousins,

I will try to write to you for the first time in three or four years. I have been out here in Capay since the twenty-eight day of May but I don't know if you knew it or not. I don't like it any too well. Aunt Ella Goodnow wrote Pa Cassity for me to come out here and he decided I could. They are very good to me.

It has been raining for two or three days and won't let up. Nobody can do much of anything outside.

I am very sorry Willie is sick. This is a bad place for people with the consumption. Where is cousin John Robert now? I never hear from him anymore. Why doesn't he write to me I wonder? Tell him to write and I will answer his letters as soon as I get them. I would like to see you all very much but don't expect I ever will. I am going to write to Uncle Jerry and Aunt Belle today. Don't they live close and when did you see them last? Tell them all good morning for me. How many children have Uncle Dim and Aunt Sally got? She has about ten hasn't she?

I do not go to school any more. I took a notion I did not want to go so I stayed at home.

Mr. Goodnow has not got his wheat in yet and this rain won't help. I do not know when he will get it in. Anna Kate do you go to school yet? Why don't Cora, Lizzie, and Louisa write to a body? They used to write every time you did but they don't write any more. Uncle Jack, are you well now? I would like to see you very much.

Cousins Pearl and Daisy and I went after the cows the other night. We were on horseback and did not get home until eight o'clock. It was fun but we did more playing than to get them in. Kate I wish you could have had such a jolly time with us.

I must close now. Will write you all a longer letter next time. Give my love to all.

Your loving niece and cousin,
Anna Page

~~~

From Robert Isaac:

Morehead, Ky.
October 27, 1889

Dear Sister, Brother, and children,

I once more take the pleasure of writing you and hope my words find you all well. But I fear not, from what I have heard about Willie. I fear he is not nor never will be again.

But live in the hopes that the will of God is done. Willie you must not give up but take care of yourself and get well with God's help.

We are having some damp weather and the appearance of turning cold. Now soon we will have plenty of wood to grind and saw. Pap's leg has not hurt him since August and he is in good health. He has gone to hunt our cattle today. We have eight nice steers and two cows giving milk. We sowed nine bushels of rye in September and we are feeding four big hogs. They will weigh two hundred pounds and I want to feed them until Christmas. Corn is not good here this year but it is good in the Blue Grass. It is worth down there from twenty cents to thirty cents. Stock is low too.

Isabel's brothers, Jesse B. Johnson and Stanton Johnson finally started to Texas last Monday, to Brownwood. Jesse said he was coming to see you all first and if Stant doesn't like Texas, he is going to Newton in California. I gave him Newt's address.

Millicent Hawkins was out to see us about taking one of her three boys. I don't know which one or whose choice it would be. It seemed a little strange as I think she wanted us to raise him. I did not get to see her. We would like to accommodate her but Isabel is not able to wait on a child.

Permelia, tell Jack I ate dinner with his sister Joanne. They are all well and I ate dinner with his sister Margaret Powers too. I have seen Aunt Lucyanne Phelps once. Tell Dim we are sill hammering on his land and will try to get it sold next circuit.

Tell all else howdy for us and will write Jerry and Belle. Isabel will write a few lines.

Robert Isaac Nickell

~~~

Dear Permelia,

I will be glad to write you a few lines although I do not write about a lot because I don't go much. I stay close to home. We were so sorry to hear that Willie was sick. I hope that he may be better soon.

Permelia, Mrs. Mead comes down often to see us. She would give anything to be back in Texas. Millicent was out to see us and she wanted to know if we had heard from you. She said she has not heard from you in some time. I hope you understand about us not taking her boy. You know we would do anything for your grandsons but we just cannot. She felt that since we had only one child it would be easy on us but I am not well this year. Millicent said her mother was so mean to her three boys that she did not want them to stay there this winter. She did not explain so I don't know exactly what she meant.

Have your girls to write to me. Tell Jerry and Belle we will write to them soon and tell James and Sally to write us. I know if Jeff Bolling ever comes to trial James will have to come to testify.[13] We enjoy your letters so much and want to see you all.

Isabel Nickell

~~~

The news of Millicent's wanting Robert Isaac and Isabel to take one of her boys shocked the Hawkins family. They were all in a dither, according to Louisa. Millicent's letters indicated she wasn't happy, but Permelia and Andrew hadn't realized how bad things were for her, or that her parents hadn't helped out more. Since Permelia didn't receive an answer right away from her last letter to Millicent, she took pen in hand and wrote to her daughter-in-law.

In those days a family member often helped raise a child. But when Anna Kate read the letter from the Nickells, she wondered how a mother could choose which child.

Louisa recalled several incidents in her brothers' lives. In November of 1889, Willie seemed to feel better and wanted to go with John Robert over east of Granbury. Against his mother's better judgment, she let him. Willie found difficulty with just sitting around the house, doing little physical work.

The boys knew to be cautious of snakes. Snakebites were common to anyone who didn't stay alert. On one trail across country, a venomous snake struck a traveler on the ankle. His friends on the wagon train tried every remedy they knew. Eventually they amputated his leg with the help of a common handsaw. His faithful wife and friends brought him on to recovery. He later cheerfully mended wagons, harnesses, boots and shoes. He even put to shame the able-bodied who were given to complaining.[14]

But as luck would have it, on the way to Granbury, John and Willie stopped to water their horses in a stock pond. Almost as soon as Willie dismounted, a snake jumped on him, sinking his fangs into the boy's leg, just above his boot. John immediately bled the wound, not thinking to find some milkweed for a poultice, as his papa had always told him to do. He just hurried to get Willie home.

Louisa reported that John and Willie came home "with Willie a mighty fever." Dr. Williamson said John did just right with what he did to help Willie.[15] His younger brother's not being stout made a snakebite more serious.

Permelia took blame for not insisting he stay home in the first place. Willie always seemed to look up to John Robert. If anything at all happened, he knew his brother would take care of him. Louisa was in her own dither, deciding she would be the nurse to take care of Willie.

All the girls looked after him, watching in turns. Anna Kate read while she sat by his bedside. The Hawkins girls loved books. They had heard tales of their great-grandfather Hawes and how he liked to read. They thought perhaps the books they left behind because they were too heavy to travel with, had once belonged to him. Alexander's wife, Lucy Fowke, came from a family with wealth. Louisa wondered if *their* children had to pick cotton.

Not many people had money in George's Creek. If the Hawkins family had more money, she wondered if Willie would be in the hospital. Back then, she thought if a person was in a hospital, he was going to die for sure. She continued to have this belief for most of her life.

Willie recovered with the tender care of his family, and was again on his horse, feeling well enough to help Andrew or mend fences with John Robert.

CHAPTER 4

A letter to Millicent - Cousin Ella Goodnow - Anna Page's adjustment – The preacher's daughter - Two are gone - Dear friends move to New Mexico - A young lady for John - Grief is difficult - Papa is seventy years old.

~~~

Pioneer women who kept diaries of their westward journeys left an insight into their struggles for better lives. They had to make their own way when husbands died on the trail. Some had one or two children, some had several. The men of the far west outnumbered the women, and frequently widows didn't remain so for long.

In the case of one young homesteader headed toward Wyoming, she lost her husband in a railroad accident near Denver. While some women, widows or single, chose "fancy houses" for their profession, this young woman plunged into hard work for her livelihood. She realized that with a mind and will, she could accomplish about anything she wanted. "Of course, I am extra strong, but those who try know that strength and knowledge come with doing." She wanted to prove her determination, and "roughing it" suited her just fine.[1]

According to Millicent's letters, being a widow back home was not as she hoped it would be. While Andrew and Permelia could assume folks would help her out financially, they had no sure way of knowing.

~~~

From Permelia:

George's Creek
Somervell County, Tex.
November 14, 1889

Dear Millicent,

It would please us greatly if you and the children are well.

Robert Isaac and Isabel wrote that you wanted them to take one of our grandsons. This concerns me as you are their mother and they should be with you. I know it is common for someone else to raise a child as long as it is family, but I cannot see why you need to do this, nor why you would ask my brother and Isabel. Although, better them than strangers.

You may be interested to know that our Willie is sick. We are praying the good Lord sees fit to make him well.

Tell me why your troubles are so great you cannot keep your family together. Can your folks not help you? What can we do? Think of what one son would feel to be the one you give away. Please write at once.

Permelia F. Hawkins

~~~

From Ella Goodnow:

Capay, California
November 17, 1889

Dear Cousin Permelia, one and all,

I will try to write you a few lines. I received your letter and one from cousin Jerry and Belle, and I must hurry and answer yours for fear you will be mad at me. Now I have just milked two cows and put the milk away. We get plenty of milk now. I would like to get one of those cream separators I have read about. It's a centrifugal separator that lets you get a lot more creamy butter than letting it just rise like it does now. I hope you get a lot of milk too. I have forty-five young chicks and had even more but some died. It has been real cold lately on baby chicks. I guess I have about twelve dozen but we still don't get enough eggs. When they do get to laying we will have enough and then you can come out here and we'll cook six dozen! How many can you eat?

We had a turkey dinner two weeks ago. My sister and family were here, Pa, and brother Tilden. Pa said for you to be sure and write him a long letter. His P.O. is East Grafton. He would be so glad to hear from you. I know it's been a long time since you've seen your Uncle James Joshua.

Now you know, Permelia, we sent for your niece Anna Page to come out here from Kentucky and we would send her to school and clothe her. Then she would help me nights and mornings and on Saturdays and Sundays. Well she came and I got her clothes and had her several dresses made so she could go to school. Mr. Goodnow got her new books and she went for two days.

Then she got mad and cried and said she would not go because she did not want to. Then I told her she could take her books and go to our other school, which is the same distance. She said she would not, so I sent for cousin Newton to come in to talk to her. He made her go but that night she came in saying she would not go back at all. Now what would you do with such a girl? Tell me. She has the worst temper of anyone I ever had anything to do with. Where did it start from? Well, wherever, she's got a mad on.

I wanted to fit her dress on her the other day and she had the lining pinned onto the goods.

The lining was too long. I told her I would measure it to her and she got mad and threw the goods behind the bed and told me I could make it all myself if I wanted to. Then she flew out of the door. I told her that I did not want to make it at all, but just to get it so she could save her cloth.

Mr. Goodnow was sitting there and didn't say a word, but her Uncle Newton gave her such a good talking to.

She has written home to her brother Clark and told him whatever she told him, and has given me fits. Now if she can find anyone anywhere who is any better to her than I am I would like for her to find them! She does as she is a mind to in everything she wants. When I get her anything she does not think it is anything at all. Now Permelia, what do you think? She is stubborn as the day is long when she gets mad. She is just as good as can be at times but they are few and far between. I have done all I can to try and get her to go to school, but my talking was just the same as the north wind blowing. So goes the world. Of course Mr. Cassity, Clark and Ella all think she is going to school where she ought to be. What will they say, do you think?

Now if you don't think I do a good part by Anna just come out here and see for yourself. She's your sister's child. Dear cousin, write me a line next time, will you? Newton will write you a few lines.

> Now goodnight from all to all.
> Ella Nickell Goodnow

~ ~ ~

From Newton Nickell, Permelia's brother:

> Capay, Cal.
> November 17, 1889

Dear sister Permelia, brother, and nieces,

It has been so long since I wrote to you at all. Cousin Ella was right. I am getting along fine. You know sometimes cousin Ella and I sit here looking at each other like two old cats but she is as good as the days are long. She never gets mad at me for anything but she knows I would take her down and sit on her!

I can never get Anna anything to please her. When she gets one thing she wants another. I gave her a dollar and some more money since she's been here. Now don't you think I have done my part? When I give her money she hardly ever thanks me and Ella is always trying to please her but all she thinks about is money.

Oh, Ella isn't finished writing. Write me a long letter and tell me everything.

From your dear little brother,
Newton K. Nickell.

One more word from your cousin Ella. Cousin Newton says his eyes are so bad that he could not see the lines so you must not think hard of him. He was writing bad words to you about two old cats. I just read his part of the letter. He is so bad. We have a bushel of fun. I wish you lived where we could go and see you for such good times we would have. Now goodbye and write soon. Tell John Robert I'll thrash his photo if he doesn't write to his ugly cousin Ella.

Newton has bought him the prettiest black horse. My, you should see him sitting up there in the saddle. He's a handsome sight he is. Write soon.

Ella N. Goodnow.

~ ~ ~

Perhaps Anna Page saw the many more material things her Goodnow cousins had, and she felt on the outside looking in. According to Ella, the girl's chores were plentiful in return for her keep. However, it is reasonable to expect Ella's own children had their chores to do.

Permelia believed Anna was not angry at the Lord for taking away her mother, but perhaps she held resentment at the circumstance. Ella Goodnow's

account of Anna's actions seemed to contradict Edmond
W. Cassity's opinion. Permelia doubted she could raise
Anna any better or offer her more, especially since the
Goodnow's large farm provided very well for them.
Permelia often wrote to Anna after she began
corresponding with her cousin, Ella. Louisa knew of the
concern her mama had toward her niece, Anna.

Newton Nickell had come through George's Creek on
his way to his Uncle James in California. He was one
Nickell brother who had a desire to see on the other side
of the mountain. He always wanted to do more than the
usual farming most young men his age did.

Newton was a nice looking man, lean and dark. His
sister said if there was still gold in California, she felt
certain he would find some for himself, although she
tried to get him to stay in Texas.

~~~

From Addie Lame, Andrew's niece:

Morehead, Ky.
December 12, 1889

Dear Cousin Lizzie,
I thought I would write to you to let you know we are all
well and hope you are enjoying the same. Lizzie, I was sorry
to hear Willie is not better. I hope he will get well so much.

I have been going to school this fall, and it will be out
next Thursday.

You know I have never had my hair cut off but once
when I was little, and I don't intend ever to cut it off again.
Some people ask me why I don't have me some bangs cut
and I tell them the reason is that it wasn't ever intended for
women to have their hair cut off. That's what was taught to
me by my papa.

I went to prayer meeting last night and there was a tolerable large crowd out. Do you have church there every Sunday morning and night and prayer meetings each Wednesday night? Well, I will close for this time. I will try to write more next time. Write soon.

Yours truly from Miss Addie Lame to Miss Lizzie Hawkins.

P.S. I have written some verses for you all. A verse to Lizzie: "When days are dark and dreary and friends are few, Remember me and I will you." A verse to Anna Kate: "Your sweet lips to my visions discloses, The birthplace of kisses and beauty of roses." A verse to cousin Eva Cora: "When you are floating down the river in your little bark canoe, May you have a pleasant journey just room enough for two."

Addie Lame

~~~

Addie's father, Lewis R. Lame, was a preacher and apparently rather strict. Preachers' children had to be careful of their actions as they would be criticized more severely. If they behaved in an inappropriate manner, they would not set a good example for their friends.

Permelia did not tell her children that dancing was right or wrong, but she thought social gatherings where dancing was the focal point, were permissible—if "strictly chaperoned."

The Cumberland Presbyterian Church didn't share those feelings where dancing and dipping snuff were concerned. The church once called a special meeting to expel a group of girls who attended a Saturday night dance. The Hawkins sisters had not gone to the dance. Apparently, many thought the church's decision was too strict, because membership began dropping off.[2]

Permelia entertained her own feelings toward preachers "doing the work of the Lord." Contrary to some people, who thought they should not be paid for spreading the word, Permelia said a preacher could do his work a lot better if he was sure to better provide for his family. A preacher couldn't support his family with preaching alone, although his "flock" often invited him—not necessarily his family—to dinner after church. His family still needed provided for since they ate on Sundays the same as everyone else.

No matter how poor the household, the wife was expected to be a good hostess to their special guest—the minister.[3]

~~~

From Addie Lame:

Morehead, Kentucky
December 12, 1889

Miss Cora Hawkins
George's Creek, Texas
Dear cousin Cora,

It is with the greatest pleasure that I seat myself to write to you.

How much cotton did you have when you got it all picked? When you said you were working in the fields I could just picture you puffing away. I guess you have lots of cotton in Texas.

There is going to be a traveling show here Friday night and some of us are planning to go see it. Cora, tell Anna Kate that Mama said to send her a picture. She wants to see if she looks like Gramma as much as she used to. Well Cora, it is ten minutes to nine and I am getting sleepy. I will close.

Write soon, from Addie to Cora.

P.S. Tell Aunt Permelia and Uncle Jack to write and tell John Robert and Willie to write to my brother John Morton. Well, I had almost forgotten Louisa. Tell her howdy for me! I will send my picture to Katie for I haven't but one good one, and it's the only one that is by myself. All of you can see it. Goodbye for all for tonight.

~~~

Everyone huffed and puffed in the Hawkins' cotton fields. Without their cotton, chances are they would have been in financial distress. All the children helped pick. Even Louisa had a cotton sack. She freckled so, her mama couldn't sew a bonnet brim large enough to keep the sun off her face. Permelia told her if she just ran after the scattering balls, she might run fast enough that the sun couldn't "light on her."

Most of the families did their own picking because they didn't have money to pay hired hands. Some people thought there wasn't enough cotton work for additional help anyhow, not if the children pitched in. However, if cotton kept growing the way it was at that time in Somervell County, they might all be prosperous sooner or later. That is what the area people prayed for.

Cotton, the principal cash crop, was known as "king." Since farmers picked the lint and seeds by hand, everyone's fingers bled by the end of the day.[4]

~~~

December 14, 1889

Willie's childhood coughing turned into "the consumption," and the doctors diagnosed him at an early age. Since he had come through so many years, his parents thought sure he had, or would, overcome the disease. One morning he just didn't feel like getting up.

Permelia thought he had la grippe and sent for the doctor. She could tell by the doctor's expression that this time it was serious. For two weeks the family prayed for him to make it through, although they knew consumption could seldom be cured.[5]

Andrew and Permelia accepted their son's death, finding comfort knowing he had no more pain and discomfort, for he had the same for so long. They laid him to rest beneath a shady tree in George's Creek graveyard.

The creek winds its way by the graveyard. Permelia called it a "friendly" place.

Springtime and summer still bring wild flowers— bluebonnets, larkspurs, and hollyhocks.

The first grave in George's Creek Cemetery was dated 1862. 1870 brought four more.[6] It is still in use.

~~~

From Emily Yeary, a friend:

Bald Prairie, Robertson Co., Tex.
December 19, 1889

Dear Mrs. Hawkins and sister in Christ,

It is with great pleasure that I take my pen in hand to answer your kind letters. We have been so very busy this fall I have hardly had time to get a good breath. We are through with our work now and the children are going to school.

I was very sorry to hear of Willie's illness and by this time I hope he is well.

Sister Hawkins I haven't much news to write. The health of the community is good. Every person has finished picking cotton and making syrup. Crops were good for this county and we made and baled thirteen bales of cotton, two hundred and fifty bushels of corn and one barrel of syrup. There was too much work for just us to do so we hired two weeks work last summer and hired six hundred pounds of cotton picked. We did the rest of the work ourselves.

Mr. Yeary has rented his place for next year. We will start to New Mexico the first of next month. We will go there with the intention of making it our new home if we like it. The children are all very much opposed to going. They say their pa has a good home here with a good living and they don't see why he should want to do any better.

We would sell our place but there is no sale for land here now. We think it will bring us more to keep it and rent it out than to sell it for a small sum. Then if we don't like it in Mexico we will have a home to come back to. But I hate the idea of leaving you, to go so far. I tried my best to get Mr. Yeary to rent this place and come back to George's Creek and settle down to stay.

Gussy can do as much work in the field as his papa can. I tell him that with the help he has got and the rent of this place, he would make enough to buy a place up there. The children are as much opposed to coming back to George's Creek as they are to going to New Mexico. They have become so attached to their schoolmates and playfellows here that they think Bald Prairie is the Eden of the world.

I regret very much to leave Bald Prairie myself, for I think I have some very warm friends here. In fact I never lived in a place in my life but I hated to leave it. I don't like this country as well as I do in Johnson County, as a general thing. The people here are not as friendly as they are there and I think it is a healthy thing to have friends.

Well, I will close for this time as I have to write a letter to my uncle this evening who lives in New Mexico. He said to be sure to let him know if we were coming so he could have a good place for us to stay. I do wish I could see you all. Can't you come down at Christmas? Let me know so I can make preparations for you. Write soon and tell me all the news.

Who is your preacher at George's Creek now? How are the girls all getting along?

My love to all and to my very dear friend.
Emily Yeary
To Permelia Florence Hawkins

~~~

Andrew and Permelia met the Yeary family when they once lived in Somervell County. After Permelia's friends moved to New Mexico, she didn't see them again.

In the 1890s, the Union Church began their services on the east side of the cemetery on land donated by James W. Allison.[7] Soon after, the Reverend Lewis Elliott (also a schoolteacher) often preached in George's Creek. Another preacher in these early times was the Reverend McKenny.[8]

Permelia depended on her prayers, letters and photographs to keep her spirits up. She thought of going home to Kentucky for a visit, but she did not make the trip. Louisa thought her mother was so lonely because of Willie's death that a Kentucky visit would help. Since they couldn't afford for all of them to go, Permelia would not go without them.

It was about this time John Robert found a nice smart young lady. After a few weeks his siblings thought he and Maggie Scarbro were "getting up a case." John had his eye on some land, but he would continue to help Andrew farm at least for a while, even if he did marry. His sisters expected him to set the date any time.

The first December after Willie's death would be a solemn Christmas for the Hawkins family. Louisa remembered they had always exchanged gifts with each other but nothing elaborate. Most of the time they included handmade presents, put together in great secrecy.

Andrew, not in the habit of purchasing gifts for the children, left that up to their mother. However, this year on a trip to Cleburne, he bought different colored scarves for his daughters. They also never suspected their mother had been embroidering collar and cuff sets to surprise them. She worked on them after the girls went to bed. Permelia also made them new weskits, but did not get Louisa's finished until the day after Christmas.

For the longest time, Louisa had asked for an autograph album. Her wish came true, much to her delight. She could scarcely wait to go to school for her friends to sign it. Little Dora Dietrich of Fairview wrote, "May you be happy each day of your life, Get a good husband and make a good wife." And this one by D. W. Styron – "Round is the ring that has no end, so it is my love for you my friend." Other friends wrote sweet verses: Alice Eddy in Buck Creek, Birdie Godfrey, Laura Cauble and more. Many descendants of Louisa's schoolmates still live in the Somervell County area.

No one repeated the verses in Louisa's album. Some of her friends said they made them up. Her sisters wrote: "When you go to a party and stay out late, Remember it is bedtime and don't swing on the gate." – Lizzie; "Sweet as a fragrant rose, Tis to have a friend, On whom in gloom or sunshine, We know we can depend." – Anna Kate; "May your life be calm and peaceful, Gentle as the flowing stream. And your life be no more painful Than the waking of a dream." – Eva Cora.

When Andrew didn't work the fields because of rain, he repaired something either in the barn or tended to repairs in the house. Occasionally he took his rocker out on the porch and watched water fall off the roof as it splattered into the rain barrel. Resting was a commodity not often obtained. The girls loved and respected their father and looked for these opportunities to visit with him. Days were short and sundown came too soon.

Once when Andrew and Permelia were talking on the porch, Louisa and Cora listened. Andrew said Millicent built her problems with her own actions, and she "needs carry some responsibility for it." He didn't want her to face her obligations at the sacrifice of her children. They discussed Millicent's not wanting their help when it was best to have it. By the time the conversation ended, they decided to find some way to pay for them all to come to Texas.

Permelia got up from her chair, saying she was going to post their grandsons a present. It wouldn't be much, but at least it would arrive with love. They had raised their children to be reliable and accountable for their own deeds, with any needed counsel from their parents. For the most part, nothing beyond sensible decisions had ever been needed.

Permelia had not heard from Millicent.

~~~

From Robert Isaac:

<div align="right">

Morehead, Ky.
Jan. 5, 1890

</div>

Dear Brother, Sister, and Nieces and Nephew,

Your letter came in hand in due time but oh such sad news as it bore to us. But we ought not be surprised. Why, because we all have to die. We and everybody else of the friends are full of sorrow. I know Willie will be missed in your home but do not grieve after him for he is in heaven. I read your letter to H. C. Mayett and they said to give you their heartfelt sympathy and best wishes. I said Willie was such a good boy. Clay Powers says Jack and Permelia had the best children on earth and you were the best parents, certain and sure.

We are having such warm weather so far and the flowers are blooming in the woods. Della goes to gather them and puts them on the table for dinner time. With warm weather lots of meat has already spoiled but we have lost none yet.

I saw George Powers the other day in Morehead. He said that he could have come by George's Creek to see you if he had known sooner that he was coming to Kentucky. He told me he would come out to the house before he goes back to Texas, but I don't expect him much. Uncle Andrew and Aunt Henrietta and all the folks said to give you their love.

Clark is turning out to be a good carpenter and gets lots of work. Pap and I have built us a big wagon this winter and about have it ready to hitch to. I have worked three yoke of our cattle to Morehead. We also have six shoats and two cows giving milk. I have not sawed much this winter chiefly because of lack of logs although there is plenty of water.

Your photos are so good. Pap showed them to lots of people in Morehead and everybody thought them so nice. Mrs. Mead could pick them all out, and said that the girls were just as pretty as the pictures were.

We have a mighty sweet little bad girl. Della figures she owns all the chickens on the place and just now came in with four eggs. She and her mama have two little pet pigs and Della can catch them anywhere.

Tell brother James that I am doing all I can do to get his land judgment this court or in February, and if I do I think I will have it sold the first county court after circuit court. I think he believes he thinks the time is long and so do I.

Now sister, excuse me for this time and tell all the friends I would like to see them. As far as I know, Millicent has her boys.

May God be with you in your troubles, and bless you all.

Your loving brother,
Robert I. Nickell

P.S. Pap's seventy years old January 7, 1890.

~~~

From Isabel Nickell:

January 8, 1890
Morehead, Ky.

Dear niece Anna Kate,
   I will try to write you a few lines this lonesome Sabbath. We were sorry to hear from you of the death of your brother and please convey our feelings to everyone in your family. I know it is hard to give him up and you will miss him. We must live in the hopes of meeting in heaven where parting will be no more.
   We were glad to get all your pictures and we think they are all so nice. Your grandpa thinks so much of them. I have a nice album to put them in.
   Did you have a nice turkey at Christmas? Your uncle Greenup was over and brought two of his children with him, Aquilla and Jessie. They are so smart and they can sing so nicely. I gave Jessie enough money to buy her a new dress. She is a real pretty little girl.
   I do not know if you can read this or not. I haven't written many letters since we got back from Kansas. I am not satisfied here and never will be. It is not like when you were here. There is no school close. Della is going on seven years and has never been a day to school. She is sweet and smart but I do not want to raise her here.
   I will close by saying write again soon.

From your Aunt Isabel Nickell
to Anna Kate Hawkins

~~~

By now, Jim and Sally (Prater) Nickell had settled in Somervell County, without selling his home place. When Robert Isaac sold his land, Jim planned to return to Morehead to finish the transaction.

The Hawkins family received many letters of condolence after Willie's death, and of course, after Daniel's as well. One concerning Willie's death arrived from a Mrs. Harrison. The writer lived in Missouri at the time but was from the east. Her family believed consumption was just being asleep. The coffin should never be closed, or the person would "come back wickedly."

Mrs. Harrison also wrote that Willie should have been carrying an onion in his pocket to destroy the germs of consumption.

Permelia tore up the letter, although Louisa remembered it well, and was somewhat scared whenever she thought of its contents. Permelia thought a superstition was just that and she never saw a black cat that did her harm. She said, "Consumption is a disease and that's all."

Jefferson Bolling has still not been brought to trial.

CHAPTER 5

An explanation – Christmas in California – A wife for Clark Page – They hung him from a tree and shot him full of holes – Letters through tears – Millicent wants a Texas man to correspond – Niece Ella Page comes to Texas.

~~~

From Millicent:

Poplar Plains, Kentucky
January 8, 1890

Dear Betsy,

I hope you are happy and in fine health since last we saw each other. The Lord knows I have had my own troubles.

Daniel died two years ago and our three sons and me came on back to Kentucky. It's all I can do to keep clothes on their backs much less give them anything they want to play with. I've been with my folks and we get along none too well. My sister says it's my fault but I don't see how that is.

I work for little wages and it's all I have. I went to Robert Nickell and asked his wife if she would take one of the boys. It wasn't like I wouldn't be seeing him as much as I could. They could not help me out. My thinking was if they raised one, I could give more to the other two. They deserve so much that I can't give them.

You are lucky to have a man to take care of you. There is so much I need and no man to provide it. Mrs. Hawkins may or may not like me and I never thought she did. I admit I gave her good reason not to some times. She was right about so many things and it seemed I couldn't do anything right myself.

I get so lonely to have a close friend to talk to and that is why I wrote you. I wonder if it gets as cold in Alabama as it does here.

Your dear friend,
Millicent Hawkins

~~~

From Ella Goodnow:

Capay, California
January 10, 1890

Dearest cousins,

To one and all, I will try to answer your last welcome letter which I received a few days ago. We are all well except for colds. I am hoping when you read this that you are enjoying the best of health.

How sorry we all were when we read of the death of Willie. But he is with the angels and we all have to die sooner or later, 'tho consumption is an awful death to die. Some suffer so much and have to die by inches.

We are having such a warm day here, although we have had the most rain you ever read of. Mud mud is all we see but the last three days have dried the ground up some. I hope it won't rain again for at least six weeks. We have not got in one bit of grain. We do not think we will even get to put any in this year. Your brother Newton is at my sister's. He is glad you liked the pretty handkerchiefs he sent.

Santa did not come to see me especially this year. He is real mean I think! What are cousins Jerry and James doing? They never write to us at all, the rascals. How many children has each and what are their names? Anna Page said she got a letter from the girls but she would not let Newton and me see only one piece of it, so I do not know what it said. She always reads my letters however!

Cousin John Robert, you old fat rascal! If you don't say something to me in your mama's letter! I know I could get the best of your photo but I don't think I could manage you. You are fine looking. Just come out here and see the girls or perhaps you are waiting on one now? Your sisters are fine looking too. Tell them to just come out and see me and Anna. We would have a fine time.

I would like to tell you about our Christmas. It saddens me to think we were enjoying ourselves at Christmas, not knowing about your Willie.

We had a dance at our house and such a time we did have. My brothers played the fiddle and my son Chester played the guitar. Then there were five of the neighbors who made up the brass band. It was all so festive and we had a jolly time. How nice if you and Andrew could have enjoyed Christmas with us. We had ham and sweet potatoes, raisins, cream cheese pie and cream cake. Newton had gone out for a turkey and brought in a big one. Everyone had such a good time dancing. You should have seen Newton swing the girls high.

We had brought in a beautiful tree from the hillside and the children made some popcorn strands to dangle on the tree. How nice it is to have a house full of laughter.

Well cousin Jack. You never say a word to me. Don't you like your beautiful cousin Ella? If I get to see you, you will have to talk to me. We could start any place on foot and I could make you trot to keep up.

I was glad to hear you have made your house bigger. We are fortunate to live in a house with plenty of room. I know how happy you must be. Your photos are all fine, and I will put them in a frame just as soon as I get one. Pa's folks are all well or they were the last time I heard from them. Excuse this poorly written letter and I will do better next time, from all to all. Also tell me your children's ages. We had a little argument about them. Write as soon as you get this.

From your cousin
Ella Goodnow

~~~

James Joshua Nickell, Ella's father, and his second wife Mary Ann Taylor and their family, moved from Linn County, Missouri to California in 1864.[1] They made their first stop in Yolo County, where they remained for fifty years, successfully farming 160 acres.[2] Many families took the same move to avoid the Civil War. James, twin of Permelia's father, William C. Nickell, never saw his brother again. They planned many trips, but never managed to fulfill their dreams.

Charlton Nickell, grandson of James Joshua lived in Woodland, California until his death in 1989. He wrote of sitting on the knee of his grandmother Mary Ann Nickell, listening to her stories of their westward journey. It took six months on the trail from Missouri to California. Rainstorms created problems when a wagon's canvas ripped, and dust storms challenged them as they crossed the plains. Cholera was a natural fear of the time, along with other ailments. Each day when this Nickell family started out, they prayed the day would be a good one, and Indians would not attack.[3]

Most travelers knew to take remedies for illnesses they were almost certain to have along the way, but they did not always use good judgment before heading west. Laudanum and camphor were mainstays but often of short supply. The travelers knew to take castor oil, rum, and a large vial of peppermint essence. They needed citric acids for scurvy, and whiskey and opium for everything else.[4] They might not have had the "everything else," but had the whiskey—just in case.

As wagon trains passed wooden crosses alongside rock-covered graves, the women often noted the number. One woman recorded more than eighty graves during their journey.[5] In 1853 another listed in her diary the number of miles covered in a day, as well as graves seen. Sometimes, traveling from nine to twenty-two miles in one day, she noted seeing from two to as many as fifteen graves. Yet another woman wrote, "I have glanced at the sideboards of the wagons, not knowing how soon it would serve as a coffin for some one of us."[6]

Letters telling of the California Christmases intrigued Permelia and her daughters. Permelia, anxious to read about her relatives' lives, passed the letters around for the family to share. It was difficult to imagine Cousin Ella's house being large enough for a band and dancing. Permelia wanted very much to take her cousin up on her many invitations to come visit. Even though Ella talked of her hard work, they seemed to have much.

J. T. Hewitt hauled lumber from Cleburne to build his house, the first complete frame house in the area. In keeping with the admirable sentiment pioneers attached to things, and since it usually required great sacrifice to obtain their possessions, this sentiment held true with their houses. They built around them rather than tearing them down and starting over.[7] Andrew and John Robert had added a second floor with lumber instead of logs. They constructed it on top of one-half the house, with stairs on the outside of the original structure. Andrew then enclosed the stairs with a kind of vestibule and door to the kitchen. This allowed for a bigger area upstairs, without sacrificing indoor space with a stairway.

The Hawkinses were proud of their new addition. Louisa long ago tired of a trundle bed she thought belonged only to small children. Space now allowed a "regular" bed.

~~~

From Ella Goodnow:

February 2, 1890
Capay, California

Dear cousins one and all,

I will try to answer your most welcome letter which I received last night, and was glad to hear that your brother James was so wealthy with boys in his family. And little Jerry is wealthy with ten cents! A child always likes to have money in his pocket. Just think, will you. Oh those rascals, I will always think they might write to me. And that John of yours! If I had hold of him, he would be willing to sit down and write.

Well listen to this. I have poison oak all over my face. It is so swollen I can hardly see out of my left eye, but then my beauty wasn't much to mar!

Anna Page has been visiting to her folks, and I didn't know if you knew. I think maybe Ella Page is married, although they didn't say so. Ella has been very sick according to the last letter Anna got from her stepfather. Also he told her that Clark is married.

Newton is trying to make himself a cart so he can drive a new colt. He is well and sassy as ever, and sends his love to all. He says to tell his nephews, James and little Jerry to write to him.

Well, Permelia, we have had the wettest winter we have had in four years. There is nothing but mud everywhere. The rains did great damage to the people living in Sacramento. The river washed all they had away, and drowned lots of cattle and hogs. It washed away houses and barns. Oh, it was terrible to see so much water and destruction.

Now Louisa you wanted to know names of my children. Chester is the oldest and is thirteen. The next is Pearl and she is nine, ten the eighth of April. Daisy will be eight the twenty-ninth of May. The baby, Raymond, will be six the tenth of November. They all want you to write to them.

Chester plays the guitar very well, and he learns music fast. The others learn well at school also. Tell Lizzie, Cora, and Anna Kate to write. If I had hold of them they would write for sure!

Now Cousin Jack, what in the world are you doing that you cannot write and say a word to me? Now goodbye to all from all. My husband John, and Chester have gone to a neighbor's to hear Chester play the guitar. Write soon and tell me the news.

Your cousin,
Ella Goodnow

~~~

From E.W. Cassity:

Yocum, Morgan Co Ky.
February 4, 1890

My dear Jack and Permelia,

I seat myself this morning to write to you a few lines. I hope they find you in a better state of health than they are leaving me. One day's work I have done since Christmas.

Permelia, I received your kind letter and was glad to hear from you but sorry for your sadness and troubles. We all have to endure at some time. We as a Christian people have to bear this land of sin and sorrow and sometimes have a hard time of it.

For myself, I am determined to stand upon God's Holy word and trust you will do the same. Then when we are called upon to leave this world, we may be prepared to meet our friends who wait at that beautiful gate to welcome us into the Celestial City.

Ella says she wrote you last week. She is well at this time. Yes, Clark is married and he lives in Clay City, Powell County Ky. I have never seen his wife yet he says she is the prettiest little creature that he ever did see, and I expect he thinks she is.

We have not had any cold weather this winter. There has not been enough snow to track a rabbit. I will bring my letter to a close by saying for you to write as soon as you get this, direct to Blair Mills, Morgan County.

> I remain devoted,
> E. W. Cassity

~~~

From Emily Yeary, Permelia's friend:

> February 5, 1890
> Bald Prairie
> Robertson Co. Texas

Dear Sister Hawkins and family,

After long delay I seat myself to answer your letter which was most kind and welcome. I hope you will not be angry with me for not writing before now. I was waiting for my daughters Lou and Annie to get their pictures taken to send to you girls. They were not good pictures, though Annie is as much like her as it can be. The one sitting down is Lou.

I was so sorry to hear about Willie and to think I wrote my last letter to you not knowing about him. We can look forward to meeting him in a better place.

Thank you so much for inviting me down to see you before we go to New Mexico. I regret very much that there will not be time for a visit. We will start next Monday, just one week from today. You need not answer this letter since I won't be here. Just address it to Socorro County, New

Mexico. I will give you the exact address as soon as I get there and write to you.

We had a tragic thing happen just recently. There was a woman killed by a man only five miles from here. The man went to the house and saw no one at home except the woman. Her husband was working in a field a mile away. After the man killed her he took all the clothing he could find, piled it on top of her and poured coal oil all over It thinking it would burn the house. It burned her clothes off and burned one or two holes in the floor and then went out.

Her husband smelled the smoke and went rushing back to the house. He got some men together who were working in the field and they tracked the man down. They caught him and brought him back to measure his tracks in the sandy dirt with his shoes, and they were the same size. He finally acknowledged that he was the one that killed her. They got him to the law and started to Franklin with him in a hack. There was about a hundred men who surrounded the hack and wouldn't let it go on. They took the man out and hung him and shot him full of holes and left him hanging there on the tree. Next day some folks got to thinking and went out and buried him right there. Tell me what your thoughts are.

Sister Hawkins, I think of you all so often. I do wish you could go with us. Give my love to Grandma Atchison and Sister Belle Nickell. Well, as I can't think of anything more I will close for this time. Be sure to write when I write again from New Mexico. Give my love to all and reserve a portion for yourself.

> I remain your true friend until death.
> Lou wants to write a note to Cora.
> Emily Yeary

From Lou Yeary:
Well Cora, I will try to answer your kind letter. I was so proud to get yours and Lizzie's pictures. I will send you mine

and Annie's in return. I regret very much that papa is going to New Mexico. We will start the eighth of April. I know I won't ever get to see you all any more and it is very sad to think of. I will write again when I get there or perhaps I will write while on the road.

Give my love to all the girls. Tell them all to write.

Lou Yeary to Cora Hawkins

~~~

From Emily Yeary:

February 10, 1890
Bald Prairie
Robertson Co. Texas

Dear Sister Hawkins,

I am somewhat rushed for time but I will write a few lines more since my letter of a few days ago. This is about that man who got hung. I can't tell you how some people have reacted to such a thing. But after almost a week passed, a man who was one of them that hung him declared he saw this man up and walking around that tree one night. He had one shoe on and was carrying the other one. Then someone else that wasn't even there for the hanging vowed he saw him still swinging from the tree. And he is no drinker either.

The girls are right scared. Some think it might be a ghost. I tell you, I don't know what to think. But how else could they still see him?

I hope you like the girls' pictures. Let me know as soon as I get to New Mexico. Please take care of yourselves and I pray health for you and your family.

Your dear friend,
Emily Yeary

~~~

From Mrs. Skaggs:

April 10, 1890

Dear Millicent,

    I will write to you these lines and hope they find you in good health.

    You will see that your letter to my son's wife is being returned. It is my sad task to tell you that she took sick with pneumonia some year and two months ago. Alas, she left her dear husband and sweet little girls. I am staying at their house off and on to help out.

    I hope you are not angry with me for reading your letter, but I thought I should so an answer could be given you. My son is planning on marrying a young woman with two little ones of her own. I thank the Lord for this union. Alas, think of these precious children having both a mother and a father again.

    Betsy always spoke of you often and enjoyed so much hearing from you when you and Daniel lived in Texas. If there is any way I can offer help to you, I wish I might. My prayer is that you will soon have a happy home for yourself and your dear boys.

Mrs. Skaggs

~~~

From Ida L. Maxey:

Ringo's Mills, Kentucky
April 10, 1890

Miss Anna Kate Hawkins
Dearest friend Katie,

    After a long delay I take the pleasure this rainy evening of answering your good letter. I was oh so glad to hear from you and this leaves all well but ma. She has had la grippe yet. 'Tis seven weeks tomorrow since she first took sick and she has not been able to do anything for a long time. She mends very slowly.

I have some garden made but no flowers planted yet. It rains all the time till people can't get anything done, not even plowing. All the farmers can do is to sow oats and it's pouring down now. For over two days the creek has been out over its banks and people can't get their grinding.

I think all the people have grown cold and careless out here and the young men all drink a heap. The older people think about nothing but making money. Do the young men drink much out there?

We have preaching only once a month here I am sorry to say. The preacher doesn't get paid very much and Pa pays him more than anybody does. Pa keeps the church up.

The Emmons you spoke about was Paul A. Emmons, better known as Bud. Your Ma knows him. He lives in the old log house where you used to live, near his Pa's. Mr. Bill Emmons married Lucy Price. The Gilmore brothers, John and Richard, keep store where we used to live. Ask your Ma if she remembers those sons of James and Mary Ann Gilmore. Mr. Gilmore is dead now and Mrs. Gilmore and her daughter Lucy, live in the old home where she used to live.

Well, I am getting toothless. I went to Flemingsburg Saturday, Laura and I. I had five teeth drawn and will have some new ones.

'Tis supper time and I will close now. Oh yes, here is your picture. You are welcome to keep it until fall but please send it back as soon as you have more taken, for I wouldn't take anything for it. Please write soon. Katy, have you any moss rose seed? If so please send me a few seed in your next letter. Have you got my picture yet?

Was Willie waiting on any girl? John Robert, be good to your sisters. You may not have them always. Life is uncertain

and death is sure. Answer as soon as you get this. I wish your
Ma had written to me when Willie was sick. I would have
given anything to have known he was so bad. I got a letter
from him in June and he never said he was sick.

I send my love to all. Your loving friend till death. Write
soon. Excuse haste.

Ida L. Maxey

<div align="center">~~~</div>

Louisa didn't remember much about the log house in
Kentucky, but her sisters recalled it well. The girls had
shared the same room, with trundle beds for Lizzie and
Louisa. They appreciated their dogtrot style house in
George's Creek, because of the open area between the
two house sections. The family dog could trot right
through, as well as finding protection in bad weather.
Depending on the direction the house faced, the
opening created a breeze-tunnel, which could still be
pleasant on a hot day—even better for sleeping during
hot Texas nights.

The fenced yard kept the Hawkins' two cows from
coming to call, or the chickens from being too sociable.
Permelia's vegetable garden inside the fenced yard
didn't deter cottontails or squirrels that scrambled right
in.

<div align="center">~~~</div>

From Permelia:

George's Creek, Tex.
April 10, 1890

Dear Millicent,

Andrew and I hope you and our grandsons are well as we
are at this time. John Robert has found himself a nice girl. I'm

not sure if they have a real case or not. Her name is Maggie Scarbro.

We had better crops last year than in the past but this year is not looking good because of the rain—rain—rain. It is too early to tell if anything will rot out or not.

Now Millicent, I want you to know that if the funds were readily available we would send for you all. God bless our dear Willie. Quite a bit of our funds went towards him, but we were blessed to be able to give him as good a care as possible. There are many folks who lose their loved ones because they cannot do as we could. We laid Willie to rest in the George's Creek graveyard. How I wish our Daniel was next to Willie. I will want to be there some day.

You did not answer my last letter and I am writing again because we want to hear from you. Inside this envelope is what I can spare for you to get something for yourself unless the boys need it more. I sent them presents earlier—some time ago. Did you get the box?

We are experiencing some bad spring weather. The heavens only know when there will be more. Hug Ban, Walt, and little Russ—you be good now. Perhaps one day we can hug them ourselves.

Permelia F. Hawkins

<div align="center">~~~</div>

From Greenup B. Nickell, Permelia's brother:

Rowan County, Ky.
April 24, 1890

Dear Sister Permelia and family,

I will write to you again and I have not heard from you since I wrote last. We are all well and are doing very well otherwise. I have been working all winter about one hundred dollars worth since last oats harvest. It has been wet here all winter and is raining now. I don't know if I can farm or not.

My little Jessie is going to school now. She talks about her mama and uncles and it would do her so much good to see you all. It would do me good too. Tell Lizzie and the girls that I have not forgotten them. I would like to be with you this summer. We would have a nice time going to singing and to church. I sing pretty loud. People sometimes turn and look. Now is it I sing good or do I sing bad?

You must ask me over to your big state. I want to see if your potatoes, green beans, and turnips are as good as I can cook them. I have been working on some rooms for twelve days now. I have worked thirty days this month at a dollar and a quarter per day. I can cook over where I work and can beat most women at that business!

Lizzie, tell your sisters they don't need to write me but tell your two uncles to write.

It is cool now and the rain isn't going to let up. I must say good-by for this time and take this to the office. May God bless us and save us in Heaven is the prayer from your uncle.

> Greenup B. Nickell
> To his nieces and his sister P. F.
> Hawkins

~~~

Greenup, Permelia's brother, was ten years younger than she. When his wife, Laura, died, she left him with three children. Laura was ill for the last part of her life and Greenup looked after his family, preparing the meals. Obviously proud of his cooking, he never mentioned baking a cream cake—a measure by which many people estimated a cook's expertise.

~~~

From Millicent Hawkins:

Poplar Plains, Kentucky
May 25, 1890

Dear Mother,

With pleasure I will answer your kind letter and most welcome it was too. It was taken out of the office and taken to Aless C. Hawkins' house and stayed there for some time before I got it. This leaves us tolable well but pa. He has been in bad health for a year.

I was so glad to read the lines you wrote for I love you better than I ever did but I know you don't think so. I can sympathize with your troubles and I think you ought to me. I love you all and would love to be with you. If God spares my life and the lives of the children I intend to make Texas my future home. If you can find me a Texas man I will try my best to correspond with him.

How sad I was to hear of Willie. Your heart must be broken. I am so sorry. I hate it so for you all.

I am staying in Poplar Plains at Mr. Jess Ingram's. Russ stays with me and they are so nice and good to me and my little Russ. I will be here seven weeks tomorrow. They want me to make my home here. Ban and Walt are with my folks while I am here. There is so much sickness here. There were four corpses last Sunday. It's just real bad. I was sorry to hear of the storm there. Did I know anyone that got hurt?

I will tell you about Martha. She lives here close to Ball Hill. She had two kids, one girl and one boy. Sam is not stout and Martha will be left just like me and then she will think of the way she has treated me and my children. Pa is the only friend I've got here.

It doesn't do anything but rain and nobody has gotten any corn planted yet. Everything else is dull too. What has become of Mr. Jay? Has Molly Graves ever married? Did the

Berry girls sell their place? Have Rosie and Lewis Elliott got any kids?

Ma please write. I read your letters through tears. It does me so much good for you to write. Write soon and don't put it off. Thank you for the dollars. I will get the boys some clothes. I spend all I make on them, but I may get a little hair comb for myself. They are so sweet and Ban and Walt are growing fast.

Has Uncle Jerry sold his place yet? How is Mrs. Myers? Has she got any more kids?

I will close, hoping to hear from you all soon. Goodby to all.

Millicent Hawkins

~~~

As people moved ahead, they could only look at the graveyards of past deeds, but there was no turning back the clock. At least the Hawkins family felt a reconciliation with Millicent could be possible.

Andrew and Permelia, desperate to see their grandchildren, would do what it took to get them to Texas. Permelia didn't think of a man for Millicent to write, so she enlisted the help of her son and daughters. They began writing names, but for one reason or the other, crossed them off the list. The girls tacked a paper to the kitchen wall for the addition of any new possibilities.

The storm Millicent spoke of did indeed cause misery. The fierce wind uprooted three trees and broke limbs on every other tree on the Hawkins' place. Large hail pounded the crops.

Several people were killed and homes blew away.

Andrew helped prepare a wagon to take clothes and supplies to the nearby community of Bono. Some people had only the clothes on their backs when they escaped the storm. Permelia added some goods to what others helped provide. The severity of the storm left some citizens, including the Hawkinses with no serious damage, yet on the fringes of destruction.

According to the *Cleburne Times Review*, the same cyclone mentioned in the letters and as remembered by Louisa, roared down the valley along Robinson Branch on May 4, 1890. It destroyed a number of homes. Members of the Griffin and Gordon families were killed. The storm in Bono pulled eighteen-month-old Isom G. Kennon from the arms of his father, Walter Kennon. He was later found seriously injured, having suffered a skull fracture.

~~~

From Millicent Hawkins:

Poplar Plains, Kentucky
May 25, 1890

Dear Katie,

I will write some to you now in the same letter as I just wrote to mother. I hope you will have a nice time whatever you are doing today. It is so rainy here. I want to go out to Bald Hill this evening to see Ban and Walt if it stops raining. Kate, Ma has planted all the flower seeds but it is so late that I don't expect they will do any good this spring. I wish you all could go up to Grayson County. Wouldn't it be better up there?

Kate, I am much obliged to you for Mr. Gordon. Give him to someone else though. I know you and mama will find a nice fellow that has no bad habits. I wish I was there today. The children want to see you and they will write to you again in my next letter. If you or any of you go to Kimbell, ask if there is a man by the name of Lee Coffman there anywhere. Write and tell me and I will tell you about it. I will close hoping to hear from you soon. Write as soon as you get this. When you write about Mr. Coffman, I will tell you all about why I want to know.

You and your sisters be good girls and don't marry, but have all the fun you can first.

Millicent Hawkins

From E.W. Cassity:

Blair Mills, Kentucky
June 11, 1890

My dear Permelia and Jack:

I hope these few lines will come on hand and that you and your family are well. I would have written to you sooner but I have not been well for some time. I am in very poor health and have been most of this year, but I am better at this writing than in several weeks.

The last letter I got from Anna in California, she had been sick but she is about well now. I got a letter from Clark last week and he and his wife are quite well. He was working at two dollars and twenty-five cents a day. You wanted to know how he comes to be in Clay City. He went out there last March a year ago and has been there ever since. He married out there and I have not seen his wife. I am going to see them before a great while, for I want to see him so bad.

Ella is well at this time and hasn't had any cramping spells for a long time. If she will take care of herself and not do too much hard work I believe she will get well of them.

Permelia, I am working for a pension from the War and am about through with it. If I have good luck with it I will not have to work so hard in my old days. Permelia, I have not thought of marrying any more and if I keep in the notion I am now I never will. I think that I will never see another woman that would suit me as well as your dear sister Elizabeth did.

I now come to a close by saying may God bless us all and bring us safely home where we will meet our dear ones who have gone before us. That is the prayer of your brother, E. W. Cassity.

> Write to me soon.
> Direct to Blair Mills, Kentucky
> E. W. Cassity

~~~

From E. W. Cassity:

> Yokum, Kentucky
> August 8, 1890

My dear Permelia and Jack,

I hope the lines that I am sending to you will reach you well at this time. I have not too much of interest to write to you except to say that I would like to see you all before a long while. My pension application is just about complete and just as soon as I can get it, I am coming to Texas if God spares my life that long. I will bring Clark with me if he will come and I think I can get him to.

Ella is coming right away. She will start next Wednesday and she wants some of you to meet her at Fort Worth and help her on. I pray God to protect her and bring her safe to her journey's end. I will come just as soon as I can get my business closed up. And then I am going to California to see Anna, for the darling little thing writes to me regularly and you don't know how bad I want to see her.

I will bring my letters to a close by saying may God bless us all and bring us safely home to that blissful abode beyond the Jordan of death, where parting will be no more. That is the prayer of E. W. Cassity.

To Permelia F. Hawkins and brothers and families

~~~

September, 1890

Dim and John Robert rode to Fort Worth to meet Ella. "Dim" became a nickname for Jim Nickell, because Louisa couldn't say Jim when she was a little girl.

Dim and Sally Nickell had agreed for Ella to make her home with them. Dim waited for his sister and nieces to finish talking. After so long a time, he said he would come back in two days after they were talked out. Ella told Permelia she had left the man named Lewis before coming to Texas, as he was not good to her. Dim drove the buggy back in two days as he promised.

Ella Page had not seen her Aunt Permelia since she was a child. Permelia was out tending Sassy, the goat, when the buggy arrived. Sassy would soon become a mama, as Louisa announced to everyone who would listen.

Later on, Andrew chuckled about Sassy and told the story on his grandfather, Alexander Hawes. It was a story many folks would keep quiet, and Louisa had never heard it before. Andrew liked the way his grandpa got out of such a "peck of trouble."

When his grandpa Alexander was about seventeen, he and his cousin Isaac stole a lamb from a family named Noel. According to Andrew's mother, Judah, her papa created quite a sensation. He received a severe sentence for the crime. He and Isaac were going to be put in prison. Many family friends used their influence to get a petition together to present to the governor of Virginia.

These friends must have flowered their petition, saying that had it not been for the bad company the boys had fallen into, they would never have considered stealing a lamb. They didn't have to go to prison, but did receive a stiff talking to.

Alexander died of cholera in 1833. Entire families were wiped out during the Fleming County, Kentucky epidemic. Andrew was only four years old at the time. His grandmother, Lucy Fowke Hawes, managed to escape the disease but died four years later. No cholera had been in Somervell County for years, but other illnesses took its place: maladies from colic, ague, croup, and catarrh to consumption.

When the Hawkinses first came to Somervell County, the *Cleburne Bulletin* carried a memorable story. A handsome fair-skinned young man with beautiful clear eyes took ill with fever and chills. He and his young lady had already set their wedding date. He was struck down with smallpox and quarantined to the Pest House.

Louisa remembered the story well. The young man survived this dreadful disease that some considered a miracle. In a number of weeks his faithful young sweetheart could be seen guiding him as they walked— his fair skin fully scarred and his clear eyes blind. The young man called his sweetheart his "morning star of memory."

CHAPTER 6

Aunt Charlotte's will – Permelia's inheritance – Quill pens – A preacher's letter – John Robert marries – Ban and Walt write their grandparents – Millicent still needs a correspondent – A wet season in Kentucky

~~~

From Robert Isaac:

Morehead, Kentucky
September 1, 1890

My dear sister, brother, nephew, and nieces,

With pleasure I once more seat myself to drop you a few lines to inform you of how we are getting along. Everyone is well except myself and I have been laid up a day or two.

Isabel and little Della have gone up the creek for a visit. They will be back tomorrow.

I shall try to go to Sunday School at 3:00 this afternoon at Siloam, as I am one of the teachers. Brother Greenup was up Friday and stayed until last night. He said all was well except David Henry Grayson. Greenup is going to send Jessie over to go to school with Della.

Della went one day to Siloam.

It has rained all day and my, don't even talk about it. I never did see of so much in the whole world. It's like it has rained for two years. I never saw as hard rains as fell from the heavens through August, and the keenest lightning and the heaviest thunder. Oh my, you should have seen it all.

We elected mostly Republicans for officers in Rowan in August. George Johnson was not. Joseph Myers was up at Morehead about the first of August. He left word for me to come down, that Aunt Charlotte Atchison had died and had willed me something. After the election I thought I would go and see. I said that a dollar would beat nothing. Her will covered thirty-two people, so a hundred dollars was the least and a thousand dollars about the largest.

I say Aunt Charlotte did just right. She gave to whomever she wanted to have her money. Newton K. Nickell got nothing. Cousins Jess Pearce and David Evans got nothing. There's no telling about breaking the will since it has been made for two years. I am afraid of Ed Anderson if it could be done. For if it is Ed's boy gets all. Now you can see do you not? She said that Newton was young and not settled anywhere and able to work.

My opinion is that we ought never to allow anyone to transact our business for us (I'm speaking generally) without our closest attention, before our business gets from under our thumb. Now you surely know what I mean. No one does much for Bob Nickell as long as he can make it out himself. Am I not right sister?

Aunt Charlotte gave away about five thousand dollars before she died but aimed to give Mother's heirs and Aunt Martha's heirs and so on, fifty dollars among themselves. Greenup got only twenty dollars I think, but I may be wrong about that. Aunt Harriett gave her to understand that her children was as near to her as the Nickell children, and that drew her attention to what she was doing and she stopped paying so much to the head. Now then you have waited a long time to hear what she willed us, haven't you?

Well now sit still and listen. She willed Robert Isaac Nickell one hundred dollars, Greenup Benjamin, one hundred dollars, Jerry a hundred dollars, James W. a hundred dollars, and for the life of me I can't say whether you were in the will or now. I rather think so for Joseph Myers said that he knew all of the folks in Texas would be very proud of their money.

Wait, I am not done. Be still. There is four thousand more to be divided proratio between the thirty-two people, which will make those that got thousand dollars about 1.13 and those that got a hundred dollars, get one hundred-fifty to one seventy-five. It will be about one hundred and fifty anyway. Now go ahead with your noise if you want to. This will not be paid before next May or June at the nearest. I believe that Joseph will do right. He said for all of you to write to him and keep him posted as to where you are, and I encouraged him and told him to do just as Aunt Charlotte wanted him to do, no more or no less.

Say, my letter is getting too long. Well I can't get enough letters around here anyway and I don't ever hear from Newton.

Ella Page has started to Texas I heard. If she gets around you and I doubt if she does, tell her howdy for us. Why I say that I doubt if she does, is that she never comes nearer than the depot. They are stranged turned children some way. I can say they don't take it after their mother for there was never a more loving woman in the world than Elizabeth, for her connection. I do not know where to lay the blame but nevertheless it's true. Maybe I'm not being fair since I don't see them too much.

I could write a great deal more but this will have to do. I want you to write as soon as you can and tell me about your crops this year. Are they better than last? Our love and prayers to you all.

Goodbye
Robert I. Nickell

~~~

From Joseph Myers:

Wyoming, Kentucky
September 17, 1890

Dear cousins, one and all,

I received your letter today and was glad to hear from you all and to hear that you were well, although I am sorry to hear that Jack is not in the best of health. I have been very sick myself for about five weeks, but I am better now. I am able to go about but not able to do anything much. I am so nervous that I won't do any good writing, so you must excuse it.

There is a good deal of sickness and a good many deaths. Charlotte Johnson died a short time ago and I will not mention all the other deaths, because you would not know them. Aunt Charlotte Atchison died July fifteenth. She died with a heart and kidney disease, and she suffered a good deal before she died.

Aunt made a will and she willed all three of you one hundred dollars each. She left me in her will to wind up her estate, but I cannot until after March, as some of her notes are not due until then. Just as soon as I can I will settle it up, so you need not be uneasy about it. I will settle it as soon as I can.

I would like to see you all so well. James, are there any black stumps out there? I would rather be with you all than with anybody else, for a week. I will close and let Mary finish it. I want you to write soon.

Joseph Myers

Dear all,

I will tell you about my children. I have four girls. One married Mr. Isaac Conyer's son. The other two are young women nearly, one fourteen and the other is twelve. The baby is sixteen months old. Then there are two boys, one

married. He married two weeks ago to Hiram Jones'
daughter. They are going to start to Illinois Thursday.

Cousin, I would love to see you all so well, so write soon
even if I can't see you. Corn crops are not very good and no
peaches. We have no fruit of any kind this year. How do you
like Texas? Please forgive my pen. It has written its last and
needs replacing.

Mary D. Myers

~~~

Aunt Charlotte Atchison left money and personal
effects to over thirty-five people—mostly family.[1] Every
penny of Permelia's inheritance could be put to good
use.

As for Mary Myers' pen, Permelia could have easily
made her a new quill. Her papa taught her how and she
in turn showed her children. The method handed down
by the Nickells was simple, provided a goose or turkey
was nearby.

First, the feather tip needed to be boiled for good
cleaning. After dry, the tip should be slit from the tip for
about an inch. Cut off the top part then scrape out the
insides and leave a neat little hollow. Slice the end with
a sharp knife, making a tip that is then slit to hold the
ink. The width of the slice determined how broad the
flow of ink. Permelia made a good pen the first try, but
Louisa made only one in six good enough to use. She
decided making quills was like rooting flowers. Some
succeeded and some didn't.

~~~

From Preacher G. W. Thompson:

Verona, Collin Co. Tex.
October 10, 1890

To Mrs. Hawkins
Dear Sister Hawkins and family,

After some delay I embrace the present opportunity of writing to you. The last letter you sent me said that Brother Hawkins was not well. I hope you are both well by now. I expect that you would write often during his sickness and tell us how he gets along.

Sister Hawkins, I am going to leave here and I would like to get a letter from you all and tell me if I could get a place, and if there is any corn raised there or not. How much could you do for me to preach for you? Next year the brothers in Jack County are wanting me to come out there and work for them. I may go but I would like to hear from you first. At best I have made but little crops and if the brothers want me to preach for them and will help me through next year I would like to do it.

Tell me where Brother Cauble is and tell him I have written often to him and never get an answer. Where is Brother Nash staying? How I will be proud to hear from you all.

I learned Brother Sims has been baptized again. I got a letter from J. D. Dossey a few days ago and he says he is coming to Texas in three months. They are all well. His office is in Briscoe, Alabama. Write to him at once. I have been instrumental in the hands of our good Lord, of persuading about ninety persons to be obedient to the faith.

I don't know how I could come to your house again and not see Brother Willie. Oh, how lonesome you must be without him. Tell the girls and Jerry to each write to me, telling me if they still live Christian like and that they are Christian. If not, when do they think that they will be obedient to the faith? Where is Brother Phillips? And tell Brother Sam Cheek that I asked about him. Don't let Jerry's and James' families forget me.

Love to all. I'm not very well right now as I stay chilling some, now and then. Let me know if I could stay with you one year.

G. W. Thompson

~~~

Brother Thompson lived in George's Creek at one time and had been a neighbor. He would require a room to himself and the Hawkins' house was crowded enough. Permelia's parents had a preacher stay with them once back in Fleming County, Kentucky. "We children had to tow the line, now didn't we?" Louisa commented.

Since no shortage of preachers existed in the area at this time, Brother Thompson did not come to George's Creek after all.

Singings were held at the churches and at the school, and then sometimes in yards of the homes, if weather permitted. On occasions, baptisms were held at George's Creek, and frequently at Berry Falls. People crowded the banks of the creek while a long line of men and women stood in the cold water, waiting their turns to be baptized. The preacher in suit and tie stood over waist-high in the water.[2]

There was little enough of a social nature available to the young people, so some "suffered" through the preaching in order to be welcomed to the socials. Since their folks did not deny the pleasures of social function of the church, suppers and singings were attended by all.

~~~

From Mrs. S. E. Godfrey:

Society Hill, Alabama
November 15, 1890

Mrs. Permelia Hawkins
George's Creek
Somervell Co. Texas
My dear friend,

I received your kind and welcomed letter last night, and was glad to hear from you although it grieves my heart to hear the sad sad epistle you were obliged to relate about my dear daughter.

I can only write a few lines to let you know that I am more than a thousand times grateful to you for your kind attention to her through her sickness. I know it will be impossible for me ever to return the favor in any way, but I hope God will bless you and yours for the kindness that you bestowed upon Della when she was in need of the best of friends.

I hope you will go to see the children as often as is convenient and assist dear little Birdie all you can by giving her good advice. Give my love to Frank and dear Birdie and Brady.

This leaves all well as could be expected under such sad afflictions. May the good Lord help us to bear them as is best for us.

I will close by saying, write to your sincere friend.

L. M. Godfrey

This is written by request of my mother-in-law, as she is almost unable to write herself. Please tell Gussie and Frank to write to Willie and myself. Tell Birdie to write to the children.

Very respectfully,
Mrs. S. E. Godfrey

~~~

As Mrs. Godfrey's letter indicated, Permelia did what she could for Mrs. Godfrey's daughter. During those times, a person could die of what the doctors called "the fever," when in reality, a severe infection might be involved. People who died of "stomach trouble," could have had undiagnosed cancer or a ruptured appendix.

By law, Texas required death certificates in 1903. Prior to that time, many causes of death were unknown unless families wrote it in the family Bible or kept records. Only occasionally did an obituary notice give reason for death. The 1903 requirement did not guarantee a record's being filed, since deaths often occurred in the country where doctors were not always available to record them.

~~~

From Permelia's grandsons, O'Banion and Walter:

Poplar Plains, Ky.
December 28, 1890

Dear ma   I will write you a few lines this Sabath day.   I hope this will find you all well we have all had bad colds. girls I wish you were all her to see the big snow   our school was out last Wednesday   we all had a nice treat   I wish I was there today.   I think you might send me a nice Christmas gift   Ma, don't you want Walt and I to come out there and live with you   I hope I will soon be big enough to help mama   I will close to let mama and Walt write some now.

O'banion Hawkins

I wrote this ma
ma our school is out   this is a bad day   I wish I was with you today I would love to see you all   I will close

Walter Hawkins

From Millicent:

Well Ma, as the boys have written they want me to write some now. This is a bad day with snow and ice. Weddings and sickness and death is the order of the day. Ban and Walt are skating on the pond now. Russ is sitting before the fire. Pa is nearly down with a cold. Cora is married. She got a good home and man. Also Minor says he wants a good Texas girl. I hope this finds you all well.

Kate, I have been looking for a letter from you but haven't gotten a line. I hope you will have a merry Christmas. I never get a thing, but the children got their treat at school. Russ says he wishes Ma would send him a Christmas gift. They all talk about you all and say they would love to go to Texas. I think some time I will send Ban and Walter there, and I could send them but I'm afraid they would never get there by themselves. Ban is up to my chin now, Kate.

I still wish you could send me a correspondent from Texas. I would be very much obliged to you if you will. I still want to make Texas my future home. Pa isn't any count the last two years. He is poorly all the time. The doctors say that he can never get well, and ma says she won't ever go to Texas. This has been such a sad winter for me.

We had a meeting at the church. It lasted about a week while I was gone. Cora joined and was baptized. He was a Christian preacher.

I must tell you what Ban said. He said that if ma doesn't write, he will never write to her anymore. Kate, Cora, Lizzie, and Lou, be good girls and marry good boys and have a home of your own. Well I will close, hoping to hear from you all soon.

Goodbye to one and all. Write soon.

Millicent Hawkins and family

~~~

Louisa and her sisters had sent hard Christmas candies with their mother's gifts of shirts to the boys. The package was mailed in time to arrive for Christmas. Mail to and from Kentucky took three or four days, so they feared something had happened to their package. It turned out the response was delayed, not the package.

January 3, 1891

John Robert married his young lady, Maggie Scarbro. John had his own responsibilities, since he had a wife and a small farm to look after. Andrew would have to manage without him, but John promised his papa that he would help him as much as he could. Andrew had enough money to hire hands during harvest time, and the girls still helped pick cotton and corn.

Andrew dug a fruit cellar years before, and Permelia put up fruits, vegetables, both regular and pickled. Some winters were so cold she was afraid the jars would freeze and burst. She covered them with old quilts and even covered the cellar door, to keep the cold air from seeping through the cracks. She placed stones on the cover to keep it from blowing off. Andrew dug the cellar next to the house on the west side so the sun would remain on it longer.

Louisa didn't care too much for going into the hole in the ground since slithery snails were in abundance in the moist soil. She disliked slugs more than a possible storm that caused them to go into the cellar in the first place.

When Permelia was a girl, they buried cabbages and apples and such. The food was buried close to a tree to mark its location. Otherwise they would be digging all over the snow. But at least they could have a good cabbage when they wanted it.

~~~

From E. W. Cassity:

Morgan Co. Kentucky
February 15, 1891

Dear James and Sally and family,

I seat myself to pen you a few lines to let you know that I am in tolable good health at this time, and hoping they will find you and family all well. At present, I am still working for my pension and hope that I will be able to come see you.

I have been working on it for three years now and I have my testimony complete, so there is nothing wanting now except to get an offer before an examining board. Then an allowance can be made for me. My attorney wrote to me a few days ago that he thought he would get an order for me soon, and just as soon as I get that, I will be coming there.

James, I want you to take care of Ella and I will see that you do not lose anything, for she is not the only girl who did a wrong. If she was, then I might throw her away. You don't know how it hurt me when I asked her if such was so, but thanks be to God she would not lie to me. She said. "Pa, I cannot lay it to your counsel, for you always gave me good advice," and she will tell you the same, but say she, "I am done."

I got a letter from Clark the other day. It was written February fifth. He is at work in Cumberland Gap. He is getting two dollars and fifty cents per day and his PO address is Middles Borrough, Bell Co, Ky. His wife is at Clay City right now. He says they will move out there in the spring.

Give my respects to the children and all the kin. I will come to a close, hoping to hear from you soon.

E. W. Cassity to James William Nickell

~~~

From Andrew's niece, Addie Lame:

Morehead, Kentucky
February 17, 1891

Dear Aunt Permelia and Uncle Jack,

It is with pleasure that I try to write you a few lines this beautiful night, as I have just returned from church. I hope you are enjoying the same good health as we are.

What has become of Ella Page? Is she with you yet? Please tell her that I saw a man who knows her brother Clark, and he said that he had seen him recently. He was working every day and getting along so nicely. Do you ever hear from Anna Page?

I went to church tonight and we heard a Englishman preach. His wife was also a preacher and I would rather listen to her than to him.

I suppose you heard that Liza Cogswell had a nice boy. I haven't seen him yet but I hear that he is real pretty.

Aunt Lucy Anne Phelps is over at her son John's. I haven't seen her in a long time, although I heard from her the other day. She was enjoying good health. My sister Emma has moved up to West Liberty, about twenty-six miles away. It's been about five months since we've seen her. I want to see her so bad but it is so far and we can't all leave home at once.

Freddie Powers has gone to Elfin, Illinois to school in order to learn how to be a jewelry smith. He was already tolable good at that kind of work when he left here. There is a new building going up in town. It is a furniture store.

Papa is going to work at a rock mill this side of Rockville. There is a large rock quarry there and he will board at Lizzie's. All of Aunt Margaret's family was well when I last saw them. I saw Mr. Bob Nickell too. Well, it is getting late and I will close.

Write soon,
from Addie Lame

P.S.—Tell all the girls to write to me and tell me all the news. Direct your letter to Morehead, Rowan Co, Kentucky.

<div align="center">~~~</div>

From Ella Goodnow:

Esparto, California
March 2, 1891

Dear Cousins one and all,

I will try to write a few lines to you to say that we are well and we hope you are the same. Now cousin Permelia you dear ol' soul, what are you doing this winter to pass away the hours? We have been housed up for about three weeks with rain and everything still looks all right. Our grain looks fine and our garden looks finer, but we don't want to get washed away. At least it isn't a heavy rain. When Anna and I get hungry we go and get a pan of lettuce and radishes and we just eat until we can't swallow any more. Wish you were here to help us eat it.

Cousin Permelia, I was afraid it was going to be a dry year but the ground is wet enough for now. Have you any rain yet? We have quite a number of young chickens. I have about a hundred and fifty old hens or more and will sell about four dozen as soon as the mud dries up. Then we can take them to town. We milk one cow and will not have a fresh one until May. Oh yes, I have a pair of canary birds. The hen is setting on four little blue eggs. They are as nice as can be. Have you any? They are so much company when they sing. The male does not sing now that the female is setting.

The wind is in the south and I do believe it will rain again. I wish it wouldn't any more for a month, but God knows best. Mr. Goodnow is up in the canyon trimming our orchard vineyard.

Newton has gone to Esparto to get me some chicken feed or he will as soon as I finish this and then mail it for me. We got a letter from cousin Robert Isaac and he sent the sad news that Isabel had a cancer on her face. Oh how sad that is. I pray that she will be all right.

He also said that Charlotte Atchison is dead. She made a will, but I think she might have willed Newton something as well as the rest. But the money was hers and she could do with it what she pleased.

Now what are the girls doing? Are they all at home? Tell them to write to Pearl and Daisy for they will be so pleased to hear from them. How are John and his wife Maggie? Where do they live? And how is Jack's health? Just tell us everything you know. We send all our love to James and Sally and family.

Pa and Ma are not well, and ma came near to dying with the fever this year. Pa's health is not good at all. I have not seen them for three months but will go as soon as the mud dries up. Now goodbye to all. Write a scratch soon.

From Ella Goodnow to all.

~ ~ ~

From Anna Page:

Capay, California
March 4, 1891

Dear Uncle Jack, Aunt Permelia, and cousins,

I will write you lines to let you know that I am well. How are you getting along? We are having a fine rain but cousin Ella and Uncle John are ready for it to quit now. It is nice and warm to go along with it. Cousin Lena, Ella's daughter, has a little baby girl but I haven't seen it yet.

Katie, when are you going to get married? You really must wait until I do so we can be married together. Do you go to school any now or are you finished? I still do not go at all. The other children do go.

Mr. Goodnow is coming in the gate now. He has just come back from the canyon.

Now tell me who did your brother John Robert marry? Did he marry that girl he had his picture taken with? Wasn't her name Maggie Scarbro? Is that the way you spell it? Tell him and his wife I wish them much joy. What do Uncle Dim's boys and girls do now? Surely some of them are married by now.

Well I must close for this time, as this is the fifth letter I have written today and I plan for all of them to be answered.

Yours with love.
Anna Page

~~~

Cousin Ella's and Anna's letters were always newsy. Permelia decided to get two canaries, one named Petie and a female they called Precious. Everyone stayed on guard concerning the cats, even though they remained outside most of the time. In winter the cats slept in the barn, or in exceptional weather, they stayed inside by the fireplace.

Robert had not mentioned in his letters that Isabel had cancer. In Permelia's listing of diseases and cures, cancer was not among them. In general, people knew little about the disease. Permelia served as her own family doctor whenever possible, knowing what to do for fevers, dyspepsia, neuralgia, and even horses' blind staggers.

~~~

From E. W. Cassity:

Yocum Co. Kentucky
March 17, 1891

Dear Permelia, Jack, and family,

I take the present opportunity of writing to you to let you know that I am well at present, and hoping that you share the same blessing.

I received your letter telling of John Robert and Maggie getting married. I wish them well and would that I could have come to Texas to see them. Please give them my prayer for all best wishes and their happiness.

Times are pretty hard here. Corn is worth seventy-five cents to a dollar a bushel and hard to get at that. Oats can't be had at any price. Irish potatoes run from a dollar fifty to two dollar a bushel and meat can be got at from six and a quarter to eight and a third per.

We have had the most rain this winter and spring that I ever did see. Permelia, you talk about having your garden made and corn planted out there. That beats this country, and if I am ever permitted to get my pension, I am coming. For it is true that I am tired of this place as ever you saw in your life. Without Anna and Clark and now Ella, it is lonesome. It doesn't matter if I stay busy or not, they all made your sister seem close by. Now that all three of them are gone from here it is lonesome certain. But I know that their lives must go on their way and I cannot begrudge them of that.

Tell brother Jack to raise a good crop so that he will have something to sell me when I come. I know that you think the time will never come but I certain and sure plan for it to be.

Give my respects to James and Jerry and families. I will conclude by saying for you to write soon. Direct to Blair Mills.

I remain E. W. Cassity

To Permelia F. Hawkins

Permelia, I will write a personal note to you. Sister, I will say that Ella went into the Lewis family against my will and she will tell you the same. I always told her that fellow was no account and she has found that out. So I will never call her by that name of Lewis.

Affectionately,
E. W. Cassity

CHAPTER 7

Quilting Memories – Money for Permelia – Millicent marries her Texas correspondent, sight unseen – Wedding bells for Anna Kate and Jim Shults

~~~

April 12, 1891

If there were clues, Permelia didn't pick up on them. One evening Anna Kate came rushing inside to help put supper on the table. She scarcely waited for her papa to ask the Lord's blessing. Louisa recalled Permelia's putting her hand on Anna Kate's arm, keeping her from another quick bite of food. When her papa tried to slow her down, she kept right on going.

Since Anna was the more reserved sister, her attitude surprised her parents. Louisa giggled and nudged Lizzie under the table. Lizzie turned to Cora and rolled her eyes upward. All the girls knew what was going on, but their parents had no hint.

Louisa broke the news in a sing-song voice, "Katie's got a beau—Papa ought to know."

Anna Kate glared and told her to mind her own business. Permelia knew of the singing that night at the schoolhouse, but she didn't know Anna Kate had plans for her new friend, Jim Shults, to fetch her in his buggy and they would go to the schoolhouse together.

After a lengthy discussion, Andrew gave his permission for his daughter's plans to proceed. This was not the norm for papas of George's Creek. He remembered conversing with Jim Shults about a month before at the Meyer's picnic. If the truth were known,

Jim probably set up the conversation on purpose after taking an interest in Anna Kate.

Jim and his brother, George Franklin, were born in Washington County, Arkansas and lived in Missouri before they moved to Texas. By this time, Anna Kate was a grown-up nineteen-year-old and surely had romance in her thoughts.

~~~

From Addie Lame:

Morehead, Kentucky
March 24, 1891

Mrs. Permelia F. Hawkins
Dear Aunt,

It is with the greatest of pleasure that I try to answer your most welcome letter which I received some time ago. You must excuse me for not writing sooner for I have been busy cleaning the yard. Uncle Walter and wife are here. They have been here since Thursday and this is Tuesday night.

Uncle Wat is blind and he can't help himself a bit. He lays in the bed all of the time. Ma says he looks so much like Grandpa Hawkins she thinks about him every time she looks at him. They are moving back to the old place. They moved up in the upper edge of Rowan County three years ago and just now are going back.

We haven't made any garden yet. It is too wet to plow it, but papa has been working at the garden today. Our apple trees are leafing out and I am afraid they will bloom out and all the fruits will get killed again this year.

You asked me if I had seen the girls' pictures and I haven't seen them yet. I wish they would all send me a picture. Anna Kate, do you have a young man?

Ma is quilting a quilt for Aunt Margaret. I piece the quilt and mama quilts them. This one is going to be oh so pretty.

She will like it I know. I was up at Aunt Margaret's when I got
the letter from you and she said for me to come in her room
and read it to her. She was so glad to hear from you. We are
glad to hear that your girls are so good and kind to you. That
is what all girls ought to be.

I am sorry to tell you that we haven't got any Morehead
paper. The man that printed the paper has left.

Aunt Permelia, write a letter to Aunt Margaret. She
would be happy to have one from you. Sister Emma's health
is bad yet, and she is still up at West Liberty. I think I will go
up there next month if I can get off. Mama can hardly do
without me.

We have had another death in town. Mr. Williams died,
but poor old fellow is better off. His son would just curse his
father something awful and would whip on him and beat him
and say he wished he was dead. We were all so concerned
for him for we always heard what was being done but there
was nothing we could do. Papa talked to him and told him it
was wrong, but he said it was nobody's business. Bless the
poor old man but he is at peace now.

Papa hurt his back today, working in the garden wheeling
dirt. There was a baptizing Sunday evening at three o'clock
and a funeral at night and I went to all of them. Well, I will
close now. Write soon. Tell all the girls to write to me.

> Goodby to all.
> Addie Lame

~~~

From Lewis R. Lame:

Morehead, Kentucky
March 24, 1891

Dear brother and sister Hawkins,

As daughter Addie was writing and her mama insisting that I should write in her letter, I therefore wish to say that I have not forgot you and yours.

I was glad to hear from you about your welfare, although we often think of former days and associates with their places, alas, now vacated and filled by another generation. We now see strangers every day. Society is not what it used to be. Strangers and foreigners and business transactions have changed the Social and Moral development of former times.

The very face of nature here would doubtless look strange to you. The railways up the Triplet Valley, with the timber take from the hills. Many old farms are grown up in bushes, with new ones cleared out. Old houses are gone and new ones are being built.

I will close with this and will endeavor to write you another letter one day.

Lewis R. Lame

~~~

Addie referred to Andrew's papa, William R, when she said her Uncle Wat looked so much like grandpa. William and Wat were brothers.

Lewis Lame seemed to have a way with words, but that may have been the preacher in him. At least he had a vocabulary. Many preachers of the time were eloquent in their delivery. It was also not infrequent that "fire and brimstone" preachin' could be heard across the acres the church stood on.

Lewis was also a Mason, and important in the organization. Isaac E. Phelps, husband of Andrew's sister Lucy Anne, was Grand Master of Phelps Lodge No. 482 in Farmers, Kentucky, outside of Morehead. In 1869, they held meetings in the Phelps' home. Later when the membership grew, they moved the meetings to the Rowan County Courthouse.[1] The courthouse had been rebuilt after guerillas entered the town of Morehead the second time, March 21, 1863, burning it to the ground.[2]

~~~

From Millicent Hawkins:

Poplar Plains, Kentucky
March the 30, 1891

Dear Mother and family,

I will write you a few lines this day. This leaves all well but pa and he is never well. I hope you are all well. I am now at Acles Hawkins.[3] His wife has had fever but she is better now. Acles says he hopes how well you may be. Pa has rented a house at the Plains, but they do not like to live there. I went home yesterday for a few minutes.

Ban has his letter written and I helped Walt write his. They are so sweet. I had to have Russ at home.

It has been raining all day. It rains every day and Saturday and Sunday for a variety. They have been holding a holy meeting this Sunday. There is a Mr. Harmon living on pa's old place. Jennie has two children and they are looking for the baby to die. Sam still isn't stout and I don't think he will be here for long.

Did I understand that you bought another place, ma? Let me know where it is, so I can tell where it is on the land I know about. I would love to see you all.

Mr. Johnson sent me a correspondent. He must be ever so nice the way he writes. I want to do the best I can so I can get someone that will be good to the children. You know that I would die for them too. Poor people pay all they make here for rent.

I want you to write again soon and tell me all about Mr. Megason. Who does he look like? Are his children boys or girls? He writes like he is a Christian hearted man. Don't let him know I wrote you anything about him, but keep it to yourself and family. I know that it is to your interest as well as mine, if he is worthy of helping me take care of my babes. I want you to do all you can for me. If you only knew the way I have to live and the way I have to be treated on account of the children. You surely would do all you could for us.

Will you tend your own land this year? I will now write Kate a few lines.

Millicent Hawkins

<div align="center">~~~</div>

From Millicent Hawkins:

Poplar Plains, Kentucky
March 30, 1891

Dear Kate,

Well, Kate, have you forsaken us? You don't say a word. I hope you haven't given in to marrying and forgotten me and my babes. They talk about you all. Russ says he wants to see Aunt Kate, and he is going to live in Denison.

Write soon. Kate, tell me all you know about that Mr. Megason. I wrote to him and hope he will write again. I will have to close. I am sleepy. It is nine o'clock. Goodbye to all. I will write more next time. Give Cora this message . . . Remember me is my best wishes when in the kitchen washing dishes. Good night now.

Your sister,
Millicent Hawkins

Dear Aunt Kate,

I will write you a few lines   wee are all well as common
I hope you are all well   I wish I could see you all today   girls
grandpapa has moved to Poplar Plains but we don't like to
live here   kate I wish I was out there to raise cotton and to
make money   mama don't stay home much now   it just
rains all the time   nothing is going on here   ma I miss my
dear papa so much ma what are Clarence and Lawrence
doing?   ma I wish I could get away from here they are
always fussing because we are here   mama don't see any
peace atall   I will close hoping to hear from you soon.

goodbye to one and all
O'banion Hawkins

Maw I will write some too   I am sleepy so I will close

Walt Hawkins

Dear Mother,

Walt says he wants me to finish. He says he is tired of the
mud. He wants to see you all so bad. I have come home this
evening for a little while, but I have to go back. Lou, Lizzie,
Walt says he wishes he was there to help you raise cotton.

Love to all,
Millicent

~~~

If Andrew and Permelia ever considered moving,
they only discussed it. They were rarely taxed more than
three dollars and usually less. Their total taxes on real
estate and personal property for 1891 were $2.74.

None of the sisters had sent Alfred Megason's name
to Millicent, but Cora mentioned her to Mr. Johnson.
He apparently gave the information to Alfred and he
wrote the first letter to Millicent. They corresponded for

a few weeks. If anything came out of this "meeting by letters," it fell into the category of a mail order bride, unless Mr. Megaon went out to Poplar Plains to meet Millicent first.

April, 1891

Andrew and Permelia were grandparents to John and Maggie's first child, born on April 4th. Permelia went to help the new mother, staying only two or three days. Maggie wanted to name the baby Myrtle Vera if it was a girl and if a boy, they had not decided. That choice wasn't necessary, for Myrtle Vera she was.

After everyone became healthy and about, Permelia returned home to find Andrew suffering from a fall. Lou and Lizzie took the buggy to Bono to get their Uncle Jerry and Aunt Belle. They thought he had a form of neuralgia, although Andrew had not been feeling well for a few weeks. He assured them that he was fine and not to go for a doctor.

Andrew told the girls he had tripped on a log in the garden, but his explanation didn't seem satisfactory. Permelia suspicioned he had a dizzy spell, which he had experienced once earlier. Louisa recalled that her papa never liked to be fussed over, and she went to sleep that night with worry on her mind.

~~~

From Millicent Hawkins:

Poplar Plains, Kentucky
May 1, 1891

Dear Anna Kate,
How are you this fine day? I feel better than in a long time.
Mr. Megason has written to me again, and I must say I like the sound of him. I will have to tell you what he said. He told me he was reasonably free of bad habits, and spends a

reasonable amount of his time in church. He said he had never written to a lady he didn't know before. And what he said was real funny. He also told me he asked what Daniel looked like. You must have told him Daniel was handsome. Then he said some folks say they don't fear his looks, so he guessed he was passable in that department.

He said he would be fixing up his home place this winter, and that it needed a new coat of paint and he would paint it. Do you have an idea of exactly where he lives? That's about all he said, but he writes back as soon as he gets one of my letters.

The boys say to tell you hello, so I am doing so. Please write as soon as you get this and tell me what you think. You know I loved your brother, but he would want me to do all I can to see his sons get cared for the best way possible.

Your sister,
Millicent Hawkins

~~~

</div>

From Joe Myers:

<div align="right">

Lovington, Ill.
June 12, 1891

</div>

Mrs. Permelia Hawkins
My dear cousin,

I read your letter yesterday and was glad to hear from you all and to hear you are all well. This leaves us all as well as common and hope it will find you all the same. We have very dry weather here and everything is backward. We should have been having some rainy weather.

Permelia, I don't know exactly how to advise you but it looks like you ought to have the right to do as you please with your own money. Jack ought not to say anything. There is no money in always moving about, and unless you come back to Kentucky you had just as well stay where you are.

From what I hear, things aren't that good back there. Personally, I would rather live in Kentucky than any place I have been, and if I can sell my land in Illinois I expect to go back there. But now you do as you please about that.

I don't know when I will get to settle Aunt Charlotte's will, as the suit for taxes is not yet settled. I got a letter from Kentucky a few days ago saying that several of the heirs had sold out their claims rather than to wait until the suit was settled. So as I promised you as I did with Jerry and James W. Nickell, I will give each of you one hundred and twenty-five dollars. You will need to sign the receipt I sent you and then send it back to me. I will send you each a draft for one hundred and twenty-five dollars. I may lose money by this but I said I would do it and I will yet. So if you can get Jack to sign the receipt by telling him anything, then you can do anything you want with the money, as it is yours and not Jack's. You understand what I mean.

Tell Jack you will go anywhere with him until you get him to sign the receipt, and when you get the money, do as you please with it if you want to buy more land there. You may think that's bad advice but a person has to do a good many ways to get along in this world, especially if other people think their choice is best.

I would not buy land that was no account, Permelia. It would be better to rent good land than to own poor land. But be your own judge and do what you think best, and you will. So I will close hoping to hear from you soon, or to see you. But you may conclude like me that Kentucky is the best and cheapest place to live and come back. Then I will come and see you all. So write soon. From your cousin.

Joe Myers

P.S.—Has your cousin Dave Evans been at your house? Let us know in your next letter.

~~~

From Joe Meyers:

Lovington, Ill.
June 22, 1891

Cousin Permelia Hawkins
Dear Permelia,
    I received your letter today. Was glad to hear from you but sorry to hear that Jack was sick. We are not well here. Mary and Connie are both sick. Mary is getting better but Connie is in bed. I hope this will find you all well. I have nothing new to write but it did finally rain yesterday.
    Permelia, you will find enclosed a draft for one hundred and twenty-five dollars. I hope it will come all right. You must write me as soon as you get it so that I will know you got the draft with no trouble. Give my love to all and don't fail to write as soon as you get this. Take the draft to the bank and they will give you the money on it.

From your cousin, Joseph Myers.
To George's Creek, Texas
Somervell County

~~~

Permelia received the $125 from Charlotte Atchison's will and deposited it in the Cleburne Bank. Andrew talked of returning to Kentucky. Perhaps the thought of being sixty-one caused him a homesick yearning. Permelia didn't discuss the use of the money with Andrew because she did not want it to go toward a journey home when they needed to put it to better use, as much as she would like to have made the trip. As cousin Joseph said, "the money is yours."[4]
    Anna Kate met Jim Shults in Texas, and as far as Anna was concerned, she wanted to stay in Texas. Her

sisters had many friends and John Robert had married a Texas girl. It would seem natural for them to stay where they were.

According to letters, both E. W. Cassity and Jess B. Johnson were not satisfied in Kentucky any longer. High prices were signs of the times everywhere. If Andrew and Permelia returned to Kentucky they would have to start all over again. Had it been put to a vote, Permelia would have the support of her children.

The Hawkins' farm gave them what they needed. Needs were surely more important than wants, but Permelia never forgot the latter for her family. Their productive farm remained at thirty acres. Cotton crops proved good each year. They raised a few hogs, and Andrew's Kentucky apples had long been replaced with peaches and plums. With the corn and vegetables Permelia put up for the winter they never found themselves lacking—they could offer company "any and all," a term of Robert Isaac's. The seasons were kind to them and Andrew saved to purchase a new Buford plow from H. S. Wilson in Cleburne.[5] It cost nine dollars and did a much better job than either of his other two plows, although they were still usable.

~~~

From Millicent Hawkins:

Poplar Plains, Kentucky
September 1, 1891

Dear Mother, Kate, and all,
I hope my letter finds you well.
My news is good as I want to tell you I am coming to Texas. Mr. Megason asked me to marry him. I am sure by his letters that he will be good to my children and to me. He writes a fine letter and I believe my decision to be right. My mother does not understand at all, my feelings. Mrs.

Hawkins you must surely understand for that is why you and
your husband came to Texas in the first place. Well, that is
my reason for coming now. For a better life.

Mr. Megason will come to meet us. We will be married
soon because there is no reason to wait. I feel our courting
was done through letters.

Please give my hello to Mr. Hawkins. I hope he is well.
Ban and Walt will not write this time but say they are so
anxious to see you. So is little Russ. I will close now.

Millicent Hawkins

~~~

Millicent and Alfred Megason, her correspondent of
five months, were married September 25, 1891 in
Johnson County. The arrangement for marriage was
made entirely by mail. Alfred did not go to Kentucky to
meet her. Marrying a stranger was apparently a
satisfying goal for Millicent. It looks to all as if her
problems were solved and she would have a comfortable
home with someone to provide for her and her children.

If Permelia put the past aside, which was probable,
hers and Andrew's relationship with Millicent would
bring only happiness for their grandsons. Ban was
eleven, Walt was nine, and little Russ, seven.

Their meeting was a reunion of embraces and some
tears. They sat and talked for a long time. Millicent
looked handsome in a deep green dress. She looked
prettier than Louisa remembered her from a few years
earlier.

Russ wanted to know how far Denison was. Louisa
wondered if he thought his papa was there waiting for
him since that is where he last saw him alive. The three
boys asked a hundred questions about Texas, scarcely
giving the girls any peace.

Finally Andrew left the reunion with his little grandsons and Mr. Megason. Louisa remembered the day as pleasant, even though the "air" between Millicent and Permelia seemed to be somewhat strained. She said her mama would "simply find the thread and keep rolling the spool," Permelia's long-time theory on sorting things out until a problem was solved.

~~~

From Mrs. Overton Maxey (Addie):

Morehead, Kentucky
October 14, 1891

Dear Aunt Permelia and Uncle Andy,

You haven't heard from me in a while so it is about time you did. Your niece is married now since September. I am now Mrs. Overton Maxey. We live in a nice little home.

Aunt, I have been sewing myself some new white window curtains. The cloth is pretty, and they fluff around when the breeze blows. You know how I like pretty things. You always wrote that a girl needs to know how to sew, and I've been piecing quilts since I was a little Addie. I have now almost finished quilting one myself. It's something I wanted to do without any help, but next time us ladies will make a group.

John Morton told me the next time I wrote, to tell you hello for him. Please write when you get this and tell me what you think about my happiness. Perhaps we could visit Texas one day but wish you could also come here too. Love to all.

Addie Lame
Mrs. Overton Maxey

~~~

Louisa had many memories of quilting stories to relate. When her mama was growing up they didn't keep the fire strong all night and it would be so cold they had the quilts stacked high on top of them. The children could have become lost so far under the covers. Permelia taught her girls to piece and even Louisa could do a "right smart" bit of work. Cora enjoyed quilting more than piecing.

Permelia learned how to sew at the age of five or six. Mostly they would "put up" quilts in the winter since there wasn't too much else to do. When they collected enough scraps, her mother would begin working a crazy quilt. It took almost as long to make a crazy quilt as it did a lovely patterned one, but they gave the same warmth, no matter the design. The stitches needed to be just as fine or a toe might get caught. Some people could be poor but rich with quilts. The expense was not great when people saved scraps and had their own cotton.

Quilts never wore out without being used for something else before they were discarded.

Once Permelia's mama cut up an old worn-out one to use for stuffing a new quilt. She found it difficult to get needles through such thick goods. It was the only time she ever used old raggedies for stuffing, but once she started she didn't want to stop. Woe be the one who had a dull needle, for it would always need sharpening with a file.

Andrew first put together a make-do quilting frame laid out on the backs of chairs or horses.[6] It slipped, the same as a similar one Permelia's papa had made. Andrew then constructed a hang-down frame from the ceiling. When Permelia brought it down, it was still too high for her, but lowering it made it too low for friends. The girls had to lean over as well. The Hawkins' daughters were all taller than their mother.

Once Permelia stuffed a quilt with wool. She and Andrew used it, having warmth without weight. They didn't have to pile the covers on, or "kivers," as some people called them. Permelia lined many of her quilts with flour sacks, but later on, she could afford regular cloth lining. Her favorite pattern was Rose of Sharon, but she had two Wedding Ring designs and a Tulip quilt. She made what she called an "apron," a loose-stitched strip about nine or ten inches wide across the top end. When that part soiled, she slipped out the loose row of thread, washed the apron and stitched it back.

Permelia invited ladies over for quilting bees, just as her mother did. The girls often joined in. Permelia helped Louisa and Lizzie work autograph quilts. Their friends signed their names on cloth and the sisters embroidered them, piecing flower squares around the names. The girls began quilts for their hope chests, with Anna Kate and Cora's first ones completed in time for their weddings.[7]

Along with the warmth of quilts, large slow-burning pine knots were sometimes lit and stuck into the jam of a big fireplace. Thick oak bark was placed under the ashes in the fireplace at bedtime, in order to keep a small part of the fire alive when the logs burned out.[8]

~~~

From Robert Isaac:

Morehead, Ky.
November 5, 1891

Dear Sister Permelia,

My hope is that you and your family are feeling well and this letter leaves us the same.

The fall is a pleasant one for us, but there is plenty to do and wood to tend to. Pap does a good bit of the work, maybe more than he should but he is feeling in good health.

I heard that Millicent Hawkins went back to Texas. Well, I hope things work out for her and the boys. They are your grandsons, so likely you are overjoyed to see them.

You said that Anna Kate is going to marry James Shults? Have they set the date yet? Tell her to write to her Uncle Bob telling me if it is true. I will write more next time. I must go into town and get back before dark. Isabel has something to say to you.

R. I. Nickell

Dear Permelia,

I do hope you are all well and we are pleased to hear that Andrew is feeling good now. Where do the Shults boys come from? Write when you can and tell us all about it. Now your first daughter is going to be married. Do the other girls have a beau?

Our Della is so sweet. She is a big help to me. Girls that help their mamas deserve good things, I am sure you will agree. How we would like to see all of you. We likely never will get to. Andrew can come to see us any summer.

Write when you get this so we will know all the news. Do you have a picture of Jim Shults?

Love to all,
Isabel Nickell

<div align="center">~~~</div>

Merry Christmas, 1891

Anna Kate and Jim chose the 19th of December for their marriage date. She wanted to be married at home. Some of the young girls in the county were married, sitting in their buggy, with the preacher standing by its side. Other couples went for their bonds, having their marriages without celebration.

Andrew cut a tree and brought in extra cedar boughs, while Lizzie and Louisa made a string of berries to hang around the tree. Cora cut strips of scrap lace, tying bows on the branches. Usually they had a small table tree, but this large one stood on the floor in front of the window. Andrew would not allow them to light candles near it.

Permelia helped her daughter sew her wedding dress. Anna's figure sometimes embarrassed her, but her mother referred to her shape as "comely." Andrew gave Permelia a cameo brooch when they married and Anna wore it for good luck. The next sister to marry would also wear it. It was anyone's guess as to which sister that would be.

The only hitch in the evening's celebration came after the ceremony when Jim's friends called him outside. He didn't return immediately and Anna worried. Everyone laughed it off, saying he had cold feet, but when Anna went out to see about him, he had disappeared. Cora, Lizzie, and Louisa were beside themselves, and then Permelia became worried because it was almost dark. They heard comments like, "He's scared," and "He's run off."

Andrew and George went out looking for him. George said, "His horse is gone. My brother's clean changed his mind about this marriage thing." They came back from the barn, saying he wasn't out there. Louisa was crying by then and took off toward the barn, her red curls flying. Jim wouldn't do such a thing to her sister. While the others tried to console Anna Kate, Louisa accompanied Jim back from the barn. She laughed so hard she almost cried, trying to brush the hay from Jim's hair and clothes. He was not too happy but not really angry. It turned out George had been the leader. He and two or three of the friends tied Jim up in the hayloft and put a cloth around his mouth to keep him from yelling.

By the time Louisa got to the barn, he had worked off the bandana. She thought Jim's dark hair and light blue eyes made him about the best looking man she had seen, unless it was George.

She never could decide.

This was a wedding day to remember. Perhaps no one else noticed, but Louisa called Lizzie's attention to how Cora was "hard at primping" on Anna Kate's wedding day. She pinched her cheeks to give them color. Would Cora be next to wear their mother's lovely brooch?

CHAPTER 8

Millicent's parents write – Cora marries – Lizzie is a poet – The Shults move to Hall County – Permelia makes a visit.

~~~

From Susan Gilkison, Millicent's mother:

Poplar Plains
December 28, 1891

Mrs. Hawkins
Dear friend Permelia,
    I thought I would write you all a few lines to let you know that we haven't forgotten you.
    This leaves all well except Pa. He is complaining a right smart. I hope when this reaches you, you are enjoying good health. We haven't had much winter yet. I suppose you have fine weather.
    Mrs. Hawkins I want you to write as soon as you get this and tell me about Millicent and those dear little children. Since she went back to Texas she has not written me a line yet. I thought I would not write first. She wrote to her brothers Minor and Charley once or twice, not mentioning my name. I don't know how she can treat me that way, for God knows I did everything I could for her and the children. As for Millicent, she can take her own part anywhere. She got mad at me because I objected to her going out there to marry a stranger she didn't even know if she would like or not. I nearly cried my eyes out after they left. It seemed like the whole place was dead without the children.
    Little Russ always thought so much of me. They seemed as near to me as my own children did. Millicent wrote to Mr.

Griffith that she had a nice home and plenty to live on. I hope she will live happy for she never was satisfied here. She wanted more, but we were unable to give more. There's nothing wrong with wanting but she was impatient.

You know I never wanted Millicent and Daniel to move to Texas when they first married. That was partly because I feared we might never see our grandchildren at all, for I didn't know if they would ever be back to Kentucky.

Our Jennie had hemorrhage of the lungs but is getting along very well now. George's little baby died in October and Dell was here with it when it died. It looks like we've had our share of trouble in the last year.

Tell Bannie and Walt that Cory's baby came out better than the tobacco crop did! He is the cutest little thing that ever lived and is as fat as a little pig. Tell Russ that I wish he was here to help set the hens for me in the spring.

Minor bought himself a beautiful $700 horse. Enclosed is a picture of them both. You need not show Millicent this letter, for I expect she would be mad because I asked about her. Tell the children to be good to that man, if he is good to them, and for Bannie to write to me. I will close this time, hoping to hear from you all soon. I wish you all a happy Christmas and a glad new year. My husband will write a note.

Susan Gilkison

~~~

From Robert Gilkison:
Permelia,

Write me and tell me if you think I could do any good out there and could get a good show in the spring to raise a crop. If I don't rent here I think I will go to Texas. Times are bad here. They would almost have to be better in Texas.

Write and tell me if you think things are better there and the prices of everything. I hear there's a lot of difference from Kentucky and wanted to hear it from you. I will thank you for your comments on the subject.

R. M. Gilkison

<div align="center">~~~</div>

Growth came to George's Creek in the 1890s. Stores and a new school opened. The postal service also improved. Young men even talked of organizing a literary society. Whatever Permelia wrote the Gilkisons about the prosperity of the area, they did not make the move.

<div align="center">~~~</div>

From Robert Gilkison:

Poplar Plains, Kentucky
March 1, 1892

Dear Permelia,

We hope you and Andrew are well, and the rest of your family. I am writing to say I have decided we may as well stay where we are. Susan has her family here and of course her own grown children. It would be hard on all if we left them. Thank you for your letter. Of course we may be wrong but we need to weigh everything against each other.

I would appreciate it if you would write now and then, telling us of Millicent and our grandchildren. Perhaps one day she will come with them for a visit.

From your friend.
Robert Gilkison

<div align="center">~~~</div>

From Katy and Jim:

George's Creek, Tex.
July 15, 1892

Dear Cousin Ella and Uncle Newton,

I once again in life take the opportunity of writing a few lines to you as I often think of you both. Cousin, we have left our home and found another that I love with all my heart. I am enjoying myself so well.

We all got back from the barbecue yesterday which was the fourteenth, all but Mama and Aunt Elizabeth Mary's daughter Ella. They stayed at home and kept house. Cousin Ella has the sweetest and smartest boy you ever saw, named Elbert, and Aunt Belle has the prettiest babe and I think will be just as smart. She was one year old in June. Her name is Junnie. She is like a little princess just as I hope to have one day.

I and my little man are going up to Uncle Jerry's and he will make molasses for us. We may stay one month. I wish you and Uncle would come and we would come and we would all have a fine time making candy.

We have our handkerchiefs yet and would not take anything for them. And I thank you for them. Mama has not used hers any yet. Uncle do you make as much money as you used to make? You never come to see us so I will close hoping to hear from you soon. I remain as ever your niece and cousin. Write soon.

Katy and Jim Shults

~~~

The Hawkins and Nickell families often made molasses candy together. The cane had to be stripped at maturity before the first frost. Jerry Nickell would grind it until the juices evaporated into molasses. Jerry kept the big black kettle convenient for when they invited friends for what they called "stiff-off." Occasionally they made blackstrap molasses, mainly for the animals, as Jerry always kept up his sorghum crop. The youngsters and adults alike enjoyed dipping their cane sticks into the kettle, and licking off the sticky syrup. A favorite breakfast was pouring molasses over corndodgers. As a child, Permelia once got splattered by the thick hot liquid, giving her a lasting small scar on her arm. She always cautioned her family to watch what they were about.

~~~

December, 1892

Another festive Christmas season—three marriages in a row. Louisa's prediction came true. Eva Cora and George Shults wed the eighth of December. Everyone expected Jim to follow his brother George's prank the year before, but for all the time he waited, nothing happened. It was a joke enough to have George expect something and not having it happen. The two Shults brothers were fine-looking men, and although their twin brothers Lemuel and Walter of course looked alike, neither resembled Jim or George.

Eva Cora wore Anna's wedding dress, with only a slight turn of the needle. She resembled her sister in her quiet nature and was very knowledgeable. Louisa often wondered if she was born smart.

No one special had entered Lizzie's life, although everyone thought she would marry before Louisa. Lizzie enjoyed taking off on a horse and go flying. When a little girl, she would stand on a barrel and climb up on a horse and go, hanging on for dear life to the horse's mane. It didn't matter whose horse, since she had no fear of any of them. She loved to feel the wind blowing against her.

The Shults' half-brother, Charles Allen, who had previously moved to Hulver, in Hall County, suggested they join him. In the spring of 1893, George, Cora, Jim and Anna Kate gathered their belongings and moved to the flatlands of the Texas Panhandle. The Hawkins' disappointment in having part of the family move was evident, as they missed them all.

They would not know until later if they would find the grass greener, or in this case if the broom corn grew better. They made the finest product in the area and sold many brooms to Chambers Store as well as to individuals. Still, they thought they could do better in Hulver, knowing its dryer land would provide better crops.

Historians would probably agree broom corn is of Southern origin, with South Carolina being responsible for sorghum as a broom-making material. This species was cultivated as early as 1791. Later on, harvesting broom corn shifted to the Midwest, to Ohio and Kansas.[1]

A business concern in Kansas rented land in North Texas and hired hands to cultivate the crops. Economically, Texas was said to be better for growing corn and labor was cheaper.

~~~

From Robert Isaac:

Morehead, Ky.
January 17, 1893

Dear Brothers, Sisters, and all,

With pleasure I read your good letter and now will attempt an answer. We are having a windy January but are certain to have some of the same in Texas although I hear it is much worse the further west you go in your state.

I saw Isaac Phelps a few days ago. He stays busy with the Masonic Lodge. Isaac says Lucy is well. You would think Morton Lame belonged in the Cassity family, the way he goes at carpentry work. He fixes the jail on a regular schedule and it seems always in need of fixing.

Jack, your sister Joanne is not too well. She seems to come and go, but Lewis had her to a doctor and they hope she will not need to go to the asylum.[2] The Lord knows we hope it won't be so. I don't know how much you hear from Lewis. I see Clay and your sister Margaret right often. They asked me for dinner when I was in town the other day. I felt guilty without having Isabel with me to eat, but I did it anyway. That kind of guilt might be easy to live with, don't you think.

Permelia, you will have to forgive your brother for not writing more. We are doing what we can to keep things moving to the best of our ability. You must tell me how Jack is, and all the rest. Lizzie and little Lou. Lou will always be a babe with red curls to me, no matter how many years she has.

Write soon.
R. I. Nickell and family

~~~

In 1881, murders in Ashland, Kentucky turned into a tragedy not to be forgotten. Twelve years later, Lizzie wrote about the killings of the young people. Modern-day references are still made to the events. Exchanging photographs and correspondence were of great importance to women in those days of little entertainment. Writing also served as a popular pastime. The following was written for Mrs. Cora Shults, by "a poor scribe, Lizzie Frances Hawkins."

The Ashland Tragedy

Dear Fathers, mothers, sisters,
Come listen while I tell
All about the Ashland Tragedy
Of which I know quite well;
All in the town of Ashland,
All on that dreadful night
A horrible crime committed,
And soon was brought to light

Three men who did the murder
Were Craft, Ellis, and Neal
They thought the crime they had concealed
But God the same revealed
George Ellis one of the weakest
Who could not bear the pain
To J. B. Powell trembling
Revealed the horrid stain

Ellis Craft who was their leader
And had an iron heart
Caused a son, two lovely daughters
From their mother's embrace to part
Poor Neal he may be innocent
But from what George Ellis tells
The crime he has committed
Will send his soul to Hell

He drug poor Emma from the bed
And threw her on the floor
And crushed her head with an iron bar
Till the blood it ran to gore
In my own imagination
I can see her little white hands
Upheld and cry for mercy
Murdered by cruel hands

Then Craft committed the same offense
And murdered the other two
And now their dear forms cold in death
Craft says what shall we do?
Then Neal proposed to burn them up
To hide their bloody stain
That some other three might arrested be
And them bear not the blame

George Ellis quaked with fear
And trembling did say
O no boys, don't do that
We had better get away
Then in a tone of thunder
Craft told Ellis to get the can
And pour oil on the children
While they stood with bloody hands

Then Craft he lit a match
And touched it to their clothes
And flames loomed up with melting hear
And the wind did start to blow
Then off they went I have no doubt
As fast as they could go
And though no one this bloody crime
Could ever ever know

Then early the next morning
The town in mourning wept
To see the children's burning forms
A sight we cannot forget
Such screams and bitter weepings
Of friends who stood around
With heart strings torn and bleeding
Tears falling to the ground

Poor little Robert Gibbons

A helpless orphan child
Died in defense of his Sister
To her he was loving and mild
Their three bodies are now buried
They sleep beneath the sod
Murdered, defending their virtue
Their souls are at rest with God

Ellis was taken by mob force
And justly got his doom
The next was Craft the worst of
Could not revel the tomb
The third is Neal
Left alone to weep
To think he murdered a little girl
Whose life to her was sweet

And while he lives away Justice
Arranged him at the rest
Their souls will tormented be
While the children's are at rest
The two dear girls and little boy
Were loved by friends around
Their mother is left a weeping
And they are in the ground

There is one thing yet
I do remember well
Major Allen with his bloodhounds
Caused tears the tide to swell
They hovered round these wretched friends
Sent death knells through the town
Caused other friends from friends to part
For Hell such men are bound

The people of Mt. Sterling
Who rate themselves so high

Ought to have favor in Justice
And say that they shall try
I suppose that they've forgot
That they have daughters too
Good and right should be their aim
And protect their children too

May law and Justice be dealt out
And spread from plains to plain
And in a future day enjoy
A mortal and a gain
Now all dear fathers, mothers
Take warning by this deed
Stay with your children
This advice you best to heed.

(Bad writing excuse, Bad spelling forgive, and love the writer as long as you live. A lonely Writer—Bye, bye, from Lizzie)

~~~

The law caught the murderers, all in their twenties. The following summer after the gruesome killings, George Ellis was taken from the county jail and lynched. Ellis Craft was hanged in Grayson, Kentucky in 1882. He professed innocence, blaming the other two men. The next year, William Neal pleaded for his life, maintaining he was innocent, but his begging went unheeded. Papers everywhere carried the story. The brutal murders disturbed everyone for miles.

The event made a special impression on Lizzie, enough to cause her bad dreams for years afterward. Reports came in that Ellis Craft, "a man of cool daring and unflinching nerve," attended the funeral of the victims and drove one of the wagons. George W. Ellis, appearing remorseful during his confession, gave the horrible particulars of their crime. Ellis and Neal were each married with children. In order to appear innocent, all three men assisted in putting out the fire the following morning.[3]

~~~

From Cora and George:

Hulver, Hall Co. Tex.
June 30, 1893

Dear Mother, Papa, Lizzie, and Lou,
I hope you are all well. We are faring well ourselves. If you were to have asked what we expected of Hall County before we ever came, the answer would never be guessed. Remember when we came to Texas and didn't have mountains like in Kentucky? We still had lots of water and things were easy grown, almost any flower seeds we planted grew with just a little urging.

Well, I'll never get used to the flat lands up here. Whatever we have we do ourselves. Our hollyhocks make a pretty sight though. Mama's favorite wild larkspurs do grow and they don't seem to mind the wind. This month is right nice.

Mama I know it is a long way up here from George's Creek but when my time comes will you still be able to be with me? It will be awfully hard for you to come but can I manage without you?

Give my greetings to all. George and I send our love. Will close now.

Cora and George

~~~

From Katy and Jim:

Hulver, Hall County
September 8, 1893

Dear Mother, Papa, Lizzie, Lou,

It is my pleasure to write to you all and I hope you are well. Perhaps I will feel better myself before too long if only that time will come. My strength is not in large amounts, but perhaps that will change when it gets cooler.

Cora wants you to come for as long as you can. I know that it will be hard for you to leave home, but if you think my sisters can take care of the cooking and cleaning then papa will sure want you to come. She would need you as soon as possible in October since her time is the third or fourth week in the month.

I would like to see little Myrtle. Give her a kiss and a hug from her Aunt Katie. Lizzie, would you look and see if you can find my lace cuffs and collar? Mama could bring them when she comes so no need sending them separate. Also there is a small amount of goods in the bottom of the trunk. It is enough to make a cover for the baby. It is that blue and white flowered and I have some yarn. I will tack a little quilt for our tiny joy.

I hated to leave Miss Fossil, but I was so afraid she would run off. Do pet her for me. We miss you all so much.

Your loving children and sister,
Katie and Jim

~~~

From Lizzie:

George's Creek, Tex.
October 17, 1893

Dear Mama, one and all,

I will try to answer your kind and welcome and good old long letter we received about four or five o'clock this evening. You are so far away up there in Hall County. We were so glad to hear from you, and I know Cora appreciates your help. I was so sorry to hear Katy was not getting along well. Oh no, Katy I do hope you will be so gayly when this reaches you.

Am glad you are all trying to find the right way to go and hope you will understand the scripture. Katy, you wanted us to excuse you for writing with a pencil. Now what are you going to do with us and us not sick, but only tired. Mama and all we do want to see you so bad. We will send this off in the morning. Oh our dear sweet little Myrtle, she is so cute.

Uncle Jerry paid me ten dollars and we paid both Strain and Rinker too. Uncle Jerry got about fifty bushels of corn at forty cents a bushel. It is high. I expect fifty cents in town now, cotton from seven to seven and a half.

Pa says to tell you no one ever gets letters but him. When he goes he nearly always gets one. I know I would love to see you all. I don't know if Cousin Willie and Fannie are going to get up a case or not. He has him a cart now. Louisa, him and me went to preaching in it Saturday night. Just a flying.

How much do you owe Sol Hoskins for the pears? The doctor was inquiring about your business the other day Jim, and wanted to know who was tending to it. Mama, we haven't been to see Mrs. Spinz yet. They go to Sunday School every Sunday now. Aunt Yine spent part of the day with us Saturday until Will W. Atchison could come here after her. We washed, starched, ironed and scoured, went after plums and made a gallon of preserves Saturday and never picked any cotton for the first time since you left.

Mama, Aunt Yine sends her love and best wishes to all. They all wanted to come home with us Sunday but there was so many they would not come. Uncle Dock was baptized at Brazos Point Sunday evening. Brother Carnes is holding a meeting at Willow Branch this week.

Oh yes, Arthur Hale was telling off on Lela this evening to Lou and me. He said she was just as ill as could be, and every time she would have a little pain she would make out like she was nearly dead. Henry Patton is in the country again. We all had a nice time Sunday. Cora, I would hardly live up there now and Mrs. Eoff gone. My, what did you let her go for. I do hate it for you sure. But don't tell any of the rest of your neighbors what I said, since I'm sure they want to help too. Give my wishes to Mrs. Revel and tell her she will feel grand I guess when she moves to town.

Mama, there was a man from Cleburne who was a collector, stayed with us Saturday night. Pa says tell you he and John killed a polecat right here at the side of the kitchen door under the sill yesterday—or the dog did rather.

Yes, we have had cool weather ever since you left. No hot days at all. Uncle Dim and Dutch W. took six bales of cotton to town for Uncle this morning.

Don't study about us Mama, for we study about you all enough and we are all doing just as well as we can—heap better than I expected we would. Now Cora, hurry and let Mama come home. I wish you all the good luck I can. Hope this will find you all getting along so well and all happy and glad. Oh, Katy, get well.

From Lizzie to every one of you, good old thoughts. Write soon. Write.

Lizzie

~~~

From Louisa:

George's Creek, Tex.
October the 17th, 1893

Dear folks in Hall County one and all,

Once more I will try to write a few lines. I have not got any news to write that would be likely to interest you at all. Oh we got your letters today. Was so glad to get them. We will have to brag on all of you. Pa settled with Mr. Strain today. We owed him nine dollar and forty-five cents beside the cotton seed. Well we were ready last Saturday night to go to meeting and there was a man to stay all night and Papa did not get to go.

Me and Lizzie went in the gig with cousin Willie Nickell[4] and there was not but a few there, so did not have any meeting. Brother Radden and family came home with us that night. The next morning Lizzie and I got dinner before we went to the meeting and Mr. Megason, Millicent and family, Mac Vansant[5], and Willie came home with us. Brother Graham is going to preach.

No you can't read this because Lou wrote it. Mama, wouldn't it be funny if you have gone to Hall County and then got fooled about her having a baby. That was a good way they had getting you up there.

George, I am getting my hands and feet ready. I put taller and glicern on them every night. Ha ha. Well I have written enough of nonsense. I will close.

I remain, Lou.

More: Saturday night and Sunday and maybe longer, we had company ever since you have been gone, and I guess we will have next Sunday too. We are picking cotton for Uncle Dim right now. Us and three Hale boys. I have my bonnet on.

Uncle Dim and Sally are just fine. George, when we read your letter and got to where your feet were so sore you could not talk, we read that out loud and had a big laugh.

Your feet being sore doesn't hinder your brain. Writing that is a poor excuse. I have got a better one that that. My lips are so sore from picking cotton they have puffed out enough to knit a pair of gloves. Now laugh. Ha ha. No I didn't pick cotton with my mouth. I mean the sun burned them, bonnet or not. But I'm not picking any more as my freckles are growing freckles.

You all must excuse our short letter but there are not but three of us and there are five of you. Oh I am so tired. This is as much as George wrote and more than Jim did. The other three have got nothing else to do but to write to us. We are getting along fine but that is no sign I don't want Mama to come home. I want to see you all. Don't let Ma kill herself running after everything.

I am getting sleepy so tired and sleepy I will have to close. I will write more next time. This is to all. I want to see Mama come home soon. Papa misses you so much. Write as soon as you can.

Lou

<div align="center">~~~</div>

From Dee Eoff, family friend:

Millport, Missouri
October 30, 1893

Mrs. Hawkins
Hulver, Texas
Kind friends,

After so long a time I seat myself to drop you all a few lines to let you know we got here all OK and have not forgotten you all yet, and don't ever expect to.

The conductor put us on the vestibule at Wichita, Kansas and it went so fast we got to Rutledge Monday night at one o'clock and nobody there to meet us. You know we wrote to them to meet us on Tuesday. So they did not come till Tuesday. It was pretty cold when we got off the train. We went to one of our friends living in town and stayed till they came after us Tuesday evening. All were glad to see us. They came out all along the road to see us before we got home.

Everybody said I did not look as bad as they expected to see me. Ma stood the trip coming home better than she did going out there. We both taken a bad cold on the road but we are better now. I feel better than I have felt for a year. Well Cora, how are you by this time and what have you got? I know you have something by this time—be it boy or girl.

Write and tell me how you are and all about it. I want to hear how your health is, Katy. I am concerned about you. How do you stand the cold weather or is it very cold there yet? We have had lots of ice here since I came home.

I would love to have another big talk with all of you. Cora, I have made our baby a nice white dress since I got home. The baby weighs eleven and a half now. He is growing fast.

Mama sends love to all. She said tell you she had made forty gallons of kraut and had enough cabbage to make another barrel yet. I wish you were here to eat sour pickles and catchup with me. Well I will close for this time. You must excuse bad pencil for you know it is not my fault that I don't write good. This is all. Answer as soon as you get it. Tell Lizzie I said howdy.

> Your friend as ever. By by.
> Dee Eoff

~~~

Dee Eoff, a long-time friend of Permelia's was apparently of considerable help to Anna and Eva Cora in Hulver. A shopping bill in Dee's handwriting, showing the prices of the times, was inside her letter.

hat $1.50
coffee $.10
veil $.25
banana $.5
gloves $.40
stamps $.10
pants $1.25
rope $.25
shoes $1.10
thread/pins $.30
ticket $8.05

~~~

During this time, Mr. Megason brought Andrew and Permelia's grandsons over for visits. The entire family looked forward to the occasions. Millicent sometimes accompanied them. Permelia commented that most of the time she looked as if she was ready to have her photo made.[6] She was always one to take good care of her appearance—and always one to take good care of her children.

CHAPTER 9

Lula Pearl Shults – A six-inch snow on in May – Junnie
Nickell and the fire – Broomcorn – Sadness for Katy
and Jim – The return from Hall County

~ ~ ~

From Cora Shults:

Hulver, Hall Co. Texas
November 11, 1893

Dear Mother, Father, Brother, Sisters,
  This cold blustery morning finds me seated for the purpose of answering your letter. We were glad to hear from you all and to hear that mama got there all right. I know you were so glad to see her, but you might have written in the last letter that she could stay another week.
    The baby is not well. I just don't know what to do for her when she is not well, but she is so sweet. She has the prettiest eyes. I have not done anything yet but dry the dishes twice. I think I will get up now and get breakfast. My back does hurt. In the mornings I feel tolable, but I could stand it if the baby would just keep well.
    Oh Mama, we are so lonesome since you left. I do wish you could have stayed up here with us all the time. I was sorry we did not get to get you a nice present before you went home, but we will get you one and bring it to you when we come down for you earned a nice one. I don't know what we would have done without our dear mother. It doesn't seem like I could ever of stood it if you had not of been with me for you were so good to me. Well I guess I had better not write much more this time and I will be able to write a longer one later.

George guesses we had better name the baby Lula Pearl. If we don't call it that we will call it Lula May.

Write all the news about everybody and give my love to them. Write soon as you all get this. My, John and Maggie you ought just to see our sweet little girl. She is so sweet and pretty. Kiss sweet little Myrtle for me. The baby grows so fast and is so fat.

George is making brooms. He is too busy to write much this time. He made four dozen and one brooms since Mama went home. He and Jim are fast at making brooms but they also make them good and lasting.

George does think so much of the baby. Jim says a word or two once in a while to her. Oh Lizzie, Carrie, and Kate took the red skirt and a piece of Kate's green worsted dress and made it a cloak. We will get it a Sunday cloak soon for her best. We are watching our money nowadays. She has woke up now. I know you would like to see her. She is in my lap now getting dinner. Write soon. Love to all. All the news.

Cora Shults

~~~

As for "watching money," the Panic of 1893 swallowed up banks all over the country. On every side people met reverses. Prices of horses and cattle had been low enough before, but they fell much lower. There was little demand for horses, and talk spread that this splendid animal was passing, soon to be found only on exhibition.[1] That proved to be only foreboding conversation.

Most of the citizens of George's Creek did not seem to be hit so bad by the depression.

At least this was true with the Hawkins family and others who did not raise horses and cattle. Prices in general went up some, but the citizens merely tightened their belts and waited it out.

Perhaps the most successful rancher of the area was A. J. Berry, who earlier had been called upon by his nephew, J. L. A., to help take care of his herd of cattle and horses.[2]

~~~

From George:

<div align="right">November 11, 1893
Hulver, Texas</div>

To all,

I will try and write a few lines. It is still dry here and no prospects for rain. Every time it looks like rain it just gets cold.

I am glad that you did not send that meal you spoke of mailing to us, but thanks for thinking of it. We will name the baby Lula Pearl. You ought to see her growing so fast she will be big enough to wash the dishes in a week or two.

We are still making brooms as fast as we can. I can't think of anything to write so guess I will have to quit. I will try and do better next time. Write soon and often.

<div align="center">George F. Shults</div>

~~~

From Jim and Katy:

November 11, 1893
Hulver, Hall Co. Texas

Dear ones,

I hope everyone there is fine. I have so many questions. I want to know if Will B. came back, where are Hank and Capy, how is Ella, and how is Granpa Barker? Tell him howdy for me. Tell little Junnie and all the rest howdy. Mama, did Myrtle know you when you came home?

Lizzie, I kissed kissed little sweetie for you.

Mama, George got about six dollars worth of groceries with his brooms. I think he got about eleven dollars and a half for five dozen of the smallest ones. He did not sell the two best dozen since the man was not there. So George did not bring his lumber at that time, as he would need to talk to the owner.

I am tired and it is twenty minutes past eleven o'clock. I will soon have to make up bread for dinner. The baby is asleep. It may not wake up until three or four this evening. I will rest until after dinner anyhow. Well it is half past two o'clock and Lula Pearl is awake.

Lizzie, have you ever written to cousin Gezzella? I will write to her next week if I can. Mama, kiss Myrtle for Kate. Jim and he got three barrels of water out of that well this time. It has been cleaned out.

I will close. Love and good wishes to all. (Lou, Lizzie said nary a word about you in her letter.) We remain as ever.

Your children
Katy and Jim Shults

~~~

From Katy:

Hulver, Hall Co.
November 13, 1893

Dear Mother, Father, Sisters, Brother, little niece and also friends,

It is with pleasure I try to answer your kind letter which we received. We were all so glad to hear from you. Were Pa, John, Maggie, Lou all there to meet our dear mother on the train? I was glad to hear from you. I know all of you were sleepy before you went to bed. Oh yes, Cora was glad to hear from you. I know all of you were sleepy before you went to bed. Oh yes, Cora and I thought you ought to have said Mama could stay another week in that letter that we got. Mama, we miss you so much especially the baby. She was not well Thursday and Friday. She could not sleep without garbling, but has cried nary a bit now. We roasted an onion last night, mashed it up and mixed some sulfur alcohol and sugar and gave it to her. She seems better this morning. Was that the way to fix the onion? We did not know for sure. We gave her two doses of oil since you left.

As for the work, we got along very well. Carrie stayed until Tuesday. She washed some for the baby Monday morning. I washed some more Wednesday and Thursday. George and I washed for Cora and the babe Friday but there won't be any washing today for there is the coldest norther and the hardest rain this morning.

The broom machine is in the dugout this morning again. They got the shed boxed up for drying the corn but not covered yet.

Mama, I haven't poured out the coffee yet and haven't hardly made any nor set the table. Jim pours the coffee now and sets the table, he and Cora. Jim has washed and dried the dishes twice. Jim also sweeps once a day for me. I just don't feel like it. He is so good to me, like he understands how I feel.

Mama, I want to tell you on George. Yesterday Jim hauled water. We cooked beans for supper. George came to the table and heaped his plate with beans and commenced eating. He spoke up in hard earnest and said "Will I get enough to eat?" So he quit and said he was afraid to eat enough—fraid they would make him sick. he ate enough for four. Well, that's all of that.

Do my sisters want to see me? I hope to see them next year. Anyhow if I just could get well I expect we would come back down there, but we can't any more tell what we will do than you can. As long as I keep medicine and take it long enough I will be up. It looks like I never can get stout any more. Oh, I do want a sweet little babe.

Mama, you remember Mrs. Drury. She is, or has been really poorly again. She sent us word that we must not think hard of her for not coming. Write next time and tell us what the rest said about their brooms. Jim and George make really fine ones.

I love you all. Papa, I hope you are well. I love you.

Katy

~~~

The Shults accepted the broom business in Hulver better than they did the winter weather. One disadvantage in making these "sweepers" was the damage to the hands. The men wore gloves to trim and bind, but not for stitching. Blisters had to turn into calluses.

Jim developed a skin allergy, and thinking the corn dust caused it, he made sure he buttoned his sleeves at the wrists. Anna sewed thin gloves for him, thick enough to protect his hands but not interfering with stitching.

When broom corn is young, the plants resemble fodder or food corn, but not when they mature. The head of the stalk has a brush end with little seeds over the top. When dry, the seeds are shaken off. Blades on broomcorn are not as broad, and as many as twenty single brush strips can lead out from each stem.[3]

The entire family learned how brooms were made, but Jim and George did the making. Choosing good saplings is the first thing toward creating good brooms. They need cutting the proper length for handles then the work begins. Some men used leather strips for tying, but George and Jim tightly wrapped the handle with wire then tied on each strip of corn wisk until they completed three layers. For an anchor, George tied one end of the wire on a small tree limb, while holding the broom across his lap as he turned its handle. That way, one man could do the work of two. He tied the wisks again, lower down so they would stay attached and not pull out.

They sold more flat ones than round ones because they covered more space when sweeping. A flat broom took stitching in and out, and more corn as well, but they also brought more money. If a woman had a shortage of money, she could always use available tree branches.

The branch could be rather small as long as its twigs were covered with thick leaves.

Often, when a couple began a new household, or when members of a church gave a donation party, a broom was sure to be a present from some well-wisher. The broom became the symbol of good housekeeping, and a model young wife needed to know how to use one properly.[4]

~~~

From Robert Isaac:

Morehead, Kentucky
November 13, 1893

Dear Sister Permelia and Jack,

It is with pleasure that I write to you these lines, with the hope that you are all well. My concern is with Ella Page. Her mother was a fine woman as ever was, and would have wanted to see Ella content. Edmond Cassity said Ella married a William McReynolds Vansant. Born in Missouri. Have you met him? Ed said she wrote that Mac was a good man, and I hope it is so. I did not see too much of them as they were growing up and that is regretful. Clark was turning out to be a good carpenter the same as Ed, and Ed says Clark has a fine little wife. Ed is still working on his pension and hopes to have his attorney get it finished up without too much further delay. Seems it takes too long.

Anna Page wrote to Edmond that our papa's brother did good with his land. Well, he had nearly thirty year to do it. That was a long way for Uncle James to go for good land, but he thought it best to get his family away from the war. He sounds prosperous. Uncle and I may never again meet on this earth and for that I am sorry.

I must write to Jim myself but don't hear from him much as I do you and Jack. All I heard about Millicent Gilkison was that she was planning to find her a good Texas man and move to Somervell County and live out the rest of her life there. Now I know she married. Are her plans going as planned? She needed a man to help provide for those boys, as they are good boys and seemed no trouble. That is fortunate in as much as they had no papa to raise them and had not much for themselves.

Della is wanting a baby brother. We will see. Isabel feels a bit better and we have a girl to stay with her. It is not easy finding a trustworthy enough girl to depend on for a regular basis, but Isabel is not up to her health. If it is a boy we will name him Johnny E.

No, Isabel did not have a cancer on her face. I can't think of anything else now. Tell the girls and John Robert hello for me. I guess I must write to the Shults families. I am glad to hear that the broom business is well for them, but am sorry to hear Kate is ailing. Tell all to write. You do the same.

Love to all
Robert Isaac Nickell and family

~~~

From Addie Lame Maxey:

Morehead, Kentucky
March 15, 1894

Dear Uncle, Aunt, and Cousins,

I hope you are feeling well. My letter is short but I wished to relate to you how sad I am over Aunt Margaret. Goodness knows, Uncle Andy, your sister was a fine woman and I loved her dearly. She was a good wife to Mr. Powers. Pa always said she had to go through some hard times when Morehead was more troubled. Pa said that Mr. Powers was an independent man that always seemed to know what he was about.

Whenever in my life I piece a quilt, I will think lovingly of Aunt Margaret. I'm not gifted with my pen as you are Aunt Permelia, but I'm desirous of writing some lines for her. Perhaps one day they will come to me, and I will try. This letter was just to express my feelings to you, Uncle Andy, as how I feel at this time. How I would dearly love to see you all.

Your niece,
Addie

~~~

From Katy and Jim:

Hulver, Hall Co.
March 16, 1894

Dear Mother, Father and all,

It is with pleasant thoughts that I write an answer to your good letter. Lula is better now and we pray she does get through all this cold weather without coming down sick. None of us want to get sick for that matter. This must be the coldest place in the world and I do feel tired most every day. I never seem to get warm.

Mama, you said you sewed a dress for Junnie. What color did you sew it? How I would like to see that precious little one. I know she is going to be smart like her brother Clarence. I wish more than anything to have a dear little girl. I would want her to take after you for there is no dearer Mother anywhere. Not anywhere. And Mama, I think I may be going to need you to come up here in a few months. I know I don't feel really well, but it may be more than that.

Jim and George have made enough brooms to sweep us all right out of our house, but I guess that is why we came up here to the top of Texas, to make brooms.

A kiss to all and a hug for little Junnie. Our love to Uncle Jerry and Aunt Belle. My, this is not a very long letter but it is time to make bread. Cora says she will write soon.

Love from Katy and Jim

~ ~ ~

Early this month Jerry and Belle's daughter Junnie reached into the fireplace to retrieve a scrap of shiny paper. She leaned too far and her dress burst into flames, the one Permelia had sewn for her. By the time Belle could rescue her, the burns were too severe for her to be saved. Jerry and Belle laid her to rest next to Willie in the George's Creek graveyard.

The custom in the nineteenth century and well into the twentieth, was to take a photograph of a deceased child. Epidemics and childhood illnesses took young lives—their deaths a common occurrence. Women of the times held fear for the health of a future child as much as joy at becoming pregnant.[5]

~ ~ ~

From Robert Isaac:

Morehead, Kentucky
May the 23, 1894

Dear Brothers, Sisters and all,

Thank you for your kind letter and this leaves us all well. I hope it will find you the same. On Monday April the sixteenth I set out to Dr. Logan's but before we got back a fine boy had arrived. Well I guess he would have weighed three or four pounds. He is doing all right. He hasn't cried any. A gentleman from Pawnee City, Nebraska told us to call him Johnny E. for himself, John Edwards, and he would send him a present. We knew them in Kansas.

On the nineteenth of the month a cold rain fell and Sunday morn a big snow was on. Just think of it. Everything is full bloom and a six inch snow on. Well it broke all the timber and the fruit trees—all the wheat and rye. Think for a moment. A big snow in middle of summer. It was the awfullest sight ever beheld I guess. It has been cold and rainy ever since. The corn tops are all bit but I think it will get all right. I have the hillside in corn below the house. it looks well. Papa is staying at home.

Lewis Lame has moved to Ditney Ridge in Morgan County, Ky. Joanne is getting better.

Isabel says tell you all she is not able to write to you this time. She thinks she has all the boy there is in the county. Well he is quite a boy and weighed eight pounds at one month old. Give our love to all.

I can't think of anything else. Write soon. They wrote about the snow in the newspapers. Daughter Della has something to say.

Love to all.
R. I. Nickell and family

Dear cousins,

I will try to wright you a few lines.   This leaves us all well and hope you are the same. I hav three little pigs and a little calf   o aunt Bell I hav got the sweetes little brother you ever saw.   little cousin my little brother is sweeter than sugar   his name is johney E.   I will close for this time wright soon

Della to cousin. good by.

<div align="center">~~~</div>

From Jessie Nickell, brother Greenup's daughter:

Young Springs
Bath County, KY.
May 24, 1894

Mrs. Permelia Hawkins
Dear Aunt,

I will try to write you a few lines to let you know that we are all well and hoping this will find you all the same.

Well we have had some nice weather. Tell everyone we have had a big snow today. This is the twenty-fourth of May. It has broken the apple trees all down nearly. I can't imagine such weather in summer.

Well I must tell you Auntie, I got my dress. I think it is a nice present and Aunt Sis thinks it is too. Aunt Isabel got me a dress the other day.

Well Aunt, tell Lizzie that she must write to me. Tell her that she must not get mad at me for I was only playing her about her fellow. Aunt Permelia, tell cousin Lizzie to come out and I will go home with her if she comes out to Salt Lick. And send me word when she is coming and we will meet her, and go over to Uncle Robert Isaac's and will have a good time. I would like to see you all and would like for you to come out. I have just joined the Methodist Church.

Well how I would like to be there and pick cotton with Uncle Andy and Uncle Jerry. We have had plenty of rain. I never told you how deep the snow was. It was five or six inches deep. Brother Quilla is a good boy to work. He was working at Mr. Cogswells. He has got eight dollars and eight dollars more coming to him.

Well I will close. From Jessie to Aunt Permelia and Uncle Andy. Write as soon as you get this.

Your niece,
Jessie Nickell

~~~

From Katy and Jim:

May 31, 1894
Hulver, Hall Co.

My dear Mother,

I hope you are well when my sad letter reaches you. I have wept all day. The good news I was hoping to tell you was that I would be having a darling little babe. Our news has turned to sadness as the child is lost. It could not have been but about three months.

We know I have not felt well for some time, but this I did not expect. Oh my dear mother, why did this have to happen, for I know we would have loved it so. Am I to believe this is God's way?

Jim says we are coming back home, and I expect George and Cora will too. It is so cold up here, and we miss everyone so much, tho we have made friends here who are as good can be. Cora says to tell you they will be glad to come back, for they miss you all too. This is all I can write at this time.

Your loving children,
Katy and Jim

~~~

Although the news that the Shults would return to
George's Creek was good, the reason was not. Anna
Kate, never the healthiest daughter, did not grow
stronger in Hulver. George and Cora could have
remained there but chose to return to Somervell County.

Louisa had been taught that she shouldn't question
God's will. With the deaths of her brothers, then Junnie
and her sister's babe, she couldn't be sure. She believed
God would take care of them, but she also knew her
mother would try making things better with the strength
God gave her. She prayed for another child for Anna
Kate.

CHAPTER 10

Brush Arbors – Margaret Romine's trunk – Katy's announcement – Anna Page's disposition improves – "Penn," the great bloodhound – Louisa's stuttering treated by mail – Uncle Moses had a close call – Survella – Lizzie and Henry

~~~

Rural communities did not always have appropriate meeting places since the church was sometimes too small, as well as being very warm in summers. The citizens of George's Creek provided the brush arbor, the forerunner to the tabernacle. Church services, funeral services, and sometimes singings took place within the arbor.

The rustic structure consisted of long poles, forked at one end, and then placed vertically in the ground. Horizontal poles stretched across the fork, with cedar foliage laid on top for shade. Straw from freshly thrashed grain was spread on the ground so when people knelt for prayer, the grain protected them from rough ground. The members of the church paid someone to replace the arbor on an annual basis, or the members did the work themselves.[1]

As in many larger towns, Cleburne's newspaper carried announcements from community reporters, who wrote about their activities, as well as the health of the locals: "The citizens of this burg met and built a large arbor, Wednesday last. The arbor has a large number of seats. A protracted meeting was begun here last night by Rev. McKinney."[2] *The Johnson County Review* carried such reports from area communities including Bono,

Godley, Burleson, Joshua, Nemo, Oak Grove, Lane Prairie, Fort Spunky and Buck Creek.

~~~

From Maggie Romine, Lizzie's future sister-in-law:

Granbury, Tex.

Sept. 15, 1894

To Miss Lizzie and Lou Hawkins

Kind friends,

It is with the greatest of pleasure that I answer your welcome letter which I received Tuesday. I was glad to hear from you. This leaves all well but me. I have been feeling bad lately. I fell riding and hurt three days.

I wish this to find you all well. Lizzie, I am not much homesick, but if I could just be with all my friends tomorrow. We can't come this month but may come before long. George has been picking cotton about two miles from home.

I have got me two new dresses and all the underclothes to wear, and if Ma won't let me have my clothes there, she can keep them, but thank her and her God for that. If Ma doesn't want to ever meet me any more I hope we will meet in Heaven when we will be at home together. She knows I love her but I did love George and would rather be with him.

I am very well satisfied up here but would rather live down there. It seems like if I just had my trunk to look at then I would be all right, but it doesn't do any good to wish. How do you suppose my Mother would keep it from me.

Lou, I haven't forgotten the last time we were together or when we were talking to Bessy.

Tell her I will come to see her when I come back down there. I've not forgotten the fun we used to have. I miss seeing my old friends, as it is not the same here.

Well I must close for this time for I am sick. I wish I could come now but I just don't feel like it. Tell Grandma Soapes howdy for me, and I will write to others before long. Good-by. George said maybe he would write if he got time. He is fixing to go to town.

Maggie Romine

~~~

   Neither Louisa nor Lizzie knew why Mrs. Finley would not let her daughter have her trunk (hope chest) and quilts. If Permelia knew something more, she never let on to her daughters. Lizzie met Henry Romine, George's brother, at one of the church singings. He had been calling on her for some time and they seemed to be serious.

~~~

From Ella Goodnow:

Capay, California
November 2, 1894

Dear Cousins one and all,
   Will write you a few lines tonight to let you know we are all well but myself. Have the worst cold and sore lungs. Hope you will all be enjoying the very best of health when you read these lines. It's true you haven't heard from me in some time. Forgive your cousin.
   Well Permelia, everything looks lovely and green, even to the people. Cousins, my children, Pearl, Daisy, and Chet have all gone to church. Have had a protracted meeting since the sixteenth of October. Will close I think Monday night. Have had quite a good many joiners. Pearl and myself hope your loving brother will join also. I know his dear mother, if she could only look down and see him join the church she would be so happy, don't you think? I would be so happy if he only would. I will never be satisfied if he does not, for I don't

know how I would get along without him. We love him so
much. Our little Willie loves him with all his heart.

Will go to bed and finish in the morning for am mostly
sick. Good night.

Later . . . Will now finish this letter. Well, our church has
come to a close Sunday night. There were four hundred or
more to see Brother Halton preach his farewell sermon. He is
a grand speaker and no mistake he got seventy-nine joiners.
Now there are one hundred fifty-three joiners at Capay.
There were twelve baptized Sunday.

Chet was baptized the eighth at night, for he had to go
away early the next morning. Pearl and myself on the fourth.
There were several more the same day. There will be
baptizing Sunday the thirteenth. Also your dear brother
joined. Oh so happy was I when he went up. He has been
baptized as his father was. Now we will have prayer meeting
every Wednesday night. Church Sunday and Sunday School
at ten, every Sunday.

I have a very severe cold yet. Most everyone has a cold.
We need rain now, but it would maybe make my cold worse.
Well, we milked three cows and make quite a good deal of
butter. Butter is thirty-five cents per roll with two pounds to
the roll. Cousin and Will have gone to pump water for the
stock. Pearl and Daisy have gone to school.

Well, Permelia, I have sixty-eight turkeys. Will sell them
soon. They are real nice. Sold one the other day and got a
dollar seventy-five for it. If I only could get that for all of
them I would be happy. Now Anna Page is working for a nice
lady down closer to Mama. They like Anna very much. Anna
is getting as fat and round as can be. She was up about a
month ago to see us and seems to be happy. She has
changed. Now goodbye to all. Give our love to your brother
Dim and Jerry's family. If you can't read this just step over
and I will try to read it.

Cousin Newton sent to Pennsylvania for a bloodhound. They sent him a white one with black nose and brown eyes. He may be real smart for all what I know. Newt has four dogs, Curly is a big dog, Prince is a shepherd, and Jack is a half-hound and the other half dog I guess.

Penn, the great bloodhound from Penn! Nevertheless he is quite proud of it.

Write us a long letter and tell me all the news about all the folks will you? From brother Newt and cousins. Send your brother greetings when you write.

Ella Goodnow

<div align="center">~~~</div>

From Maggie E. Romine:

Glen Rose, Texas
November 13, 1894

To Aunt Belle and Aunt Permelia,

Well, I have written about all I know to the rest, but I haven't forgotten how good you have all been to us. I am very sick but hope this will find you both well. Aunt Belle, you don't know my troubles but I am not in as much trouble as I was. I feel like a bird let out of a cage even though I haven't been anywhere since I have been here. But several women have been to see me.

Aunt Belle, you told me to write Ma a letter. I don't feel like it would be welcome if I had written it. I feel like my parents have forsaken me. But I still think of home and to think how hard I worked for my trunk and quilts, and now can't get them. But we can live without them. I don't see how Ma can have the heart to forsake her daughter. It makes me cry to think of how they have done. Well, that is enough on this.

I have pieced one quilt and made me a dress and George a shirt and myself some under clothes. I lost my pretty hair pin but George got me another. Sometimes if it were not for George. . . .

Maggie E. Romine

~~~

Maggie called Belle and Permelia "Aunt" as an endearing reference. Perhaps Permelia did not inquire as to the problems between Maggie and her mother, or if she knew, she never mentioned it to Louisa.

Lizzie and Henry indeed had a "case." They married on December 20, 1884. Permelia's cameo was again worn for good luck. As soon as Anna and Cora returned home, another child left the nest. Henry's folks lived in Bosque County, and he decided to try farming there.

Henry began calling Lizzie, "D." No one knew the reason—perhaps it stood for dear or darling. Louisa had nicknames of Lou and Babe. Since she was a little prissy when a child, Anna Kate often called her "Prissiky." And the girls called John Robert, "Bud."

From an early age Louisa had a tendency to stutter. A woman named Maggie Cribbs was a friend who once lived in George's Creek, and with her Science and Health books, she offered to cure this speech impediment.

While Permelia was not familiar with the Science, she and Louisa decided to let Mrs. Cribbs try to help.

~~~

From Maggie Cribbs:

Matador, Texas
January 28, 1895

Mrs. P. F. Hawkins,

My dear sister in Christ. It is with a great pleasure that I perused your short and welcome letter. I was so surprised to hear of Sister Belle's dear little Junnie's death. Yes, it was hard to give the dear precious one up. I do wish I could come down and be with you all a while. And I will come too some time if it is God's will for me to come. I am anxious for all of my patients to get Science and health with the Key to the Scriptures, and read it all they can, and the Bible.

What is the matter with Katy? If it is a cough caused from anything you may think has caused it, I will treat it for fifteen dollars if she wants me to. She must write to me and state the cause of it.

I would love to see Cora's little girl. Really I want to see all of you. I know you were lonesome after Lizzie married. But you have one child left yet.

Many thanks to Lou for this stamp and envelope. Stamps are scarce with me for I am without any money now; except a little I am saving to buy a sack of flour with. No, do not be anxious about your daughter. She will talk all right. And never fear for God is all presence all power and all knowledge. There is nothing that can overpower all power. You think yes, she can speak plain. God is here and there is no fear. All of you think that she can speak plain and say that she wants to speak plain.

Do not doubt or be afraid. All is well when we put it in God's care which is good. God is the giver of every good and perfect gift. Give Him the praise for all blessings. Do right and help Lou to see and do right. Never get mad. Acknowledge God's presence and power at all times.

I send my love to all and kindest regards to inquiring friends. Ma is well. Pa and Ma both look better than they have in twelve years. All join me in love to all of you.

Lovingly your Sister in Christ
Maggie Cribbs

~~~

From Maggie Cribbs:

Matador, Texas
January 28, 1895

Miss Lou Hawkins,

My dear Sister in Christ: I have received your letter and this is the first one since the one I answered and sent in your Aunt Belle's letter before Christmas. I have answered all of your letters I have ever received.

I cannot tell the cause of you not improving any. I have treated you thoroughly: and will treat you a while longer. If you want to be restored to your natural speech you must do as I ask you to do. Now do not be afraid to speak but speak as others, without hesitation. God had made all that was made and all that He made was pronounced good. So your voice is all right and you can speak if you are not afraid and others around you are not afraid. For I have treated you.

You must not doubt God's power. There is nothing impossible with Him. God is love. All power all presence all knowledge. You must reflect God by being so good, so kind, so true and so loving to all. Love God good, with all of your mind, soul and strength and love neighbor as yourself. Speak ill of no man. Do unto others as you would have them do unto you. All that is not of God or good is discord. So you stuttering is discord and so unreal. Now in the name of Christ, all that is not of God or good to depart from you. Be good and you will get the good.

Do not think that you cannot speak as plain as any one. There is nothing that can keep you from speaking. God is all in all. Trust Him, dear one and you will receive the blessing and give Him the praise. You say get thee hence Satan. Thou cannot bind me any longer. I am free and can talk plain. God help me. The next time you write tell me that you can talk plain.

I am your loving Sister in Christ.
Maggie Cribbs

~~~

Louisa tried her best to follow Mrs. Cribbs' advice. She tried to speak without thinking—everything. She could sing without stuttering, although she admitted she couldn't carry a tune. Permelia spoke with their friend and preacher, Brother Elliott, asking if he knew about the science book Maggie Cribbs used. He knew something of them, and told her it was a faith called "Christian Science."

Dr. Williamson thought Louisa would outgrow her stuttering, as he had known it to happen. As for curing Anna Kate's cough for fifteen dollars, Permelia did not accept the offer. She obtained Dr. Williamson's help for Anna's ailment and gave her "Ipecac and squills" with a little wild cherry syrup at a fraction of the cost Maggie Cribbs asked.

~~~

From Robert Isaac:

Morehead, Ky.
February 3, 1895

My dear Sisters and Brothers and all,
    Well after a long delay I will write. We are all tolerable well and I hope you all are. Our little Johnny is getting along very well. He is so good and smart and pretty.

I haven't seen Greenup since I got your letter with those good pictures. Just like you all I know. Now let Dim and Sally send in theirs. I may get my mill photograph taken this summer and if so, I will send you one.

We are enjoying some fine weather and snow. Oh my, we have had some cold days.

Jack, I failed to tell you I saw your uncle Walter when he came through Morehead that time. He and his wife and son stopped off at the general store. It had been a long while since I saw him. His family seems to be taking real good care of him, and even with his blindness, he seemed in pretty fair condition. He was sitting right up there on the seat with his son.

Tom Johnson who married cousin Jane White has gone to San Antonio, Texas for his health. He has consumption and I think will die. if he does not get better in Texas he said he would go on to California to Newton. I have not heard Papa say anything about coming to Texas. He is still with us of course and is as well as usual. I must write to brother Newt. If I do not write very much this time you will excuse me I hope.

Jack, I want you to know I tend your folks' graves over at Siloam. It's kept up fine.

Belle, Henry McNasby is working in Morehead. Says he has not heard from you all for a long time.

Give our love to all and write soon. Reserve a share for yourself. Della will write a few lines.

Your brother,
R. I. Nickell

dear aunt

I hope you are well well aunt Johney is a grate big boy he is so sweet

Lizzy I would love to see you I got some oranges and an arithmetic and some lemons at Christmas I got a new dress too there is a big snow on now Lizzy I wish you were here to ride with me well I will close for this time Wright soon from Della to aunt Lou you ought to be hear and ride down the hill and skate on the ice with me we would have such fun.

good bye to all
Della

~~~

Ponds often froze over in Kentucky winters, but the Hawkins children had never been sure of the safety of small ponds in Texas. When younger, they slid down snowy embankments near their house, and Louisa once sprained her wrist trying to slide on a flour sack down a bumpy knoll.

Andrew's folks, as Robert Isaac mentioned, were William R. Hawkins and his wife, Judah Hawes. William was the eldest and Walter R. (Wat) was the youngest of five brothers, including John R., James R. and Moses R. They each had the middle initial "R." Caza Wilcoxin, James R's widow, stated in her deposition for a War of 1812 pension, that James made up the initial so he wouldn't be confused with all the other James Hawkinses in Northeastern Kentucky. This is a fact confusing to family researchers, if all the brothers did the same.

Moses R. married two of Permelia's aunts, first Melvina, and then her sister Martha Jane. During the War Between the States, they lived in Rowan County. Only one battle was fought in Rowan County during the War.[3] However, Morgan's Raiders created more worry for the people.

One of Moses' young neighbors slipped home from the Union Army to visit his family. Morgan's Raiders found it out and as he started back, they shot him many times in ambush. Moses heard the soldier scream with every shot and said, "That's Ben Ivins. I'm going to him."

In spite of the protest and fear of Aunt Martha Jane and the rest of the family, he followed a mountain trail and found Ben barely alive. Moses came home for a wagon and a feather bed. Somehow, alone, Moses managed to get him into the wagon and home. They nursed him back to health.

Some months later when Moses was alone in the house, two of those rebels returned to kill him for aiding Ivins. He stalled for a time so he could wash and get ready to die. He rolled up his sleeves and lay on the floor and said he was ready. One of the men wanted to shoot him, but the other suddenly overruled him, so they left, much against the protest of the first man.

Whenever Moses left the house again during the strife of the war, he was always where he could look back at the house, fearful that the renegade would return to kill him.

Sometime after the incident with Morgan's two men, Morgan himself came along the mountain trail with a small group and happened to stop at the door of the blacksmith shop while Moses prepared a shoe. He said Morgan was an imposing looking man, and Moses walked up to him, blessing him out for sending those two men to kill him. He said, "Open your mouth to lie and I'll brain you. Never come near this shop again!"

Morgan left without any problem. They never knew why Morgan didn't attack him or why he stopped in the first place, but Andrew knew Moses would have gone after Morgan as long as there wasn't any trickery from the other side.

Moses was a good blacksmith and was well respected. Once while he was repairing a two-wheel dray for an old skinflint who lived a few miles distance, the man asked to pay for it with hay. He returned with what hay he could put on a one-ox cart and unloaded it where Moses told him. The man came back to the shop and expected to get the work done on this day, plus about four or five dollars more for himself for all the hay he brought.

Moses kept right on shoeing the horse and said, "This will just about even the debt you owe me." He had done other work for the man and somehow he always got off without paying, so this time it worked out. While Moses shod the horse, the animal kicked the nail, ripping open Moses' finger to the bone. He poured the wound full of turpentine and wrapped it. He then finished the job.

Moses and Aunt Martha Jane's youngest daughter married William George. He served in the war and had fifteen captured men left in his charge one time while he was guarding a long wagon train of ammunition and supplies. The wagons were moving slower than the army ahead. All day he and his men followed the wagons. Tired and weary, they topped one hill after another, and could see the wagon train far ahead, topping another hill. The men wanted to guard the wagon train first. As he left them and hurried ahead, he caught the last wagon. He laid down his gun and held to the tailgate to keep going—a lone guard for all those wagons.

The next morning Morgan's Raiders took their camp while the men slept and they paroled them, which meant death if they were caught again. One day William ran the top edge of a ravine all day, back and forth, throwing shells to the fighting men below. Bullets cut the brush and small trees from the path he followed, but none touched him.

By this time he was weak and sick and took a short walk, coming to a rail fence. He leaned on it a while and tried to pick up apples from the ground. A burly Dutchman with a large white bulldog came up, with the dog jumping from side to side. Dutch, with fists drawn back, was cursing the young man. William was too tired to defend himself and said, "You can destroy me but if you do, that camp down there will destroy you and all you possess." Dutch then helped him over the fence and gave him apples.

When William George told the boys about it, he had a hard time holding them from going to get the Dutchman.

But back to Moses: When the railroad came through Hillsboro, Kentucky after the war, Moses had a large white house. It was an inn where people would eat and sleep while waiting for their train. Moses obtained permission to operate it as a tavern. Being a blacksmith became secondary to his business as an innkeeper.

Moses R. Hawkins died of cancer of the jaw, and he would let no one dress his wound except his daughter, George Ann. One day as she started to replace the dressing his whole cheek came out in her hand. Such was the courage of some of the old folks of the times, with no available medical help.[4]

February 1895

At long last Anna Kate and Jim had a little girl. They called her Survella Irene, born on the eighteenth of February. The baby weighed only four pounds and exhibited a good set of lungs. Anna remained weak, and Jim waited on her with no complaints. Louisa was happy since the baby's birthday came the day before her own. By this time John Robert and Maggie had their second child, Orbra.

~~~

From Lizzie:

Cyrus, Texas
March 9, 1895

To one and all:

This morning finds me seated for the purpose of answering your most kind and welcome letter we received yesterday, and were so glad to hear from you. But real sorry to hear Cora's little Lula Pearl was complaining. Hope all are well now.

Katie, we were glad to know you were able to write this time. Hope you will continue to improve. Pa, I hope you are well now and able to plow.

Yes Mama, I have beat you. My garden that is planted is about up. I have peas, lettuce, mustard, kale, raddish, beets, onion, cabbage and tomatoes. I want to plant some more in a few days. I have six hens and a rooster. About four or five are laying.

Lou, Mr. Tol Darden is here now. He told me to tell the girls up there if any wanted to marry to come down here. There is going to be a law passed that men have to marry when they are thirty or before or pay a five hundred dollar fine. So he says it is time for him to hunt a woman. Now you can believe that if you want to.

George, has Lou and Johnnie got a brand on the press today? Now Sis, I don't allow that. How do you like Johnnie's company anyway? You're the only one left now. Oh, I would love to see little Orbra walking and little Lula Pearl trying to. I guess Myrtle is as sweet as ever. Howdy to Maggie and Buddy. Ha! Bud, I don't know why you don't write to your sister. I'll remember that when I come up there.

Cora, Bob Darden's writing to May Shofner. I gave her to him. Don't tell it though.

Jim, if I had of had any idea you would name that little sweet thing what I wanted to, I would sure have sent it a

name. I was sorry to hear about Mr. Scarbro being poorly.
Henry wants to say something. He's taking the pen right out
of my hand . . . .

Now he wants to write something smart in my letter.

Sister I want you to send me some of my flower seed. I
left everything nearly. If you have any moss rose send some
seed and cypress, zinnias, and other seed you can. I want to
plant them soon. Yes I will write again before I come. Cora, if
you all move to the Atchison place will you wait until Mauda
marries? What does Joe do? Tell Mauda howdy for me.

Did we write in the other letter about an artist being
here close to us? I cooked bread for him all the time he was
here so he took our photos. We haven't got them yet. I guess
he will send a dozen to us. And will certainly send you one.

We have had a right good shower this morning and it is
still drizzling. Henry is going after a cow this morning across
the river.

Katie, I have pieced me a spool quilt, only one spool half
nearly as large as four of yours. I pieced it out of red, green
and white all over the bed and 'tis pretty.

Lou, I am going to try to get Miss Dell Hogan to come up
there with me. I don't want to come alone. The smallpox is in
the convict's camp near Fowler and I will have to come
through there. Jim, you must write next time. I will close.
Write as soon as you get this letter. Henry will add some
now.

> Good bye.
> I remain your daughter, sister, and
> Aunt Lizzie Romine

From Henry:
Hello everybody,

Lou, I wish you would come and help your sister for she
has so much to do she's in trouble. Ma, D has decided to
come up there the fifth Sunday in this month if you will meet

her in Walnut Springs. She can stay as long as she will if you all bring her home and if not, she must come back the next Sunday. I can't afford to lose much time. The train goes to Walnut Springs at ten fifteen in the morning. She can leave Whitney at nine and get there in a few minutes.

Well as it is raining and I can't get out, I will try and write some. Ma, Lizzie said she wouldn't milk and I traded off my cow. But now she says she will milk and churn and pour coffee too if I will buy another cow. She has got more to do than anybody I guess. She has got six hens and a rooster and she gets seven eggs every day. The old rooster won't lay in one nest. He just struts around.

You let us know what works best for you.

Henry

~~~

From Ella Goodnow:

Capay, California
March 24, 1895

Dear Cousins one and all,

So glad to hear from you and that you got your dress. I thought it was real nice. Send me a piece of it when you cut it out. This Sabbath day is just as fine as anyone could wish it to be. The sun is shining so warm. We had a nice rain last week. The grain looks so fine. Cousin Newton is plowing and will get through next week he thinks. He is awful tired at night and I believe a little cross too.

Cousin Newt and Pearl, Daisy, and a friend, Miss Mary Zimmerman all went to church. I would like to have gone but I thought my dress was too old so had to stay at home. Poor me has a hard row to hoe I can tell you. Work from four in the morning until nine at night. Oh am so tired! Only get scolding when everything doesn't go just so. You know how men folks are. They do not think a woman ever gets tired. Perhaps I will get a rest when I'm dead. There is no pleasure on this earth for me. If you were to stay here a month you would say so too. No more on that subject as it doesn't amount to anything anyway.

I and Chet are herding horses today. Those that plow, plow sixteen head. Well cousin I have got ninety-nine turkey eggs setting and about one hundred twenty hen eggs. I wish they would all hatch. Have six more turkeys to set. I put fifteen eggs under them—twelve under a chicken. Hen eggs are only worth eight cents a dozen. Butter twelve and a half cents per pound.

Mr. Goodnow is plowing on our other place up in the canyon. Has not been home for most a month. How is your husband's health now? Oh, you and your brothers Jerry and Dim come to visit us will you? We would be so proud. Come the last of July and go with us camping. We stay until the last of August. It is fine.

I would like to see Katy's and Cora's babies and oh I wish we had the means. We would come to visit you some time. What would a ticket from here cost do you know? I am sure I do not. You could visit Pa's. Oh such a jolly time we would have. Have not been to Pa's for over a month but heard from them. They were well. Wrote to Robert Isaac the other day. Uncle Will is with him as you know. How I wish I could see Uncle Will. Wish Pa could see him once more on this earth, as twin brothers should be closer.

Pa has a nice little home. He owes a little on it yet, but will soon be out of debt. That was what put us behind in buying land. Some men never know when they are well off. It is buy buy all the time. Hope some day we will be out of debt. It looks rather slim now. If these hard times had not come, everyone would have been better off. I can tell you it is good for the rich people I suppose.

Now Permelia, answer this letter and will you tell me all the news? Your brother sends his love and best wishes. He is proud to think you like your dress and kerchief. Now give my love to all your girls and cousin Jerry's and cousin Jim's families. Tell them to write to me. Now goodbye for this time from your ugly cousin Ella to you all. From your brother also. Oh we had a very heavy frost that ruined most all the fruit and almonds, tomatoes, and everything that it could take a bite of.

Ella Goodnow

~~~

With each letter from her cousin Ella, Permelia spoke of the jolly times she would have with the Goodnow family, brother Newton and her Uncle James Joshua. Permelia often discussed going there, but it was make believe. She never saw California.

CHAPTER 11

How does your garden grow? – Burrs, burrs! – Seven doses of Black Draught – Digging a well – It's much too cold – Survella is sick (with a tick) – Smallpox – Lizzie's first baby – A big fight

~~~

From Lizzie and Henry:

Cyrus, Texas
May 8, 1895

Dear parents one and all:

I will try tonight to answer your letter received several days ago. Lou Babe said the rest of you would write in a few days, so we just kept waiting and have not heard from the rest yet! So we will write anyway and not wait any longer. This leaves us tolerable well. Hope all are well up there, and sorry Katy has the sore eyes.

Mama, have you heard from cousin Ella lately? Katy, why doesn't cousin Gessella write to me or have you heard from her yet? It would be nice to go to Clinton County for a visit, but what a long way to Missouri it is. Cora, are you and George and the little Pearl getting along? Why don't you write to us? Now if you have written when you get this letter just answer it right then, and we won't write any more until we get an answer from these scribbles.

Jim, do you know we haven't got a Herald paper since I came home, and our time wasn't out then, but it is now. I wrote to that man two weeks ago but still haven't gotten any paper yet. I wish you would tell him as soon as you can and we will pay him, for I look forward to the news.

Pa, how are you feeling? Have you had plenty of rain? How does your crop look now? Be sure to answer what I want to know.

Sis, Miss Dell came and now she is going home Saturday. She said tell you she would be thinking about coming back again before you come. I don't know how in the world I will get along without her, as what would we do without friends? She came so often to see me and the other girls are all out hoeing. She wants me to spend the day with her tomorrow, but I must wash in the morning.

Well, Mama how is your garden? Mine is a dandy. I have got about two hundred cabbage plants living, one hundred tomatoes, fifty peppers and lots of beets, potatoes, beans, cucumbers and radishes. Well, everything that grows in the garden nearly. Will have peas to eat before many days and Katy, what a watermelon patch we are going to have.

Katy, I would have had your quilt done long ago if I had worked on it. All the time I have quilted on two quilts lately and quilted one by myself in two days. I will have yours done by the time you read this letter I guess. Bud, I guess you and Maggie never aim to write. Kiss the little shuggies for me. Myrtle, have you forgot Aunt Lizzie yet? Good by to all and write soon as you get this. Henry wants to write more.

Love to all from
Lizzie and Henry.

~~~

From Henry Romine:

May 8, 1895

Kind people one and all,

A line or so from me too. As I don't think you are going to write I will try to answer your kind letter we received some time ago. This leaves us well and with plenty of work to do. I have plowed nary a day in the past two weeks. It has rained nearly every day and everybody is behind as well as myself. I will begin laying the corn next week if it doesn't rain too much. I am chopping cotton now. I want to get half of it chopped this week. Cotton looks mighty pretty.

Ask George and Jim if they would say "su-y" if the hogs were eating their crops up and see if they say they would. And ask then why they don't write. I must close. Write soon. I remain as ever.

R. H. Romine

From Lizzie:

Well, I guess this is all for this time. Henry's cotton just came up since it has commenced raining and he has it plowed over once and going over it again. His hired hand is chopping cotton too. He will plant the other half of his cotton some time next week maybe, if it stops raining.

Lizzie

<div align="center">~~~</div>

From Henry Romine:

Cyrus, Texas
May 12, 1895

Kind people, to one and all,

This rainy morning finds me seated for the purpose of answering your prompt letter that I received and have just read with pleasure. You must have answered as soon as you got our letter. And was glad to hear you were well. D is complaining worse.

Rain, rain, burrs, burrs! Shut your mouth about burrs and rain, for here is the place to find all of them. I am sure it has rained four days out of every week for the last seven weeks, and certainly it hasn't been dry since last I wrote to you.

There isn't anybody hardly that has got all of their cotton planted yet. I think it will rain again tonight.

R. H. Romine

~~~

From Lizzie:

Cyrus, Texas
May 12, 1895

Dear folks, one and all,

Tonight I will try to answer your letter. We were glad to hear from you all. I am not feeling well tonight and you must excuse my writing.

Oh how glad I would be to see you all one more time. We got a letter from Katy and Jim yesterday. Jim said to watch out for them soon. But I can't believe any of you will ever come. Just think, only a little piece down here and we have been down here five months and you all haven't come yet. Come some of you by the nineteenth of next month and we will go to the negro picnic. Just a short distance from here. Mama, you know that was the day the negroes were freed. What an important thing for them.

Well, I don't know what I would do down here if the people weren't so good to me. Mrs. Hogan came up here yesterday and brought me some tea cakes and Mrs. Alexander sent me a glass of butter. I surely ate this morning. I had beets for dinner. Come down and we will have some more. Jim, don't you think Cretia is as pretty a name as Survella?

George, Henry is coming up there after his brooms. He will be glad to get them.

Well now talk about somebody being surprised, we were when we got that long letter from you. Poor little Myrtle got wasp stung. Maggie, did you make a paste for it? I will kiss you honey and make it all better. Little Lula Pearl, if I had hold of you I would nearly smother you with hugs. Tell little Aubry Aunt Lizzie loves him too. Well, it is morning and not raining, so I will finish here so I can iron. Come baby Cretia Irene and I will kiss you if you will help me iron. I guess I'll call Survella that name for a time.

Mama, what is the matter with Millicent—has she come down there yet? I wonder how her little girl Cora is. I hope you get to see her boys often. I would love to see them all. Cora, someday when mama gives you extra butter you slip off and bring it down here and I will help you eat it. Papa, have you got your crop laid out yet?

Well, I must close. I asked all the questions I can think of to ask. I will write more news later. I can't have another babe until I have this one, so it won't be that kind of news. By by. Here, Cretia, is a piece of Aunt Lizzie's new dress in the envelope.

Love to all,
Lizzie and Henry

~~~

From Henry Romine:

Cyrus, Texas
July 6, 1895

Dear folks one and all,

This night I will try to answer your kind letter I received today and was glad to hear from you all. D has a large garden and everything is up. I have just begun planting corn. I will have about two or three acres in corn I guess.

Jim, I have traded for me a cultivator. I guess I can manage my crop all right. I got another plow and that has set me back some though. It is ready for work this morning. Lou, you must come down and eat peppers and spuds with me.

We have got spuds enough to do forever the way we planted them.

George, it is raining this morning. We need a good rain now since this month has started off so dry. Has it rained up there since the last snow? We haven't received any rain hardly this month. There is some sickness in the partoaks. The smallpox is all around us. It's a bit scary, as I don't know how close you can be to someone and not catch it. Not that I plan to get close.

D can come up there the first of next month if she will come, tho' I don't think she will.

Well breakfast is ready and I must close. Write soon.

R. H. Romine

~~~

From Lizzie:

Tuesday morning
Cyrus, Texas
July 8, 1895

Dear parents, one and all:

This dark cloudy rainy morning I will try to answer your kind and gladly received letter. Henry wrote his letter Sunday but as I did not feel able to write I waited until today. I don't feel much better now though I will try to write a few lines. Two weeks tomorrow I commenced taking pills—taken twelve and did no good. Then taken seven doses black draught and it just made me so sick and weak I haven't done much since. Then Thursday night I took a sick headache and threw up, and haven't got over that spell yet.

Mrs. Hogan came and stayed Friday eve and Saturday all day with me and did the work. She was so good. She and Mrs. Darden bring me milk and eggs or something every time they come. They are so nice to me. Mama, how do you put up cucumbers and how many will it take to do us and have plenty?

Lou, I have some fine tomatoes now if they ever get ripe. And plenty of them if the chickens will not get to them first. And my nice heads of cabbages too—the little old rabbits just eat in the heads and then let go. Henry cut seven the other morning. Sent three to Mrs. Darden, three to Mrs Alexander and we ate ours. They are sure nice. How are yours?

Yes, you found I was glad to hear George joined the church. You all wrote like he and Cora had written to us but they haven't. So we don't know when he joined or anything.

Well, I wish you could have come down last month on the nineteenth. I went to the Negro meetings. Several of us whites went. They didn't mind us being there, for it was a big celebration.

> Love to all.
> Lizzie

Katy's babe must be a dandy!

~~~

Black Draught,[1] a popular medication in liquid form in the nineteenth century and granules or tablet in modern-day. Seven doses could easily make Lizzie weak, or be harmful to the baby if the strength was the same as today's.

Lizzie's garden was not unlike most of the gardens in the area, as she followed her mother's plan for growing vegetables. Permelia and Louisa, the only women present in the Hawkins household, still put up canned foods. Permelia always put up cucumbers. For serving, she sliced them in a dish of thick cream, along with small chunks of tomato and a little green onion. She had no recipe for catchup but prepared it by how the mixture looked as she progressed.

This particular summer, Andrew hired a young man to help with the crops. His name was Ed Barnes, from Tennessee. He had freckles like Louisa and a shock of wavy red hair. He was a "Christian boy" and a hard worker. Ed planned to stay the season, then work his way to Colorado.

~~~

From Maggie Romine:

Nemo, Texas
July 16, 1895

My dear Henry and Lizzie,

This morning I will write you a few lines to let you know we are all alive. We were glad to hear from you all but sorry that you have both been sick. Lizzie, I am at Edna's for the first time since that day you left. She has got on a hubbard.[2] I told her that I was going to tell you she had to wear it.

You asked me about my quilt. I have not got enough to finish it. I haven't got the money to get any more goods. When I come I will bring what I have got done. George can't spare the money right now.

Oh Lizzie I made my dress. It is sure pretty. Mrs. Johnson says I look like a bride so you will just have to excuse me this time. I will be down there before long. Henry I am sorry I missed the colored picnic last month. There was one here that day too.

Well I must close. Write soon.

Maggie Romine

~~~

From Lizzie:

Tuesday morning
Cyrus, Texas
August 24, 1895

Dear people one and all,
   This morning I will try to answer your letter received
Saturday. Were so glad to hear from you and to hear you got
home all right. It was so good to have you here. This leaves
Henry well and me just able to get about and help do the
work. Henry has gone to dig Mr. Hix's well this morning. I will
be here all day by myself now since you all helped me so
much.
   Mama, Henry's mother cooked that soap two or three
days while she was here and put two or three buckets of
water in. There was still lye in it so I just cut it out anyhow. It
looks like good soap. I feel so bad I will rest a while. If Jim
was here now, Henry would give him a dollar a day hauling
manure for Mr. Hix while he is at work on that well. I do
want him and Kate to come so bad. How are all getting
along? Henry can't write this time.
   Buddy, I want you and George to read every word of this
by yourselves. I must close my letter. I have been lying down
and now I have a chill. I can't sit up to write. It is almost mail
time so I will just send these pen scribbles on today as I have
them written. Will sure do better next time if possible. Oh I
do ache so bad and am nearly frozen. We have plenty of
wood and still I am so cold I surely will break if I moved.
Haven't written half enough.
   Now you remember, whenever you possibly can come
down here even if it's just for a short visit. Write soon.

Bye bye.
Lizzie

Old Gray is dead.

~~~

Jim and Anna Kate planned to go down to Cyrus for a visit, and maybe stay longer. Old Gray was a horse Henry had since long before he married. Permelia's horse in Kentucky was named Billy. She assured everyone Billy could carry on a conversation with her. No one seemed to believe it, but no one questioned it either.

~~~

From Katy:

Cyrus, Texas
August 30, 1895

Dear folks at home, one and all,

I will try to answer your good letter received yesterday, but don't know whether I will ever get it done or not for this babe. I don't believe there ever was a babe that cried as much as this one.

No difference where I put her, Survella is going to get hurt. She has fallen off the bed twice. You can't let loose of her a second but what she is just going rolling. This morning I left her on the bed. Put all the chairs around the bed and tucked the mattress up. I ran out to the fence and drug the kettle up to the porch to catch it full of water. Just as I got to the porch I heard her hit the floor but it did not seem to hurt her. She fell out of her box on the bed and rolled off.

If I put her on the floor she bumps her nose and I don't want her to get her nose bleeding. If I tie her in the chair so she can't possibly fall out, she will tear a hole in the quilt and choke on the cotton.

Last Wednesday she was fretful and did not sleep a bit good. I wondered what was the matter with her. It did not seem like she was sick so that evening I took her and sat

down in the kitchen door to watch her, to see if I could find
out what was the matter. I watched her about five minutes
and she would flinch like something was hurting or biting
her. I raised up her dress and put my hand on her and looked
to see if her little tummy was swelled. And would you
believe there was a tick on her. We got it out after the
longest time and she hasn't fretted a bit since. She has a
terrible cold and is coughing a right smart though.

I am giving her some of my cough medicine. My cough is
better and I am on my second bottle of medicine. I was
getting uneasy. I had that rattling in my throat and my lungs
hurt after I washed two weeks washing for Lizzie and two for
myself. I don't expect I will wash very much more myself. Jim
told Henry he expected some of these negroes would do
most of my washing. Jim has to carry all the water from the
gin. I thought I could go down there and wash but no one
else goes there and we don't expect they allow fire down at
the gin.

It is raining now. I have two tubs full of water and the full
kettle. Jim, a man from Whitney and six negroes are at work
putting up the cotton press. There are two or three bales
ready to gin next week. Henry has had fever ever since
Wednesday. It is six o'clock and my letter not finished yet.

We've had company. Miss Ella White has been here all
evening—that is the White whose pa died. And it has also
rained all evening. Cora, Mrs. Alexander stayed all one
evening. Her mouth had fever blisters all over—all of them
had the chills and Mrs. Dike did too. I hope it isn't smallpox
because we were with them all that time. Oh isn't that awful
about Lillie Mary, to die from it. There have been three or
four died over across the river with that disease. Mr.
Alexander ate dinner here today. He said he had the sore
throat and had it about ten days and it wouldn't go away. I
wonder if he had a doctor to look at him or not.

Aunt Belle, I'll kiss Survella for you and whole lots for
you, Mama. Now you must kiss Lula Pearl, and John Robert
kiss Myrtle and Aubry for me. Well, I must finish this
morning. That man working at the press mashed Jim's finger
and he can't write. I forgot to ask him what he wanted to say
but he can tell you more maybe what he will do in the next
letter. I sure love to live in this house. It has six windows. If
there is any air we get it. Lou, I cut the curtains in two and
made blinds. Little Sis, tell me more about Ed. Have you take
a liking to him?

I hope we can get more butter and milk soon. I would
rather have that than any of the other good things to eat.

Mr. Shults went to Whitney last Monday. Got him an
alarm clock that he gave a dollar and a quarter for and also
some medicine. John Robert, what time that Saturday did
you get home? George, tell Sister Cauble that I cannot go in
the wagon so far to church and so often, but I do hope how
soon it may be we will have a church close to us.

We remain as ever your loving children, brother, sister,
also uncle and aunt.

Katy

<div style="text-align:center">~~~</div>

From Lizzie and Henry:

Cyrus, Bosque County, Tex.
September 4, 1895

Dear people one and all,

This evening I will try to answer your most welcome
letter. Oh Buddy you little scamp. I was so glad you came
down but you made me want to see the rest so bad. I did
want you to get across the river so bad. Buddy, were you
scared? The water was so high. You just went flying. I was

scared to death for you. Did you get home with no trouble and when did you get there?

You sent some of my last letter back. Did you mean to or couldn't you read it?

Mama, you never said a word about coming. I have just begun to think the rest of you are not coming at all. The time seems awful long for me to sit here not able to do much and study about you all being up there going to preaching and no good meeting here to go to. Well that's all right I guess. Do I sound like I'm feeling sorry for myself?

I do miss Katy and Jim while they were there. It is so good to have them close though.

They need to write to us. I guess they will slip in on us again. If any of you do aim to come you had better hurry if you want anything to eat. The cabbages are all burning up and tomato and cucumber vines too. But if it will rain soon maybe they will be all right. I never saw things burn up so quick in my life. It looks like just one day of this sun does it.

It has been looking like rain all day but hasn't done it. Cora, are there any peaches on those trees? I wish I could make some peach preserves. When have you ever heard from Mrs. Eoff, for I wish she would write to me. Well this is Monday evening and I will finish my letter. It is finally coming a good rain. It will help everything so much.

Henry has gone over the river to get me some medicine. I feel right bad today. One of Mrs. Romine's stepfather's nephews is here. He hoed for Henry this morning and will continue for a few days since he has nothing else to do. It is well enough Maggie, that I didn't get across the river or I would have spanked your little ones. We haven't got any letter from Ma Romine for six or eight weeks, and we don't know what to think. She has always written just as soon as she got our letters. Goodby. Write soon.

Lizzie and Henry

I would write some though you would probably send it
back. Guess I haven't time to write any more today. We are
sure glad to hear Ed's working out good. –Henry

~~~

From Lizzie:

September 20, 1895
Cyrus, Texas

Dear parents one and all,
    This morning I will try to answer your most welcome
letter. This leaves me getting along very well, but Henry has
been sick one week tomorrow. He took a round of calomel
yesterday and last night a big lot of salts, and this morning a
dose of oil and turpentine. It has not acted yet.
    I guess it will take another round tomorrow or next day.
    Lillie and Nettie Hix professed at the Methodist meeting
on the creek the other night. Tib and Dollie, Walter Whiddon
and Birdie, Mr. Cambell and Nettie, Sam Alexander and Lillie
went to church in the wagon. Mr. Cambell is going to stay on
this side of the river for a while. He is making this his home
and feeding and tending to the things while Henry is sick.
This morning they hitched to his cart and are taking a ride. I
think they will take me to Katy when they come back. I want
to see that little Babe Survella so bad. By the way, Fannie M.
is married.
    Henry and I washed this week. Kate can't keep coming
over here to help me wash, that's for sure! She's not able by
rights to do her own washing. Bud, you all write to us again.
Kiss those children for me.
    Mama, I have two hens setting and five laying. Papa, do
you like rabbit? If so, you ought to have been here this
morning and helped us eat. Miss Ella White is at Mrs.
Dardens now. Mrs. Hix stayed all day with me the day Katy

came. First time since before I went home. Yes, you know those chills hurt me and I had three.

Mama, Mrs. Romine left her feather bed with me until we go up there. She wrote to us to send her money to get cans and she would can us some peaches as I just don't feel up to it. I don't know whether Henry will send it or not. Thank you for all the good peaches and the new broom. Mama, Mrs. Alexander has been sick and is salivated. She does look so bad. I hope she doesn't get the smallpox. I guess for sure now I don't have it or I would have been long gone by now.

Mama, when had you better come? You know the nine months will be out about the twenty-fifth or twenty-seventh, some where along there, but Katy was saying I might be sick two weeks before. I was aiming for you to come about the twenty-fifth but maybe you had better come before then. Now answer as soon as you get this and tell me what is best for you, for you know I don't do anything hardly (and I sure want you to be here.) Write soon so we can write again before you come.

Lou, would you send me one or two of your G. E. newspapers to read. I wish you were all here today. This letter is to all of you and all of you write back.

Love to all,
Lizzie

Tell George and Cora to write and beat on Lula Pearl for me.

~~~

Permelia was on the scene for the birth of Cora, Anna, and Maggie's children. She would be there for Lizzie. Cases of smallpox appeared in isolated incidences, and the Romines worried about the smallpox in their area. The news of the disease in Katy's letter was not one a mother would want to hear.

~~~

From Henry Romine:

Cyrus, Texas
October 19, 1895

Kind people one and all,
On this lovely Lord's day morning I will try to write you all a few lines. D had another chill this morning and she is mighty sick right now. I coughed all night and she hurt all night. The baby is fat as she can be. She doesn't cry much and hasn't ever been sick since you left here. Lizzie will write when she feels up to the task.
Kate, Jim is a batching without you. He has run the gin one day since he came back. Well I will close for this time and let Jim and D write some. I will try to write some more if I have time.

R. H. Romine.

Tuesday the 22, 1895

I will write you all a few more lines. This leaves us both sick. D had a chill Sunday morning and had four yesterday morning. She is up this morning and feels very well. I have had the worst cold I ever had. I coughed two months. I had fever yesterday though I feel some better this morning. Jim is ginning again and he is all right as far as I know.
Ma, if you want to you can buy one pig from John Robert and I will get you one if two will make you meat. I will fatten you two wives up. It was good to have Lou down here as well as you. I will close now. Not yet.
Sorry to hear about the fight there. We had a fight down here last week. One man beat the other nearly to death—beat him on the head and hurt his breast. He has been

spitting up blood ever since and it isn't coming from a tooth. It will go mighty hard with him in court I'm afraid.

Lou, there is going to be a big picnic the twenty-fourth. Come down and we will take that in. Ma, come and I will give you all the cucumbers you can eat, and potatoes, cabbage and tomatoes. I gather a water bucket full of cucumbers ever other morning.

When have you heard from my folks? I haven't heard in a long time. Well I will close by asking you to write soon. Maybe D will write before I send this off. I remain as ever.

R. H. Romine

From Lizzie:

I will write a little now. Everyone tell us about everything. Kiss the rest of the little chaps for us. Hope Maggie and John are getting along well now. I want them to come down this summer. What did Dutch and Burl fight about? How is Dutch?

Henry had pulled a lot of our little white beans and is trying to pick them off the vines.

The vines were awful green but lots of the beans have rotted with so much rain and some haven't matured. Maybe we will save some and will have beans this winter. They aren't my favorite food but aren't so bad cooked with bacon grease. One good thing is we will have plenty of other good things to eat. I just need to have it ready.

Bye, bye. Write soon.
Lizzie

<div align="center">~~~</div>

Permelia and Louisa made the trip to Bosque County, staying until after Lizzie's baby was born. They named her Jewel. This was Louisa's first experience in helping with a newborn. Actually, she was no help at all, by her own admission, but she enjoyed rocking the finished product.

An old superstition back in Kentucky was to place an axe under the bed, with blade up, and the delivery would be made easier. Permelia put no such stock in it. However, she liked to believe a child born on Christmas day would always be happy and have the power of understanding animals. Permelia was not born on Christmas but loved animals. She would never believe a black cat was bad luck.

When Louisa and her mother returned home, Permelia told everyone about Lizzie's garden. They had made poke salad (sallet) with dock, field mustard, wild pepper, dandelions—that and more made up the dish—as many tasty wild greens one could find. Lambs quarters was another choice, but Louisa thought it was bitter.

CHAPTER 12

*Books and buckets went flyin' – Cora's baby, Silas –
Newton marries his cousin, Pearl Goodnow – Sadness
back home – Bread for photographs*

~~~

From Ella Goodnow:

Capay, California
January 25, 1896

Dear Cousins one and all,

We received your most welcome letter and were so glad
you like your dress. I got Pearl and myself one just like it. We
are all well but my little William. He has such a bad cold. His
eyes are also so sore—I guess it is caused from cold. I need
to make up some rose water. He had ulcers in his throat.
They are gone now but he has taken another cold. Am afraid
they will come back. Oh when he is sick I am so uneasy for he
will not tell us how he feels. He is so sweet. Cousin Newton
loves him so much and he thinks just as much of cousin.
Newton got him a goat and William is afraid of it. It will rear
up on its hind feet and shake its head at him.

We have had such a stormy time for about two weeks.
Will be glad when it clears up so William will have a chance
to walk outside and play. The girls and Chet go to school.
They like their teacher very much.

Oh I wish you were only here to stay all winter with us.
We would just enjoy to hear you tell us of your young days
and of Uncle Will.[1] How was he when you got a letter from
Robert Isaac? Who does your papa live with now? We wrote
him a letter and he does not answer. Wish he would. How is
he now? I am going to send him a present one of these days.

Why does Lou not write to the children? They would be glad to get a letter from her.

We are milking two old dry cows. Make enough butter just for our own use. Now you tell all the folks down there that we would like to see them. Belle might write me a letter once more. She writes the nicest letters. Wish I could see her.

I have not made any garden yet. We are having church at Capay. I have not been for a long time. I guess I will not know how to behave when I do go.

Now do write Pa a letter will you, for they will be so rejoiced to read a letter from you.

Don't forget now. His PO is East Grafton, Yolo Co, California. Do write me a long letter too.

Cousin Newton says tell you he would love to see you the best in the world. He has not forgot you even if he doesn't come to see you. Now Jack, you do not ever say a word to me. If you only saw my ugly face you would like me a little bit.

Ella G.

~~~

From Daisy, daughter of Ella Goodnow:

Capay, Cal.
Jan. 26, 1896

My dear Cousins one and all,

As Mama has got through writing to your Mother, I thought I would scratch you off a few lines. How are you all? We are all well except Little Willie. He has been sick for about two weeks but he is better now.

Well I will tell you what I got for Christmas. I got an autograph book, a silk handkerchief, and two scarf pins, a book from my teacher and two little ornaments. They are just awful pretty. My sister Pearl got a gold watch and other things. Little Willie got a little horse, a pistol, a horn, and candy and nuts. We all got a few presents. I want you to write and tell me what you got and all the news.

I had two new dresses made this winter. One is a black sateen and one is brown. Lilly Perkins made them. Pearl had two made. Mama had three.

We had more fun than a little. We got to school and had a fine old time. Mary Parker is my schoolmate and she is the funniest girl ever I saw. Pearl and Eva Parker ride the horses mornings. Mary and I ride them at night. We have a race nearly every night. One morning Mary came to school and didn't have a bridle on her horse, only a rope across his nose.

Henry Taylor was riding behind us talking to Pearl and Eva. Pretty soon he just came flying up behind us popping his whip. The old horse just lit out. The rope came off his nose and I told Mary to jump off, and she wouldn't do it. We lost our buckets, books, and hats. Then I jumped off backwards and the old horse stopped. Then I jumped up and grabbed him. I just laughed until I was sick.

I will close as it is late and I am sleepy. This is especially to Miss Louisa Hawkins. Answer soon.

From your Cousin
Daisy M. Goodnow

~~~

From Lizzie:

Cyrus, Texas
April 3, 1896

Dear ones at home,

I will try to write you a few lines now. We got to Whitney at three o'clock. We hired a buggy and got to D's at five o'clock. The man charged two dollars and fifty cents. Henry will pay it.

Jewel is so sweet. She had not cried a bit. She laughs all the time and is not a bit afraid of us atall. She is a great big thing. We have got an invitation to a party tonight at Mr. Porter's. I guess we will try to stay until before three Sunday. Jim, I don't guess you will have to meet us.

Mama don't buy that lard till I come home. I hope you all will get along all right without me, Sis. The mail has come. Lula and Cora have come now. Goodby. Write soon. Isn't Silas a little man though?

Kiss to all
Lizzie

Just a note the next day before mailing. With the girls here, I have not time to write more. I am so glad they are here. Lou tells me Ed went to Colorado. I thought they might get something going. Can't tell how she's taking it. Howdy to everyone. Send the note on. Jim, I guess you were glad to see Charles Allen. Katy, I am so sorry you are feeling poorly. Mama, you all write as soon as you get this. Maybe we will see each other soon. I may have to stay at home. I have forty chicks to look after.

Love to everyone. Must quit now.

Write soon.
Lizzie

~~~

When Lizzie said they might stay until three o'clock on Sunday, that seemed to be a normal procedure. Friends invited to a gathering at someone's house were graciously welcome to spend the night if going home after the party meant a long buggy ride. Usually there were not enough beds, but the hosts would make the guests a pallet on the floor, or sleep on the floor themselves and give their bed to the guests. After a big breakfast the next morning, they said their goodbyes and were on their way. A reciprocal invitation would soon be issued.

Lizzie had only forty chicks to take care of. Her Aunt Belle tended many more, and Permelia had as many as one hundred. In winter she kept them in a closed porch off the kitchen. Selling them could bring in hard cash, but it was a risky business keeping them warm in cold weather. On occasion, methods of keeping them warm resulted in burning down the house.[2]

Cora and George named their new baby Silas Allen, for his grandpa Shults who lived in Missouri. Lula Pearl spent a lot of time watching over him, and George was apparently a doting father. Louisa was now busy being auntie to all the children in the family. Cora asked only one thing of George and that was not to smoke his pipe close to the baby.

~~~

From Ella Goodnow:

Capay, Cal.
April 11, 1896

Dear Cousins one and all,

Your most welcomed letter just arrived. Was glad to hear you were all well and hearty. I do not feel well today, as my stomach has experienced such miserable pains for about a week. I do not know what makes it unless it is indigestion. I sent and got some medicine this eve. Well our grain looks just fine. Yes, your brother is running our place of five hundred ninety-five acres and it is all ours. There is no mortgage on it. The mortgage was outlawed last fall and it was a great thing for us. A mortgage is the worst thing that ever was invented. I only hope there will never be another one on our land again.

Your brother is well. He is sitting by the stove and smoking his pipe. We have had the finest rains this spring we have had for years. The grass is fine. Oh, my mare has the finest colt. It is a mare also. Now you send it a nice name in your next letter. I have about thirty-five little chickens. How many have you?

Brother and wife was up and stayed all night. Pa was well. I have not been down home for a long time. Anna Page was over and stayed all night. She is as plump as a dollar. She has a fellow now. His only bad deed is drinking. He will get on a booze ever once in a while.

How many babies has Ella VanSant? Tell her I name her babe Raymond Edsel. That was my little darling's name that died. How I love that name. I was over to his little grave about two weeks ago. I love to work there and I could stay all day. The I.O.O.F. is going to have a meeting over there the twenty-sixth of this month. If it is nice we will all go if we are well.

I will be married twenty-one years the twenty-sixth. Pearl was sixteen the eighth of this month. Daisy will be fourteen the twenty-ninth of May. Chester will be twenty the third of June. Little William will be nine the twenty-fifth of August. Now Permelia, guess I will have to close for this time.

There are two young men here tonight. Chester is playing on the violin. He plays fine. The young man is playing on the guitar. Daisy is playing on the organ. They play some fine pieces, Wish you could only be here to listen to them.

Our school will be out soon. Do you have school close to you? Do Jerry's children go to school? How many babies do James and Sally have? Tell them to write me a long letter and I will answer it just as soon as I can fetch a piece of paper. Tell them just to try and see. Give my love to your girls and the kinfolks. Tell them Anna is just as good as they make them. I love her.

Give my love to Jack. Tell him I often think of him. Now good night to all. Write as prompt as I do of late. Your brother said tell you he would be through plowing Tuesday. He sends his love to you and all the family.

Now listen here, Permelia. I hope you are fit now, hear? You take care of yourself. If you were only out here, we could have a gobbler for dinner. Just step over and help us eat it, will you?

Ella G.

~~~

By this time Ed Barnes decided to take off for Colorado. Louisa had taken a liking to Ed from the first time he began working for them. She thought if he felt the same about her, he would stay in Texas. But this wasn't the case. He stayed longer than he planned, and since he left, Louisa was sure she would be an old maid.

~~~

From Robert Isaac:

Morehead, Kentucky
August 18, 1896

Dear Brothers and Sisters,

O can I tell you or not. Poor Isabel is no more. She died the twelfth of August in Lexington. I cannot tell you anything yet how she died. But they sent her back dressed awfully nice. They had a white shroud on her and we never changed it. O she was so natural. Poor little Johnny knew his mama and kissed her. I thought I never could stand that.

Isabel knew everybody when she left. The label on the coffin said she died of consumption. We buried her by her

father at the Queen City.[3] Brother Button preached her
funeral at the grave.

The children are only tolerable well. Papa is about well,
too. I cannot write anymore. Belle wrote down a piece of
poetry some time ago. Put it in my pocket for me to find
after she died. I found it before she died. I had Brother
Button to read it at the grave. Everybody said it was so nice.
Here it is.

Love chimes may be broken and friendship may die
Harsh words may be spoken by lips that now sigh
Close veiled is the morrow the future none see
In joy or in sorrow Think kindly of me.
The pathway of duty may often look drear
The bright eyes of beauty be dimmed by a tear
What fate shall divide us and youth shall flee
What 'er may betide us Think kindly on me.

I have no fears of poor Isabel not being in Heaven. I think
she is saved if anyone is. She prayed all the time day and
night.

Write soon. If we never meet on earth again I pray God
we may meet in Heaven. She was willing to die, but would
rather have lived to raise her sweet children she said.

Good by
R. I. Nickell

~~~

The news of Isabel's death engulfed the Hawkins
household. Robert Isaac and Permelia had always been
close, and weeks passed before Louisa thought her
mother had gotten over the initial shock. Andrew said
they would manage some way for her to go to Kentucky,
but she knew it would be a hardship. She consoled her
brother and his children with frequent letters.

Frank Button received his theological degree from Transylvania University and came to Morehead in 1887. He founded the Morehead Normal School with his mother, Phoebe.⁴ This school later became Morehead State University.

~~~

From Newton and Pearl Goodnow Nickell:
<div align="right">

Woodland, Cal.

January 19, 1897
</div>

Dear Sister Permelia one and all,

Your kind letter was late getting here and came at last. We are so happy you like our wedding photographs. We were awfully glad to hear from you, and that you welcomed me into your even closer family. We are well and hope you are the same.

I thought your dress was pretty too. Well I will tell you what a nice Christmas we had. Mama, Daisy, and little Willie all came down and mama brought a great big cobbler with her and Newton went to the turkey shooting and got a young turkey hen. Then he went to town and brought three small cakes and a great big paper sack of cookies. I made a cream cake and we had a fine dinner and plenty of everything.

My aunt, Mrs. Jacobs and little girl, my aunt Mrs. Tilley, Mr. Tilley and four children and two working men were all here. We had a Xmas tree in the parlor and had a great time.

Now I will tell you what all we got—two little picture frames to sit on a center table and I got a pink ruby drop. I gave Newt a cigar holder and he gave me a twenty-five dollar cape. It is so pretty. I wish you could see it. And we got a wine set and a set of glassware. Newt got a silk muffler. He gave Mama a nice Bible and Daisy a beautiful heart that opens, all lined with silk. I have my gold watch a year Xmas. Newt gave me that too.

And Willie got a new little shovel, a rake and a hoe, and some jumping jacks, candy and oranges, and I believe that's all. Oh yes, he got another little horn. There's a lot of music in our house, but this particular little horn doesn't add too much. Don't tell Willie I told it though.

Newt said that if he made three thousand dollars this year, just to keep your eyes open or you may see a couple of packs coming it. We will have three hundred and forty acres of wheat and barley when we get done this week. There are about a hundred and seventy-five acres all up and growing. It looks awful nice. Wheat is one and a half now and barley is one cent, and if it stays up we will be right in the swim. We are turning the ground under and our expenses are twelve dollars a day and have got three hundred acres of summer fodder to plow in February. That's to put in next.

What's the matter with Robert Isaac that he never writes since Isabel died? Has he broke up housekeeping or not, and what's become of papa William that we never hear from him? What's brother Greenup's post office? We never sent him our wedding picture. We have to send him one of the next ones we have made. Is Greenup married again or not? That's enough questions.

Well, will close for tonight. This letter is to everyone.

Love and kisses to all.
Pearl and Newt

~ ~ ~

Newton and Pearl's getting married completely surprised his sister. Wedding pictures came as the first announcement. Their marriage could have surprised Ella as well, since she never mentioned it in her correspondence. Not describing the marriage and wedding seemed unusual; however, this particular letter could have been lost.

Newton was twenty-two years older than Pearl. Permelia let it be known she didn't take to the idea of his marrying Pearl, but Louisa said she kept her thoughts in Texas.

~~~

From Henry Romine:

Tyson, Hill County
February 6, 1897

Kind people one and all,
This lonely night I will try and answer your letter we received some time ago. We are all well and hope you are the same. I haven't plowed but one day. I am hauling ties now. I will commence plowing as soon as the ground dries. George, I can sell all the brooms you can bring. Can sell them at the store or to anybody who wants them. Come as soon as you can. I have got one thousand ties to make and haul.
Now George, tell me how many times is the word seven used in the Bible and why is it used so much? You may have to study to answer this.

Goodbye
R. H. Romine

~~~

From Lizzie:

Tyson, Texas
February 9, 1897

Dear People one and all,
Tonight I will try to answer your kind letter. This leaves all well. How are you all by this time? Well George, I have been looking for you tonight but you haven't come now have you?

Jim, where are you and Katy living exactly? I know the PO number but I mean where is your house? Mama said you were contented, but let us hear from you. And how is little Vella?

Lou, I have been to Mrs. Fuller's today. I like her so well and Will Johnson is here tonight for the first time. Since we have moved over to Tyson, we do like it. I liked it before too, but I like this house much better.

Jewel is as sweet as ever. But you wouldn't hardly know her, she has fallen off so since she has been sick. When will school be out? Katy how are you by this time? Isn't your time in April? I do hope you are feeling well, and take care of yourself.

Lula Pearl pet, kiss your little brother Silas for me and mama can kiss you in return. Are you coming with your papa down here? Come and you may have the little blue pitcher. Henry is plowing today. I have been here all day by myself. Bell Wooten stayed twelve days with us.

We have cold weather. Mama, I got my chickens home at last—eight hens and a rooster. George, when you all get here I will do in a chicken. Lou, I am piecing a goblet quilt for Nannie B. She wanted one and since she has been good to me I am surprising her with it. If you are getting any eggs, bring me enough to make a cake. Anyway, I am starving. I don't get any eggs yet. Myrtle, looks like you could come and stay with us like the other little girls.

Mama, I use juggles for stove wood all the time. Everyone come now. Papa, I thought of your birthday and am just sick I didn't write on that very day. I will have a present for you.

Jewel is sixteen months old. Well I must get on now. Write soon.

Lizzie

~~~

From Pearl and Newton:

Yolo County, Cal.
February 18, 1897

Dear Sister and Brother and Cousins,
   Your kind letter was finally received and we were awful glad to hear from you. We are all well and hope you are all the same. Well, Sister Permelia, it is all on our crop whether we can come and make you all a visit. If we have a good crop and get a good price for it we will come and if nothing more happens than we know of now.
   I haven't heard from brother Bob since his wife died, poor man. I guess he is all broke down and we never heard a word from father. If you hear from Brother Greenup, ask him if he got one of our pictures. I hope I had the right number. We are going to have some new ones taken before long.
   Don't mention rain to California for it is so rainy and muddy I don't hardly know what to do. Yes, I have somewhere up around forty little chickens but it is so cold for the little things. Yes, we have all of our grain in and will commence summer plowing as soon as it gets dry enough. You tell Anna Kate I answered her letter and I am waiting for an answer. How many children has she got now?
   I got some lovely silk to fix lounge pillows. They will be quite pretty when I get them made, and I got some more goods. It is lovely with great flowers in it to make rocker chair cushions.
   It is awful cold today. Is it cold in the summer back there? Do you dress in thin or heavy goods for summer? Newt said it was warm and nice and I guess he remembers it pretty good. We got a letter from cousin R. M. Johnson. We have a Chinaman cutting wood for us and we will have about twenty-five or thirty cords of wood.
   Mama and Daisy, Will and Mable Burns were down to see us last Friday and stayed until Sunday afternoon. Newt

and Uncle George Tilley are out to the barn moving bailed hay. Well, as far as news goes there isn't any out here.

Cousin Anna Page has got in a good humor and now we correspond. She is coming down to see me the first chance. Well I will close for this time.

Write soon. Love and kisses to all. Tell Lou to write and Happy Birthday to her.

From your Brother Newton and Sister Pearl

~~~

From Lizzie:

<div style="text-align: right">

February 19, 1897
Tyson, Hill County

</div>

Dear ones,

Well I will scribble a few lines. I aimed to write lots last night and went to bed and forgot it. Katy, Jim didn't know why, but he said you cried. I don't blame you either. But I'm sure all is forgiven by now.

I will send you these two blocks to put in your quilt. Jim said you wanted some pieces and I haven't any. I can piece me some more. Cora, if Silas does beat Jewel walking I will beat on him good. Lula Pearl, you and Survella come and stay with me a while. We would have lots of fun.

Cora, I could just give it to Lou for going back and not coming to see us any more. Lou, you're having a birthday and don't get too bad stuck on Mr. Scott and not go after Mr. Williamson. He's nice too. Lou, I want you to tell me what all you and Mama have to do. It will run you all to death to do so much work. Can't you get anybody from outside to help?

Katy, I will quilt your quilts. I find myself still excited about your expected babe. Please take care of yourself, and I hope you have a little brother for Survella.

Love to all.
Lizzie

<div align="center">~~~</div>

From Robert Isaac:

Morehead, Ky.
Feb. 21, 1897

My dear Sister, Brothers, and all,

I will answer your kind letter. This leaves all well but Johnny. He was sick last night but is better today. Oh he is a grand boy. He is getting better. Just as pert as can be but cannot walk yet.

We have a girl staying with us for five months but she has left this morning. I have to keep a hired girl. Our Della is not stout. It is so hard to get a good girl to stay and take the right kind of interest.

Well sister, Clay Powers has been dead for about two months. Lots of people died in this county this winter. Fred Powers lives in Ashland. Sister, I can't get over Isabel's death at all it seems. Of course I am satisfied she is in Heaven. Oh I miss her so much.

We are about to sell out and buy property in town. I am going to apply for a government job—Whiskey Inspector, and I guess I'll know pretty soon after the fourth of March. If I don't get that I have the promise of another job in town. Pap says he is coming to Texas this spring if he sells his land. I do not know whether I will come or not.

The creek is up and it has rained all day. Our hogs are all dying with cholera. And Bob Basford and son were bitten by a mad dog. Some think not enough to hurt.

Pap says he would like to see you all and here is his photo taken last summer. I can't write much this time. I do hope Sister we all may meet again on earth. If we do not I pray we will meet in Heaven. I always pray for you all. I will write to the rest of the folks soon. Our love to all.

Do you see Millicent and the boys? What of her little girls? I sure hope they are happy and contented.

—February 24. Clear and pretty. We had high water. Back water from the river at the dam this morning. Pap is poorly today, but he sends you his love.

> Your brother,
> R. I. Nickell

~~~

Henry Clay Powers, second husband of Andrew's sister Margaret, had been an upstanding citizen of Morehead for many years and one of its earliest residents. After his house was mobbed for the second time with considerable damage done, he was convinced he would be killed if he remained in Morehead. He gathered up his furniture and family and moved temporarily to the small town of Covington.[5]

Robert Isaac's desire to be a whiskey inspector could hold an element of danger. Stills operated all over the Kentucky hills, and whiskey inspectors would not win a popularity contest.

CHAPTER 13

Raccoons in the chicken coop – Try smoking mullein – A letter from niece Jessie – A beau for Louisa? – Andrew visits Lizzie in Hill County – Pearl Nickell writes of their farm – Clark Page in the Spanish-American War.

~~~

From Pearl and Newt:

Woodland, California
March 22, 1897

Dear Sister Permelia and Brother Jack,

Your kind and most welcome letter was received yesterday and we were awfully glad to hear from you. We are all well and hope this will find you all in the best of health. We will try to come for a visit. It depends upon our crop. If it isn't destroyed we will be right there.

Well when you write to Uncle Robert—I guess he's my brother now too—ask him why he doesn't answer my letter. I know about how he feels, poor fellow. What is he talking of doing now? If we make you a visit I hope your father will be there. I would like so to have one of his photos. I do wish he would come out here and live with us.

Well sister, the coons have been taking my chickens and I can't stop them. Do you have raccoons in Texas? Our grain is almost knee high. Almost three hundred acres. Just think of that and smile. Newt is just like an old night owl.

When we have working men we get up at four o'clock and rush things right through. No monkey business on this ranch! When we have work, they have got to get in and work it out that we may pay one dollar a day wages.

Newt had trouble in his nose and he has a little thing that he pumps oil in his nose with. He is just pumping away.

Mama is going to give me a cow. She is a young heifer but will have a calf next month. This will be her first calf. Well I will close.

Love and kisses to all. Write soon.

From Pearl and Newt

~~~

For a man with a stuffy nose, smoking mullein was a sure cure. The plant needed to be crushed, then rolled like a cigarette or put in a pipe. It cleared the head in no time. For the children, Permelia relied on her own remedy or the doctor's prescription.

Anna Kate and Jim's son was born April nineteenth. They named him Loyd Bruce, and he was every bit as small as Survella was. Even though Survella was only two years old, she tried to help take care of her little brother.

Permelia helped Katy with chores for some time before the baby was born, was there for the birth, and continued to help until Katy was stronger.

~~~

From Jessie Nickell, daughter of Greenup:

Young Springs
Bath County, Ky.
June 28th, 1897

Mrs. P. F. Hawkins
My Dear Aunt,

I received your letter the fourth of May and read it with much pleasure. It found us all well. Pa was here last week and brought Uncle Newt's and Aunt Pearl's picture to me.

Uncle Bob is all well and so is Grandpa William. Uncle Newt ought to come and see us when he comes this fall. He surely will.

Yes Aunt, Pa is farming for Mr. Ed Myers on Licking. Oh Aunt, why don't you come out? We would like to see you so well. You must come this winter. I would like to go home with you and see the Texas country. We are going to have our pictures taken and send them to you all. Pa said tell cousins Lawrence and Clarence to send me their pictures. Do they go with the girls any?

Well Aunt, I will be seventeen on October the twentieth, and I thank you for your good advice. And Aunt Sis gave me some advice too and I expect to keep it. Aunt Sis says it did her good to hear from you. She said she never saw you on earth but she hoped to meet you in Heaven.

Aquilla lives with Mr. Cogswell and Freddie lives with us. Well I would like to see Louisa and sing with her for I sing when I am washing dishes. Sing at the top of my voice. I am so glad you are having good meetings there. We have had good meetings here for several days. Church Sunday and Sunday School and prayer meetings Wednesdays. I wish you all were here to go with us Sunday.

Louisa, anyway, my brother Freddie is fourteen years old the 18th of May and he is the best little boy in the country. Aunt Sis must have raised him till he was thirteen years old. She said she couldn't do without him. She loves him like her own and he loves her too.

I was talking about going down in Fleming County near Grange City to a Sunday School picnic Saturday. Me and Cousin Laban and two of his cousin girls.

Well Aunt, I think this is all this time. I will send Lizzie's letter in yours. All from your niece to Dear Aunt Permelia. Aunt Sis sends her love to all. Good bye.

Jessie Nickell

~~~

From Jessie Nickell:

Young Springs
Bath County, Ky.
June 28, 1897

Dear Lizzie and Cousins one and all,

I will try this evening to answer your most kind and appreciated message I received and read with much pleasure. It found us well but Aunt Sis.

Well I will tell you how we are getting along. Pa was over last week. He has been sick. I haven't seen brother Aquilla for some time. I am living with Aunt Sis yet. I got a letter from Aunt Permelia and have just now answered it. Katy and Cora must write to me and send me pictures of all the children, and you must send me Gladie's picture and yours and Mr. Romine. Aunt Permelia said she would send me her picture by itself. I got Uncle Newt's and Aunt Pearl's picture last week—it was so nice.

You said for me to write you a great long letter but I don't know what to write. There has been a great deal of sickness here this summer.

Well I will tell you all about going to church Sunday. Had a nice time. My fellow was here. You asked me what his name was. He is Mr. Simpson Karrick. He is Mr. Hue Karrick's son. He didn't come that Sunday. The waters were up and he couldn't come.

We have a nice garden and lots of beans to eat. I wish I was there to pick cotton when it gets ripe. O we have had lots of rain lately. We will send our picture as soon as we have them taken. Pa said we would. This ink is bad. Pa lives at Mr. Myers. He hasn't ever married again and I don't think he will. I hope not. I will have to finish with a pencil.

Well Lizzie I think someone might give me a birthday present October the 20th. I think an album would be nice, don't you? I think I have written enough such as it is. Write as soon as you get this. Don't do like me. I want to hear from you all, and about your children.

From your cousin Jessie to Cousin Lizzie Romine.

Good bye
Jessie Nickell

~~~

Everyone shared letters in the Hawkins household, and then placed them in Permelia's letterbox. Anyone who wanted to reread them could.

Louisa said that in the old days, whenever a pen was bad, it was much better to read a letter written in good pencil. When Permelia was growing up and they were out of ink and a pencil would write no more, she had the solution. She would go out to a slate ledge and break off a thin piece. By filing a point at one end, this makeshift pencil sufficed until she could get a real pencil. The idea did not work in George's Creek since there was not a handy slate quarry.

~~~

From Lizzie:

Aquilla, Hill County, Tex.
August 26, 1897

Dear ones at home,

This beautiful Thursday evening I will try to answer your good kind and welcome letter we received and read with pleasure. This leaves all of us well as could be expected. One of Jewel's eyes is trying to get sore again.

I do want to see you all so bad. Are you coming atal? Aren't George and Cora coming either? How long will you stay here? How are they all getting along? I know you are

anxious to get back. Mama, Henry's folks never did get here
nor we never have heard from them since the next day after
we left up there. I do wish some of you would come. I don't
know how I will stand it from now on. I have to stay right
here and Henry off over yonder picking cotton. He hasn't
worn a shoe on one foot now for three weeks from that
spider bite until today.

Jim Barrow's folks came to see the children. They went
on down to where they were but they don't like that woman
atal, keeping their little ones. They said they wished we had
of kept the children until they got here. They will start back
tomorrow. They were eleven days coming from Greer
County.

Jewel can talk right along. I wish you could hear her. Lou,
you did write a good long letter this time. I would have
written sooner but we went over yonder to see they came
home with us, and I just couldn't get to writing sooner. They
want us to come up there to live so bad.

Mama, my feet were swelled awfully and I commenced
taking that cream of tarter and sulphur and they aren't
swollen one bit now. I am getting along all right, but would
feel better if we could see you more.

Lou, how is Mr. Scott getting along? When will his school
commence? Papa, how are you standing the times? Why
don't' you rustle Cora and George down here, but if you all
don't come now, come as soon as you can for sure. When
you see Ban, Walt, and little Russ, tell them I said hello. I will
close. Love to everyone.

Write soon for I will want to hear so bad.

From Lizzie and all

~ ~ ~

The spider Lizzie spoke of must have been a
dangerous species if his toe was so swollen. Since no one

wrote about it later, Henry definitely lucked out by whatever treatment he administered.

Permelia learned from experience what doctors would prescribe for various ailments, and in many cases she provided her own remedies. She wrote them down in a small tablet. Having the book, *Valuable Prescriptions*,[1] came to her aid many times. It contained a valued "Collection of Successful treatments, used by the Leading Medical Men of Europe and America, giving the Latest Formulae which Brains, Time and a Liberal Use of Money Could Obtain."

Permelia didn't have all the ingredients on hand, but at least she knew a medicine was available through a druggist or physician. She always kept Rose Eye Water because sore eyes among children, as well as adults, were common. She kept some supplies on hand, since it was a lengthy buggy ride to the nearest druggist.

Her prescription book did not have a specific remedy for a spider's bite, but Permelia used turpentine and camphor. Her papa once bled a spider's bite as if it were a snake's.

Permelia's small wooden medicine chest sat high on the cupboard out of reach of the grandchildren. In it she kept limewater and linseed oil. She shook four ounces of each, and then applied it to burns and scalds. If the ingredients were not at hand, the old remedy of one tablespoon of cooking soda dissolved in a cup of water was the next best thing.

The remedy for a headache was one dram of menthol and one ounce of chloroform. According to her book, "Rub it over the seat of pain until it begins to burn, and make the eyes water." It continued, "This prostrating, enervating, mind-destroying trouble can be modified and soothed at once. We have known thousands who have been cured by this prescription." All the family decided they would rather have a headache.

~~~

From Lizzie:

Thursday 12 o'clock
Aquilla, Hill Co. Tex.

Kind Mother and Dear Little Sister:
Now I will try to write a few lines as Papa is talking of
going home tomorrow if Henry gets back from Waco tonight.
So he can go as far as Whitney with him. Paw has been
aiming to go with him all the week until after he got up this
morning, and he said maybe he had better not go or he
would not be able to go home this week, after such a long
ride. We would not let him go until Henry got some money.
I do hope he will get home all right. You write just as
soon as he gets there. He has been very well satisfied or
seemed to be. He sure has been a heap of company to me.
He has stayed right here all the time and nothing he can do
will make Jewel mad. She thinks he is all of it. He is sure he
can hear her say Pa. I have washed out his clothes but I did
not boil them, but maybe they will do for him to wear home.
I will not have any washing done this week as the negro
is so busy. She goes every day to wash and said if I possibly
could, to put off my washing this week. And I never thought
of Papa's clothes then and never thought he would want to
stay this long.
Lou, what time did you get home? Are you picking
cotton? Papa went over to see the Fullers today. How are
the little children getting along? Kiss them for me.
Mama, I wrote to Henry's ma to see if she can come the
first of next month. I would try to do without you as you are
so busy, but she may not let me know right away. And I will
write to you, and you can just count on coming for we don't
know about where she can come or not. If you come how
will you come? Have you got a new buggy yet? If you have to

come on the train, Henry said you could come to Hillsboro and he could meet you. It would be cheaper.

The way this old preacher woman counts for me, I will not be sick before the fifteenth of October or later. I will do without you as long as I possibly can.

Love to all,
Lizzie

~~~

From Pearl and Newt:

Woodland, Cal.
Sept. the 9th, 1897

Dear Sister and Brother and Nieces,

Your kind and welcome letter was received and were so glad to hear from you. We are well and hope when you read these few lines you all will be the same. We are having lovely weather nowadays—nice and cool The north wind is blowing quite strong.

Well the first news is I have sixty-six cans of fruit. Five jars of pickled grapes and a half a tub of grapes to preserve tomorrow. Friday evening and my preserves made.

Am still taking vocal lessons. I went down today and took a lesson. I think a young lady does well to sing and sing the right way, not that I would ever want to go into concerts. Of course, Woodland is having a new opera house.

Oh yes, got a letter from my cousin in Nebraska. She is to be married this month. She sent me three pieces of her dresses. They are all silk, blue and white, and will be lovely I'm sure. She is going to marry a butcher by the name of Lewis Kennedy. She is awful busy sewing. I don't know if she is making her wedding dress or not but I rather suspect so, since she is quite talented in that direction.

As I have my morning's work done I will try to finish your letter. Daisy, Mama and Willie were down and made us a visit of eight days. Had a fine time. Why doesn't Kate answer my letter I wrote so long ago, and what is the matter with Robert Isaac? It has been six or eight months since we heard from him.

A school mate of mine, Eva Parker, is going to be married a week from Sunday. They are going to be married in Woodland.

Well as news goes, there isn't any more. we haven't got our money so I guess we won't get to come and see you all this Fall. I am so disappointed.

Newt bought him three lovely big work horses. Now we have to have one more and then will have another full team. Newt and Will Cramer are out looking for our hogs. I guess they had good luck. I hear Newt calling them along.

This letter is to dear Lou also. I would have written her one but the news is the same. I do want to put up a lot more fruit tomorrow. Tell her anyway and ask her to write. I have ten little chickens. Mama gave me two lovely roosters.

Wish Newt would come on in so he can tell me something to write. He said to tell you he would write some next time. Well, I will close for now. So goodbye. Love and kisses to all of you. Write soon.

Yours truly,
Pearl and Newt Nickell

~~~

</div>

The family was disappointed that Pearl and Newton did not come to Texas, especially since they had never met Pearl. One photo of Pearl is of her as a young woman, with hair down to her knees.

Alfred Megason died the eighth of March. Millicent, again widowed, was left with the three teenage boys and two little girls, Cora and Eunice. Millicent had always been a strong woman. Everyone could be sure she would work it out some way. She knew how to come through the hard spots in her life.

~~~

From E. W. Cassity:

Morgan County, Ky.
March 16, 1898

Dear Sister,

I seat myself with the thoughts of writing you a few lines, and with the hope that God is looking over you and yours. It has been many months since I have written. You are not forgotten and are in my prayers.

Yes, Clark, Anna, and Ella are missed but at least Ella is settled with her own family in Texas. Clark has a mind to join up for the war. He has no ties any more since he is without his little wife, so a young man can do as he pleases. He has already been a long way from home. He will sign up in Fleming County in a few days. Permelia, you never made it back to Kentucky. You always said you would come for a visit. It is more peaceful a place than when you left it. I wanted to stay in touch if only by letter. It looks like I am having luck with my pension, but it has taken long enough to get settled.

Give love to your family, as I still think of you.

God bless you all.
E. W. Cassity

~~~

From Lizzie and Henry:

March 29, 1898
Menlow, Hill Co. Tex.

Dear People one and all,

I will try to answer your good long letter we received some time back. This leaves all well but colds, and Henry's back has been hurting him some lately. He sat up last night a week ago with a young man, Brother Jones' son. He died at two o'clock. Henry stood right over him as long as he lived and then shaved him and helped lay him out without any help hardly, and has been nearly laid up ever since with his back. But he has been out today rabbit hunting.

Boys, Henry has two gray hounds now and he sure catches the rabbits. Well our crops will be late won't they? Henry hasn't planted any cotton yet. Aimed to plant this week but it has been such bad weather. I don't guess we will have to plant corn over. We had plenty to get killed and lots left. Some right across the road from ours looks nice, but ours was the prettiest in the country. The field looked green all over but it doesn't now, and my garden is sick. My beans were so nice. I thought I would have early beans but I have planted again. I have cucumbers up. I guess they will get killed if it stays cold. We have commenced eating on our onions. The bugs or something ate all my first mustard and raddishes up. Part of my garden got killed and part never got hurt.

Mama, last Friday two weeks ago our friends Jim and Emma came over and stayed until Monday. We went home with them and stayed till Thursday. We all sure had a lively time and I am looking for them over again Friday or Saturday. We heard from them Friday and they were all well. They have sweet children and they sure make them mind too. Henry has something to say to you. . . .

Lizzie

From Henry:

See here what the dogs and I caught. Thirteen jack rabbits today. I have had the dogs ten days and caught twenty-eight. Those rabbits may have caused me to lose an entire crop. Scarecrows work for the birds, but they sure don't scare the rabbits.

Ma, tell us something about your cousin that came to visit. Is he from the backwoods or Arkansas and if you are not ashamed of him, tell us something about him. Where is he from? D doesn't know anything about him. Now don't give us a hint about your cousin. Tell all or none. I can't guess right every time. That's the same as saying a man died. Guess what his name was? Don't be afraid to tell us about him—just let it all come out or none.

George, you said you would show me when those people in the Bible were baptized. All right, now give it in full. This was to be done in a few days, and one day is a man talking. One day is twenty-four hours. Can you show me now or a thousand years from now? A man needs to know his Bible.

Henry

From Lizzie:

Well, Henry got that straightened out, so you be sure and tell it all, George. Jim, I know you would love to go rabbit hunting with Henry, so just come on down.

Katy I would love to come to see you and see how well you are getting along. Are little Survella and Loyd still precious? Yes, I know how lonesome you can get. Know all about it. I like here fine but I still get lonesome for you too. Lou babe, I'm glad you're stuttering less. Mama thought you would outgrow that. Yes yes, Cora, just send me a mess of greens. I know they would be good and I haven't had a bit.

Well Mama, you kiss every one of the kids for me. The little dress came all right. Many thanks Miss Lou Babe for the spoons and the Enterprise. I have two copies of it, and flower seed. Also tell me all the news. Papa have you planted cotton yet? We have prospects of getting milk now. A young calf. Next time we will tell you of a young colt maybe.

This is after we got the letter from you—yes, we wrote to you, but we have been going to see the sick and have never sent it off. You guessed at it about us being out of stamps but we thought every day we would get some but failed so far. Yes, I would love to come awful well but Henry hasn't planted any cotton yet and is trying so hard to get it done tomorrow. He has to go to that trial and I don't know, as he hasn't said where we could go. I would love so well to come after we get our cotton planted. We will be up with our work then.

Yes Lou Babe, you are right about that marrying business. It takes two willing. If I had of never lived for mama to come last Fall and stay with me, I never would have known how to appreciate her the way I do now. You don't have any idea how good she was to me. I never will forget on earth. I could write the rest of the evening about her, but Charlie Alexander is here and is going to Menlow so here is a chance to send the letter.

I have never got the paper yet. I will be so glad. So sorry of all the deaths. Tell everyone howdy. I just seem to be lonely even with dear Henry and friends here. Hoping to hear from you or see you all soon. Let us know how Lula Pearl is getting along.

Lizzie

~~~

Louisa remembered both squirrels and jackrabbits causing trouble in equal amounts. The squirrels scared the crows from the corn, and then the rabbits ate the corn. Squirrels chased the rabbits, but the rabbits ran in circles, coming right back to the meal they could find close to the ground. Squirrels ate the tops right out of the corn. A more common type of scarecrow made of crossed wooden strips with a hat bothered the crows, but didn't scare the other critters, just as Henry said. They decided the rabbits won the award for pest of the year.

~~~

The Spanish-American War

Thomas Clark Page enlisted in the United States Army on April 9, 1898 at the age of twenty-seven-and-a-half years. Clark decided to enlist before the war with Spain actually began. Permelia kept up with the war through her *Weekly Enterprise*, reading aloud that Theodore Roosevelt had led his Rough Riders up Lettler Hill. Clark served in the Philippines.

No one in the Hawkins family had letters from Clark. His stepfather, E. W. Cassity, would be the one to hear and surely would inform Permelia if anything had happened to him.

Interestingly, business increased with the coming of the Spanish-American War. Roosevelt and his Rough Riders left for Cuba, and wartime conditions seemed to better the economy. A more prosperous Somervell County awaited the veterans.[2]

CHAPTER 14

Who slows down? – A Civil War pension – Making soap – Our personal tragedy

~~~

From Robert Isaac:

<div align="right">

Morehead, Ky.
June 26, 1898

</div>

Dear Permelia and all,

I once more take pleasure in writing you. Well your children all have families and I take it are experiencing good health. Is little Lou waiting on any beau at this time? As you might say, she is some used to having her own way so she may be particular. Would that be right sister? I heard from Lizzie and she and Henry are faring well. She says it is not too far from you, but my you still like to have your family close I know.

I'm glad Jack is feeling better but you are doing too much to make up for his general health. I fear for your own good. As we get older we need to slow ourselves. What Jack cannot do, does John Robert help out? Then I am certain he does. How many do we know that slow down unless they are forced.

What do you hear from Clark? I know he enlisted. Do you get any letters from him from the Philippines? I guess E. W. hears. Tell Jerry and brother Jim to write. I will try to write more often. There is no news to speak of. Give love to all.

I sure am sorry to hear of Mr. Megason. I hope Millicent is managing all right. I must close now and will write more later.

<div align="right">

R. I. Nickell

</div>

~~~

From Addie Lame Maxey:

Morehead, Ky.
August 29, 1898

Dear Aunt Permelia and Uncle Andrew,

It is with the most pleasure that I answer your welcome letter. Excuse me for waiting so long but we have been very busy. I guess I know how much Mama always had to do even if there was my share to take care of. Nothing told me as much as having my own little home how busy a body could be. I'll vow Katy could keep up with me.

Where are all the girls now? Katy wrote to me when they lived up in Hall County. I was so sorry to hear about her babe then. Are they back home from there? I have not written her in such a time and know she must have children by now. How many do Cora and George and Lizzie and Henry have?

I have just made me a new cook apron and you will never guess what I did. I made a lace inset at the top. Overton wants to know if I plan to wear it to church. Ha! I had finished cutting and trimming curtains with lace and the idea came to me. I am also piecing a quilt. It just makes me think of Aunt Margaret. She so loved pretty quilts.

Generally my work is hardly ever done. I never want you to think I forgot you or any of my cousins. My hope was always to see the Texas Country but that wish may not come true.

When Anna Page left for California, one day I thought I would go across the Mississippi and whatever other rivers there are, just like her. But maybe I will not see more of this world than right where I am. That satisfies me enough I guess as we have a happy home.

I will send you all my love, dear Aunt Permelia and Uncle Andrew. Write soon.

Your niece, Addie Lame
Mrs. Overton Maxey

~ ~ ~

From Robert Isaac:

Morehead, Ky.
October 3, 1898

Dear Permelia, Katy and all,

Here I am writing this letter to you and hoping you are all well. I will always think we will meet one day. Katy, your little Loyd must be growing like a weed. I was sorry to hear you are not well and fear you work yourself too much, judging from your letter. Survella must keep you moving fast. I'll say she will be helping you before long. Pap is fair and slowed down not just a little this summer. Pearl sent me her and Newt's wedding photo some time ago. They make a fine looking couple. I still wonder how you feel about it? You never said.

We have had a right smart of rain for October and should have the cold weather coming around the barn any day. Morehead is taking on the appearance of a good place to live. I must tell you E. W. Cassity finally got his pension. The time was long to wait for it wouldn't you say? He says he would still like to visit Texas.

Tell all hello for me. Love to all. Do you ever see Ella Page? Vanzant isn't it? Now tell me about yourself. I hope you are in better health now.

Your brother and uncle,
R. I. Nickell

~ ~ ~

From Ella Goodnow:

Woodland, California
December 14, 1898

Dear Cousin Permelia and all,

Was so glad to hear from you and to hear that you are well. As for my health I have good days and bad days. Pearl canned fruit all fall and knows how to conduct a house. She is still interested in her vocal lessons and sings so well. At least I think so. We went down to visit her and Newt for a few days earlier this year. Their house is as neat as a pin.

Well you know how inclined my family is to music. Not me so much but I do like to listen to it all. Did you ever get an organ or piano for Katy to play? We are looking to a real nice Christmas as always. But it is so cold here. Please step over and have some plum pudding with us. I keep thinking you will come some time, but if I settle my own thinking it will never be.

Pa was so glad to have a good letter from you. Write him whenever you can. I hope Jack is well. I got a letter from cousin Robert and he said Uncle Will had felt better than now. He is exactly as old as Pa is, now isn't he? That is almost eighty don't we know. How nice if they could celebrate their January birthday together.

I have not grown any prettier as I have grown older but don't let that keep you from writing me a nice long letter. Tell Lou to write her cousin Daisy. Has she found a young man since that Scott fellow or is he the big one now? Give my love to all and I know you would like to have your children all with you.

It is time to stop now. My eyes are tired.

Ella Goodnow

~~~

From Lizzie:

Menlow, Tex.
February 9, 1899

Dear Mama and Papa and Lou,

The cold is biting into all of us. Little jewel is fine but does not like the cold atal, even when she is dressed all warm it is still not enough. She is sweet as candy.

I thought we would have seen you before now but I will send this letter anyway. We are of a mind to go to Galveston County. It seems like the end of the earth but it may be better for us. The worst part would be leaving you and my sisters and brother. How can I ever do such a thing. I don't know if I could stand being away from you all. It wouldn't be like you could just come over any time. It is so far. It is bad enough just down here.

Mama, do you feel well now? I know Lou can look after you—still I worry about you. Mama, that soap recipe—is this all there is in it? One sixteenth of a bar of soap, one tenth of a teaspoonful of indigo, one tenth of a teaspoonful of ammonia, one teaspoon of powdered Borax, two teaspoonful of powdered lye. Now is this supposed to make a gallon of washing liquid?

Well there is nothing more to write. Henry has come home and is ready to eat. I am feeling some better now and will let you know. Tell Uncle Dim and Aunt Sally to write. Do you keep up with their children? Give love to Uncle Jerry and Aunt Belle. I wish they could come down. Clarence and Lawrence too. What do you hear of Millicent?

Love to all,
Lizzie

~~~

The winter of 1899 hit with exceptional cold all across the country. Permelia's *Enterprise* reported a coal shortage in Northeastern Kentucky, with a supply to last no more than twenty-four hours in the entire state.

Mines flooded, making it impossible for the men to get the coal out. The temperature continued to drop from eight degrees on the day of the report. The bad weather didn't skip Somervell County.

~~~

From Robert Isaac:

Morehead, Ky.
February 9, 1899

Dear Permelia and family,

Your last letter was good to read and my news will not be good, for our Pa has now left us. In January he departed this life as we know it on earth. We did all we could for him, but he was ready to leave. Pap had a good year on the whole but the winter cold seemed to get to him more than ever before. He was tired and had only wanted to see all his children once more.

Don't grieve for Pa because he did not seem to suffer. That is the important thing we all know. Reflecting on it I was the most fortunate for having him near me throughout my life. Greenup was here when Pa died.

We have had winter snow and it's much colder than usual. There's been flooding around the state and coal is in short supply. The only good thing coming from it is the ice allows the children to skate, but they have to bundle up. Remember the icy ponds Permelia or is that too long ago? I doubt that Texas has ice ponds for skating.

I don't know what else to tell you because we all have to go to our Maker one day. Give my love to all.

Your brother,
R. I. Nickell

After twenty years Pa is now with our dear mother.

~~~

According to Louisa, Permelia never returned to Kentucky during the years she lived in Texas. She regretted not seeing her Papa Nickell again.

Each year Louisa thought she and her folks would return for a visit, but when summers came and went, they had not made the journey. Permelia often said, "There's no right way to do a wrong thing." She possibly thought those words were appropriate when she put off a Kentucky visit one last time.

Other reports in the *Enterprise* announced clashes in the Philippines. On one day the Filipinos advanced to attack on the eastern side of the city of Manila. They were ordered to halt by the Nebraska regiment, after which a real battle ensued, lasting for two days. Two hundred Americans were wounded, and more than one hundred Filipinos were taken from the trenches to the American hospitals.[1]

At this time no one had heard information concerning Clark.

~~~

George's Creek

In Louisa's reminiscing of the fourth day of July, 1899, she said the family had no warning, only that her mother felt very tired for two or three days. Permelia lay down for an afternoon of rest, something she rarely did. It was a rest from which she would not awaken.

She had not felt so bad as to call the doctor ... and then she was gone. Although the cause of death was unknown, Dr. Williamson later accepted it as heart failure. Permelia Nickell Hawkins departed this life at the age of fifty-four.

Eva Cora and Louisa were with Andrew at Permelia's bedside, but by the time their sisters reached home it was too late. They all expressed their feeling toward their mother, saying they should have done more to make her life easier. Louisa was shattered still to be single, saying they would be without a mother to see her marry or to have children. Cora professed it was "God's way," and they should turn their concerns to offer their condolences. A funeral parlor was not available so the community took care of its own. The next afternoon the families climbed into their buggies, leaving for George's Creek Graveyard. They gathered by the tall trees, next to where they laid Willie to rest ten years before.

Preachers regularly reminded those present of their obligations to their Maker, and they should always be ready for their last day on earth. After the service, friends carried the coffin from the tabernacle to the site, lowering it with ropes into the ground. The family followed the custom of staying until the dirt had covered the coffin and the last of it was patted down with shovels.

Andrew placed a fruit jar of bright zinnias from Permelia's garden against a small mound of earth at the head of her grave.

The family said goodbye to their friends, then lingered until sundown, as Andrew did not want to leave. John Robert finally walked their father back to the buggy. Louisa accompanied them and noticed her papa didn't say a word the entire ride home.

While walking up the curved flowered path to their old house, Anna knelt to pluck a weed from the garden. "Mama would have had a hoe to it as soon as it popped through that soil," Louisa asserted. The Hawkins' house did not have tall white pillars, but it had a white porch swing the girls shared with their beaus.

After entering the house, Anna Kate prepared tea while everyone seemed to be waiting for someone else to say something. Andrew began by saying he was an old man and it was their turn to "pick up" and make their own dreams where their mother left off. Louisa admonished him that he wasn't old, and he could still plow and pick cotton. He reminded her that seventy wasn't young.

George and Cora encouraged Andrew and Lou to live with them. Then Andrew could help George and not have responsibilities for his own land. George told him he had worked hard enough and besides, he needed Andrew's expert advice for their own farm.

Lizzie and Henry announced that they planned to leave for Galveston where Henry wanted to try his hand at dairy farming. Lizzie insisted Andrew study on taking turns staying with each of them. Jim, Anna Kate, and everyone agreed. Louisa was relieved since she would be the only one left at home and was not confident she could take care of her papa and a household, even with the others close by.

Andrew said he would consider their suggestion. Then he asked them to choose from their mother's things, something holding special remembrances for them. The only specific was he wanted Anna Kate, the eldest daughter, to have Permelia's letters.

CHAPTER 15

Anna Kate cherishes her mother's letters — The Romines are ready to leave — The turn of the century

~~~

From Katy and Jim:

West, Texas
August 2, 1899

Dear Cora,

My tears take the place of unfound words. Here I sit, writing my sister who I don't see nearly enough. Our dear mother has left us too soon. Perhaps we wanted too much to have her with us until we ourselves were no longer here. Better we grieve than Mama.

I guess Papa is broken. You and Lou can look after him all right. I know you said George tries to get him to leave the work to him, but Papa is determined as long as he has the strength.

Please help him with his grief. It is good to know John Robert and Maggie are so close.

Oh Cora, will you be all right come December? Of course you will. Lizzie wrote that she is feeling well. Her time is early December too, and without Mama there for either of you. I could not take our dear mother's place, but if I possibly can I will be there to help you both.

Would you believe I had a card from Uncle Dim and Aunt Sally? I owe so many letters and must write Lizzie. Hug Lula Pearl and Silas for me and I will kiss Loyd and Vella for you. I must stop now for it is time to fix supper as I'm baking a cream cake for Jim this evening.

Love to you dear ones,
Katy and Jim

~~~

From Ella Goodnow:

Woodland, Cal.
August 10, 1899

Dear Jack and all the family,
    My heart is full of sadness and I can't tell you how hard this writing is for me. Newton is heartsick I'm sure. Permelia was my friend as much as my cousin. I could tell her all my troubles when there was no one else to tell. Her letters meant much to me and how I looked forward to reading them over again. Now will you write to me. You girls could take turns. What do you think of such an idea?
    Jack, there was always the hope you and Permelia would come for a visit. We would have liked that so well. Especially at Christmas did I yearn to see my cousin. Are you going to stay where you are or break up housekeeping there? In her last letter Permelia said Henry and Lizzie were thinking on moving to Galveston County. She did not say when. Where is that exactly? She said it is a long way from you. I wonder if Henry's folks live there. That would be lovely if they are.
    Jack, don't let the girls stop writing for I want to keep up with you all. Lou, do you have a man of your liking? We are all in good health and Papa is doing very well. Anna Page comes down to visit ever so often. Her young man is named Lewis. She is changed a lot since first she came to live with us. The good Lord saw fit for that.

All our respects and love,
Your cousin Ella Goodnow

~~~

From Robert Isaac:

Morehead, Ky.
August 19, 1899

Dear Jack and family,

It is with a great deal of sadness in my heart that I write this letter. I am not sure it can be done. Like Clay Powers once said, you and Permelia were the best parents to your children certain and sure. And I agree.

Jack there was no better woman for a wife, sister, or mother than Permelia. There is no other way to put it except to say that is the way she was. She has God to look after her now and we will all be together one day. I would say the next life is joy with God forever. No cause to ask for more. This is enough.

Katy, you are the eldest daughter. See that you and your sisters take after their mother and raise their children as they raised you. You will find gladness in knowing your mama was a caring woman who loved her children. See that John Robert reads this letter. I will write Jim and Jerry but I don't feel like writing more at this time. You understand.

Write when you can. It pleases me to hear from you. My grief is passed with only your own.

Love to all.
R. I. Nickell

~~~

From Cora:

Nemo, Texas
December 19, 1899

Dear Jim and Katy,

I hope everyone is feeling fine, and the children are well too. Katy, I misplaced your last letter. My, I don't know where that could be. There aren't enough places for something to be hiding.

Papa and Lou are well. Papa didn't want to leave the old home place at first. We can understand that but Nemo is only a handful of miles away.

Our precious Golda is one week old now and is the sweetest thing. We see John Robert often as we are neighbors. Charles Allen is with us now and he and George built an extra room on our house.

I remember you asked about Dim and Sally. My, I don't think I could handle seven little ones. I am thankful Henry and Lizzie moved back to Hood County, temporarily. I did so miss Mama's loving care but the care of my older sister is very dear. I hold sorrow that she didn't get to see either of her little grandchildren.

We don't hear much from cousin Ella Goodnow. We always had a good California letter to read. Mama was so good about writing and Uncle Robert Isaac writes less.

Katy, don't worry about Papa. He will be fine. Right now he is out on the porch swing with Lula Pearl. The sun is out and it's right pleasant. I suspect the cold will be coming back before long.

Jim, do you know yet if you all can come Christmas? It would so please us to see you.

Our love,
Cora

~~~

From Katy:

West, Texas
March 5, 1900

Dear Papa, Cora, Lou and all,

I hope my lines find everyone well. Little Loyd has the sniffles but not a cold I think. Survella wants to help me make supper. It's hungry time for her. If I don't start to feeling stout again she might have to put my apron on all the time. Can you imagine she thinks she can cook as well as anyone.

Cora, I am going through Mama's letters. One day you must read them all. Remember when Willie brought home the kittens and dumped them in Mama's apron? I didn't know if we could keep them or not. Guess Mama didn't want to hurt Willie's feelings. Little Miss Fossil lived a long time. I still miss her.

It turned out to be such a cold winter. It's no wonder I can't get well and I have a bad sore throat. This druggist down here told me what to mix up for a gargle. I take a handful of sage and he sold me some alum. I use one teaspoon of that and add it to boiling water to make a pint. He says it's good for tonsilitia and bronchial problems too. Is that the way Mama made it up for us?

Thank you for the seeds. If I feel like it I will get them planted as soon as it's time. Cora, did you ever hear from cousin Gessella? I wrote her a letter some time ago but never heard. All I know is she married Edward DuVall three years ago. I addressed my letter to that effect in Clinton County Missouri and I supposed she got it.

I do wish you could come over for a few days. What do you think of George's Creek being moved across the Creek? I never heard of such. When do they get started? If it all happens, then the mud had better stay behind or it will be for no good reason.

A hug for the children. How I would like to kiss baby Golda. Silas and Vella can sure have a good time together. Loyd chatters about Silas all along. I think that's what he is chattering about. And oh, Lizzie's little Drewy. Won't Junnie and Jewel have a time with their little sister. Maybe there will be four like us.

The people around this place made us feel welcome. They are real friendly and Survella is invited to a birthday party of a special little friend. I sewed her a precious little dress to wear—at least I think so.

Come see us. I must stop now for Jim is riding up the road.

> All my love for you.
> Katy and Jim

I love you Papa.

Part II
AFTER SUNDOWN

CHAPTER 16

Clark Page's Army discharge – Louisa marries – The move to Indian Territory – Aunt Maud Shults writes to Survella – A divorce in 1903 – The San Francisco earthquake

~~~

Nearing the end of Clark Page's three-year enlistment in the United States Army, he became ill and was confined to quarters in Manila for six weeks. After convalescing in a Corregidor hospital for another month, he was transported to San Francisco. He recuperated in a hospital there until well.

His discharge papers read, "Thomas C. Page: twenty-seven-and-a-half years old, five feet seven-and-one-quarter inches high, ruddy complexion, blue eyes, brown hair, and by occupation a bridge carpenter, was honorably discharged at Presidio, San Francisco Cal, this eight day of April, in the year of our Lord one thousand nine hundred and one."

In early 1902, Henry and Lizzie moved as they had planned, to Arcadia, Texas, Galveston County. Henry traded his crops for cows and accomplished his goal of beginning a dairy farm.

Jim and Anna Kate lived south of George's Creek for a time, in West, Texas, and then to Bartlett, where Jim found work. Anna Kate was not a complainer and kept tending to her house and family. Her letters to her sisters lessened, and she fell ill the fall of 1903. Her condition could no longer be ignored, and Cora and George went to Bartlett to see about her. The doctor said she probably had TB for a long time, without being diagnosed.

~~~

From Cora Shults to Lizzie:

Bartlett, Texas
October 21, 1903

Dear little Sister and Family,

Poor little Katie is at rest at last, at last, after this long old toilsome life she has had to live how glad we ought to be to know she doesn't have to suffer any more. She died this morning at about 6:30. You know I told you yesterday she would live till about daylight. And sure enough she had a drowsy spell about like yesterday.

Jim woke Lou and me about 2 hours before. But she did not talk any. She tried to shut her eyes a few minutes before she died. How bad she did want to live. She just seemed like she was going to live anyhow. She died like she was sleeping. I was so afraid she would die hard.

I heard Jim and Lou talking so I think she is going to keep the children till he gets done this job here. We will keep her until 9 in the morning. There is several offered their teams, buggies, hacks, free of charge. Her coffin cost $25. So much company since Saturday. I will write to Brother John.

Her dress is cream nuns veiling trimmed in lace ribbon and lace. I saved you some of her hair. Oh how poor she is. It is now 1 o'clock. She is turning dark fast. How sorry I am for Jim and these little ones. I do hate for us all to go and leave Jim.

Well I have lots of others to write to so good by and let's try to live better every day to meet our loved ones.

Cora

~~~

Anna Kate died at the age of thirty-three. Jim blamed himself for not helping out more, blame he continued to carry. George wanted him to come to the

Territory, but at Henry's and Lizzie's urging Jim took the children to Alta Loma in South Texas.

John Robert and his family started for Indian Territory, followed by George and Cora. On the north side of Red River, they set up camp for what they planned to be a short rest. They especially hoped it would be short because the hundreds of grasshoppers annoyed them day and night. However, a few days turned into weeks.

John Robert and George registered for the lottery in the land office at Guthrie. Each homesteader's name and address was placed in an envelope. Land officials then drew out the envelopes, and according to the number on the envelope, the homesteader could "stake his claim."

George later returned with a smile on his face, having won a patent for land in what was then Kiowa County, including Snyder, about sixty miles from the Texas-Oklahoma border.

The families parted company, with John Robert heading farther west to Hollister. He and his family stayed a short while in Hollister before opening a wagon yard in Faxon. The children helped with the business and lived above the wagon yard and livery stable. They eventually moved to Frederick.

From their Red River camp, the Shults family headed for their new homesite. Theodore Roosevelt signed George's original land patent. Once in Snyder, he constructed a dugout for their living quarters while making plans for their permanent house. The dugout had a front outer section of wood.[1] "Quite comfortable for what it was," Cora reported.

George drove his wagon to Vernon, Texas, to purchase three hundred dollars worth of lumber to build his grand house. He installed white pillars across the wide front porch. Cora knew her mother would have liked that. Just outside the kitchen door he placed a cistern, surrounded by a wooden floor. He enclosed it with a screened-in porch, and Cora hung buckets of plants from the ceiling. He placed the storm cellar just outside in the back, so if needed, they could get there in a hurry.

Another luxury George provided was a water pump, which he connected to the cabinet by the kitchen sink. It had a drain allowing the used water to flow into the yard. While many New York residents from 1842 on, had piped-in water, most rural families continued to haul and pump throughout the nineteenth century.[2] George's version of "running water" made washing dishes as well as clothes convenient.

After Clark fully recovered in California, he stopped in Texas to see his family. Perhaps fate determined his decision, because after going home to Kentucky for a while, he returned to George's Creek and courted Louisa. They married in 1905 and moved to Wichita Falls, where Clark began working for the Gulf, Colorado and Santa Fe Railway. According to plan, Andrew would divide his time living with the children's families. Fortunately, Clark could provide a railway pass for his father-in-law.

~~~

From Robert Isaac:

> Morehead, Ky.
> December 10, 1903

Dear Cora and family,

This cold December day brings a letter hoping to find you all well. But I cannot bring myself to believe Anna Kate is no longer with you. God bless those dear children as I know what it is for children to be without their mother. I wrote Lizzie my sympathy for her Junnie. That's two little Junnies gone. We have had our sadness in this present year but the time will come when we will all be together with no more sorrow.

How I would like to see John and you all. Guess their little Opal is a bright spot. I will write him and Maggie if you will send their PO.

Now my news may be considered good to you all. You and I both know I did not have to ask permission but I want you to share my happiness. I have married again which I never thought would happen. Her name is Ellen Skaggs. She is from Lawrence County. No one could replace Isabel and that is not what I am trying to do. Loneliness is not a good thing and you understand I am certain. Ellen is a fine woman.

Well this is all for now. Give my nieces and nephew a hug from their Uncle Bob. You must forgive me for not writing all this time, but it was not an easy thing to do without my sister to answer it. I hope this reaches you.

> I remain your uncle,
> R. I. Nickell

~~~

From Maud Shults, Jim's half-sister:

> Sullivan, Missouri
> March 12, 1904

Dear little niece Survella,

How are you? Well I hope. We are just tolerable well but your grandpapa. He has to sit in his chair all of the time. He hasn't been in bed since Thursday night and only about two hours then. I don't see how he can last much longer. So much water now that is the reason that he can't lie down. Guess he will have to be tapped soon. He is so drowsy and doesn't talk much.

Your Uncle Walter came home with brother Oscar
yesterday and went home since dinner. They are well and
your Uncle Lem stayed here Friday night. We have lots of
company today. We've been sitting up with papa for nearly
six weeks. I feel sorry for him. But he doesn't complain
much. He can't even raise himself from his chair.

Yes the picture looks like us. I got a card from Mrs.
Romine. We certainly miss George and Cora since they went
home. It was nice to have them visit. Heard from them last
week. How are you getting along in school? When are you
going home? How is your papa and Loyd?

We have some jonquils in bloom. Will send you one. I
don't know very much to write. Looks gloomy here today. So
I'll close. Answer soon. By by. Love and many kisses to all
from your Aunt.

Maud Shults

Monday—Papa is about as usual today. He never rested
very well last night. —M.E.S.

~~~

After George and Jim's mother, Elizabeth
Springston, died at the age of thirty-one, their father,
Silas Allen, remarried. Being twice a widower, he lived
with his daughter, Maud. She was a few years older than
Survella, and she began writing to her after Anna Kate
died. Survella was a young child at the time she received
Maud's first letter.

~~~

From Lizzie:

Galveston County
December 27, 1904

Dear Lou—this is yours strictly,

Yes, Mrs. Hicks still lives at Cleburne, 601 Sabine Ave.

I am just sick three times since November but you send that remedy in next letter of course. Why hadn't you thought before and is it a good one? So many fail you know.

Lou you know that it has been a year now since Katy died and Jim cannot get hold of himself. He just talks about her all the time. Long ago he has let his Woodmen dues fall through, unless he has renewed right lately of which I am sure he has not.[3] We did not know it for the longest. Yes and worse still how it breaks my heart. He's been drinking since Christmas. Was down Christmas Eve night at the depot and poor little Loyd standing over him crying. Our friend Reese took him to his house and put him to bed.

After the Christmas tree George took him home. They kept it from me as long as they could. Oh how it tore my heart when I found out he was drunk and had been drunk twice before, and how I wanted to tell you and Vella but could not take the courage.

Jim promised Henry so faithfully he would quit. But I found out through a close neighbor he has been still drinking and oh how it hurt me. Just as soon see my own dear brother in that condition as him, for those dear children's sake, but he can't get over losing Katy.

Mr. West lives close and he has charge of the livery stable there, so it's different and Jim doesn't have to go to town every week like he did while selling milk. He doesn't come down so often and I know now that's why. He is ashamed. He came Wednesday to borrow some money. Henry could not let him have it. Then he sent Loyd with a note to sign so he could get some money at the bank. So

Henry could not refuse. But I tell you Jim must help himself.
Now send this to Cora when Vella comes home. If you want
to you can tell her. Do as you please.

Lizzie

Oh yes, Lou, you might write Henry a letter about me
coming up there to visit. I can't find out anything from him.

From Lizzie:

Galveston County
April 2, 1905

Dear Lou, Clark, and Papa,
I take this time to write a few lines in answer to your last
letter which was received some time ago. I am glad you did
not tell Vella about Jim for as far as I know she never knew. It
is a blessing that Jim has gotten himself straightened out. He
has not had a drink since that time. Looking at another
Christmas without Katy must have gotten him started and he
couldn't stand the thought. Seemed to think that drink was
the answer. We know it doesn't answer much. But thanks be
to God it didn't take hold of him permanently.
Now you must tell me, how is Papa? I know he misses the
country but are you all getting along fine? Do you still like
living in town? It's quite a change what with no cotton. Now
what do you think of that? We generally are all well. I do get
blue when I think about Junnie. That's most all the time so I
have to keep up for the sake of everyone else. They all have
feelings too.
Henry likes his dairying and Jim has picked it up.
Oh if Katy were here. They would all have a good life.
Vella and Loyd are fine. It's getting late and I must put on
supper. Write soon. The children send their love.

Your sister,
Lizzie

~~~

Permelia's brother Jim died in 1905.[4] His obituary notice stated, "J. W. Nickell, aged sixty years, died at his home across the river Monday (10/16/1905). He was a member of the Christian Church and leaves a widow, five sons, two daughters who have the sympathy of many friends in their bereavement." The obituary printed in *The Glen Rose Herald*, October 19, 1905.

~~~

From a hospital nurse:

San Francisco, California

To Mr. Jerry Nickell
Dear Mr. Nickell,
    My name is Miss Harrison and I am a hospital nurse. In the personal belongings of Mr. Newton Nickell, a patient here, we found your name and address. It seems to me that you may be a relative. The doctor has asked me to write to you telling that Mr. Nickell was injured in the earthquake. The extent of his injuries is not known at this time.
    I can tell you Mr. Nickell has a head injury and has not regained consciousness since he was brought in for care. He has a broken arm and a twisted knee which is yet quite swollen. His head injury is a concern, as it is possible he will not wake from his sleep. I am sorry to relay this information but feel it is my duty. Please write and we will keep you informed.

My prayers,
Nurse Harrison

~~~

From Lizzie:

Arcadia, Texas
May 12, 1906

Dear George, Cora, and all,

How are all of you this bright day? There are many bright days lately. The dairy is keeping Henry and Jim busy.

Uncle Jerry wrote that he heard from Uncle Greenup and he has a wife now by the name of Anna Burton. But my, twenty-five years is a long time for a man to mourn a wife. His children are grown up and they shouldn't mind if he married again. Uncle Robert said Aquilla gave Uncle Greenup a grandchild so that's at least one I know about. Oh, Uncle Jerry also said Amos Russell married Ada Love. I guess you knew? I guess Lou is the only one who gets to see our kin in George's Creek.

When is Papa thinking of coming down? Just whenever he is ready we are ready for him to stay. Lou and Clark want him to visit with them first. Bless his soul. I sure do miss having him around and miss him so much as soon as he leaves.

Well this is all so will close for now. Papa are you all right? We sure will be glad to see you. It's so good for Vella and Loyd to come visit you. They love Oklahoma too. They talk about the country for weeks when they come home. They are the best children and don't give anybody any trouble atal. Too bad Lou won't have little Loyd come visit. She's my sister too, but she doesn't want to have to look after a boy. Much as I hate it, it does hurt his little feelings. He's a sensitive sweet child as it is.

Love to all.
Lizzie

~~~

From Newton K.:

San Francisco, Cal.
May 19, 1906

Dear Jerry and Belle,

Here I was on that cot in the hospital, not knowing if I was alive or dead. I decided when the nurse came in with my dinner. It was a simple stew but smelled like food for a king. I hadn't eaten for three days, maybe longer as I haven't figured out the calendar yet. I got hit on the head and got my arm broken as a afterthought. The arm was the easy part and if you can't read this it's because I'm writing with my left hand. They said I was lucky as they didn't know if I would wake up. My head still hurts. It got cut bad but it was mostly on the inside. I've been staying with one of my motorman friends and his wife. Their place wasn't damaged at all, but then I have to get a place of my own as soon as I can.

It's been a long time since you heard from me. How I would like to see my brothers once more. I've been in Frisco some time. Got a position as a motorman for the railroad. I spect I still have it but the tracks need a lot of work. You know I never was short on words but there's words to tell about the earthquake in this place. I lost most everything which was not much but it was what I had. The destruction through the city would make you sick. I can't tell you as you would have to see for yourself. I went back to my place and there wasn't a place to go back to hardly. I am alive and I thank God for it.

People helped everybody once they got their ownselves together. Jerry you wouldn't want to see the ruin for anything. It will never leave my mind. You would not believe it if you saw this city. I will come back to this later. I drift off to sleep even when my eyes are open.

May 20

This next is owed you and I regret it wasn't given sooner. I thought I had found it all in California. My years with cousin Ella and her family brought me contentment I did not know was there. The farm was hard work but what crops we brought in. It taught me to run a real farm of my own.

The furthest thing from my mind was to ever marry Pearl. She was a child when I came out here and before I knew it she was a grown woman. Life meant a lot to her and then one day she was the love of my life.

Something I never told Permelia was how we married. Looking back on it now it was not the right thing to do by Pearl or by Ella. Pearl deserved a nice wedding at home with her family all there. I took her to San Francisco and we went out on an excursion boat and had the captain marry us. Would you ever expect that from your little brother?

Ella never let on that she minded we got married. Ella and me, we got a long fine. Always did.

I confess I never should have married Pearl that way but she readily agreed. It was a good marriage and I got her about everything she ever wanted, but as times went on things changed.

After a while she changed. I will deal myself most of the blame maybe. Who knows maybe she married ol Newt on that boat because it was a romantic thing to do.

Three years ago we had a divorce the likes Yolo County won't see again for a long time to come. They said the marriage wasn't legal done by this captain and Pearl was too young. She was sixteen though. We had no children so we went our separate ways.

Tell Lou I asked about her. What is George and Cora's PO number now? And who is Andy staying with? I haven't written since you told me brother Jim died. Do you know the cause of it? It sure hurt me to hear the news.

This may be all you hear for a while. I wanted you to know I am all right and please pass the word. I would sure like to see all my family. Give your boys respects from their Uncle Newt. I hope Texas crops are doing good. Let me tell you driving a motor car is a lot different than driving a team.

Your brother,
Newton K.

<div align="center">~~~</div>

From George and Cora:

Manitou, I. T.
May 30, 1906

Dear Clark and Lou,

I will only scratch a short letter as there is a world to do. I hope everyone is well as we are at this time. Kiss those children for me and an extra squeeze for Lizzie's little Mavyce when you see them.

My, we are still shaking over the earthquake. Uncle Jerry sent me his letter from Newton and I can't hardly hold my pen steady enough to write. He was spared but lost most of his belongings. God was with him through it all don't we know. I don't have to tell you all that the earthquake and Pearl too in one letter was almost too much news at once. I will go ahead and mail Newton's letter to you if you haven't seen it, but you may have heard from Uncle Jerry.

Well this must close as I have to sort through the lard to see what I need. Am so afraid I don't have enough flour for the rest of the week. And we must have bread and more bread.

I wish you could see the children. Little Golda is growing so fast. Silas teases but he's a help and Lula Pearl is sweet as ever.

Love to all,
George and Cora

~~~

This year was not a happy one for George and Cora. Their daughter Lula Pearl became ill with the fever. The doctor was summoned immediately, but no amount of help he offered was enough. Silas and Golda were too young to understand, then neither did George and Cora know why a beautiful child was taken from them at so early an age. Lula Pearl had long dark curls and big brown eyes that her mother would not look upon again, except for the large portrait hanging in the parlor.

CHAPTER 17

Deputy Sheriff Jim Shults – Andrew and his cotton sack – An interesting lawsuit – A white stripe down its back – The storm – Papa was eighty

~~~

From Jim Shults:

> Arcadia, Texas
> Galveston County
> June 12, 1907

Dear George and Cora,

    These lines should find you all well. George, your farm sounds mighty good and was glad to get the photo. Who rides that bicycle by the side porch? I thought it might be the teacher's if Silas does not ride it.

    Your barn is bigger than most houses—like Katy and I were going to have. A house with two stories and a big porch. I'll never get over Katy and will never marry again.

    Loyd and Sis would like to come up this summer and thanks for asking. They are ready to come right now as they are anxious. Lou won't have Loyd visit. She lets it be known she doesn't care for little boys much but I would rather she did not take it out on her sister's boy.

    Well maybe more next time. Days are long but I stay busy. Stay well.

> Your brother,
> Jim

~~~

From Jim Shults:

Arcadia, Tex.
June 19, 1907

Dear Vella and Loyd,

Hope everyone up there is well. I hope you are having a good time and do your chores to help. Well you would not believe what kind of job your daddy got his self into now. Had to go to Galveston on business and got into a fight with a sailor, but ended up with a new job. I stayed the night as I had to tend to business early in the morning. It was terrible hot that evening, and supper was over at the boarding house, so I told my landlady I was walking down to the waterfront café.

She asked me did I have a weapon. These places are full of rough crazy sailors from all over the world, and she said I would be smart to have a little protection. I carried my papa's gun he gave me in Missouri. I put the gun in my belt and struck out for the waterfront about a mile distant.

I had just pushed back my plate and stood up when this big sailor moved to me and asked if I was going bear hunting, or maybe elephant with that gun. He grabbed for it to see how heavy it was. I slapped his hand away. He took offense at that and drew back his hand so I hauled off and slung my coffee mug. Whacked him good upside his head and down he went.

I headed for the door when another man stood in my way only this one had a badge on. I thought now I had done it for sure. But he asked if I knew who I put to sleep on the floor. He said that was a good exhibition of avoiding a real fight. He said he thought I was the man he had been looking for and asked if I had ever been a law man. I told him I'd never come close to even shooting a man before and wasn't in the habit of wearing a gun.

He said the way I handled big Otto proved what he had just said and he wanted to hire me on as a deputy. I told him I lived in Arcadia with my two young ones. He said it was his loss but I should be in the law somehow. So I took on being a deputy sheriff in Galveston County and can live where I'm at for a while. Now what do you think of that? No more time now. Yes I will be careful.

A kiss,
Papa

~~~

From Jim Shults:

Arcadia, Tex.
June 19, 1907

Dear George and Cora,
Just a short one this time. Thanks for having the kids. Appreciate you doing this. It means a lot to them. Being a deputy carries a different day but most times are calm. You never know for sure I guess.

I wish one day we could all get together. It's been too many years I would say we been together at the same place the same time. Say hello and give love to the children for me. I miss them when they're not here. Come down whenever you can.

Jim

~~~

From Cora and George:

Snyder, Oklahoma
June 20, 1907

Dear Lou and Clark,
Your welcome letter was received Friday but I couldn't get to answering until this afternoon. We are all so busy. George has hired hands to work and I make dinner for us all.

That's a good kind of bother for the more hands we have the better the crops are.

Loyd and Vella are having a time. Silas and Golda don't want them ever to leave. Papa is feeling fair. He does like to help pick cotton. George takes him out a little chair and when papa finishes picking from one plant, he takes his chair to the next plant and picks some more. He just pulls the cotton sack along. Lately he's taken to the rocking chair on the front porch. It's cool out there and he's partial to Rusty the dog. Rusty likes to have his ears scratched and papa obliges.

The men have just built us a new outdoor house. It is closer than the other one and with a rock path all the way from the kitchen door. Will never forget the story told on Anna Page when she went out to the little house at night and left the door open when she thought a cat followed her. She found soon enough it had a white stripe down its back. She came flying out of there. Surprised she even told it on herself. Anna also married that man named Lewis. She sent their picture. You will have to see it if she did not send you one.

There isn't much news. The weather is fine as long as the sun shines, then so does everybody. Papa sends his love. We all do the same.

Cora and George

~~~

Andrew lived with George and Cora for six months the spring and summer of 1907. He sat and talked, reminiscing of tales the family never heard before. Survella and Loyd spent a few months with their uncle and aunt in Okahoma then returned to Arcadia.

~~~

From Survella:

Arcadia, Texas
Galveston County
June 24, 1907

Dear Golda,

I thought I would write you a letter. Now you try to write one back to me. We are having fun down here, but not as much as on the farm. We sure had a good time.

Aunt Lizzie is so good to me. She is teaching me sewing and that's what I want to do, make me some dresses. She says it doesn't take any cloth at all hardly for me a dress. Well tell me what you are doing since I was up there. Say hello to Silas and love to Uncle George and Aunt Cora.

Cousin Ban and his wife came up to see us and we all went out to the lake when I was in Wichita Falls. We all had our bathing suits except Uncle Clark didn't go. He was working the day we went out. The water was so cold I couldn't stand it when I got out. It wasn't so bad while I was in the water. We had watermelon and it was really good.

Answer soon. Love to all.
Survella

~ ~ ~

From Survella:

Wichita Falls, TX
July 10, 1908

Dear Golda and all,

Received your letter and I could read it just fine. I forgot all about telling you about the little chest Uncle Clark brought home from Manila. It has brass corners and handle and is full of things. I'll tell you what it has in it. Some carved wooden sandals with a leather strap, some wooden combs, some embroidery slippers, some real pretty silk handkerchiefs. Some shoes are for grown ups and a pair for children.

Some gun shells and things like that he had in the war. Aunt Lou lets me take the things out every once in a while but is afraid they might get hurt or something. I don't know how you can walk in the shoes. Anyway, you can see them when you go to Wichita Falls. Uncle Clark brought his rifle home too, but I don't touch it. He took buttons off his uniform and brought some shells and that metal thing off his helmet.

There was a fourth of July celebration here. The band played. Did you have anything there? Not in the country I guess. But there was quite a bit here in town.

Write as soon as you can.

Love and kisses,
Survella

~~~

From Cora:

Snyder, Oklahoma
July 12, 1908

Dear Lou and Clark,

I will take time right now to write you any news. Of news there is little however. What do you hear from California? Uncle Jerry lets us hear when he does get a letter. I wonder what Cousin Pearl is doing now. Aunt Belle is good about writing. They are thinking of going up to Delta County and may yet. But I don't know what is calling them up there. Do cousin Clarence and Laura get up to Wichita Falls any? Would like to see them.

My, the barn is going to be full to popping. We have another crop of kittens too. I will tell you our crop of mice is low.

Well we get down to church all the time of good weather. If not, we have our family prayers. Papa Shults isn't doing well at all. I think it so nice that Maud writes to Vella. She has kept her up on his health and I think Survella must hear news before George does. How nice if she and Loyd could ever meet their Grandpa Shults but won't ever be a time now I suppose. I must close for it is getting late and I am a little weary.

Love to all,
Cora

~~~

From Lizzie:

Alta Loma, Tex.
July 20, 1909

Dear Lou and Clark,

I will write you a short letter as I have delayed writing too long. It has been uncomfortably warm the last few days but the air seems to be changing. Maybe rain is coming. We are finally settled here, and grazing for the cattle should be good.

Oh dear sister, Drewy cut her second toe a few days ago and I thought sure she would bleed to death or lose her toe whichever came first. One of the girls accidentally stepped on it and it hurt her so bad she fairly swooned out. I could scarce stop the bleeding. I just reached in the rainwater tub and drenched her with it. She came to after that but poor child, her toe was cut so bad. Couldn't wear a shoe. Reminded me of that time when Henry got bit by a spider.

Tell Survella that Loyd misses her. He's having a good time helping his papa and Henry. Says when he grows up he wants to be a deputy too.

Papa is still feeling poorly and doesn't have much strength. Likes just to sit outside under the shade tree. I wonder what he studies about and sometimes think it must be mama.

Well it looks like rain. I have some sewing to do and must get on with it. Vella, I have that piece of goods we talked about. When you come back we will cut and sew the dress up for you. Write when you get this. You write a note to your papa sweet Vella. Love to all.

Your Sister and Aunt
Lizzie

~~~

In 1909, the Romines' cattle had grown considerably in numbers. The land had dissipated, so they moved to nearby Alta Loma where grazing land appeared more abundant.[1]

~~~

From Lizzie:

Alta Loma, Tex.
Galveston Co.
July 22, 1909

Dear Lou,

Oh how sorry I am you are not here, and under the circumstances can't let you even know. Oh how it hurts me that I even can't send a telegram for the wires are all down. Can't get anywhere. Two hundred feet of bridge washed off across the bay. Can't get an undertaker from town to embalm Papa. Can't take him without, to George's Creek. Oh how bothered we are. Lou, poor Papa died so easy at 2:30 a.m. today.

Jim Adams Locke went after his coffin and suit in Alvin. No trains across the bridge. Your letter came today. I was so glad to get it. Henry was aiming to wire up to Uncle Jerry. Ask John Robert to talk to Cora over the phone. Can't keep looking for you but of course you may not start until you

hear again. Wrote you a card yesterday morning. Hope you
will be here in the morning.

Will bury at ten tomorrow by our little Junnie. Will have
to move later on unless all are satisfied.

Don't grieve. We can't possibly do any better. Love, a
kiss, oh am so sorry you are not here.

You know Papa always called mama a little doll and he's
been mourning her for ten years. I can see the old fellow
right now with his gloves on out in the shade. The good
shade leaves have fallen just like after frost. That's strange
for them to fall like that. I guess it must have been the storm.
The yard is a sight. Will try to get it cleaned up a little before
you come.

Yes I got a pretty letter from Clarence. He and Laura will
visit us I guess. So I wrote him to come next week. I am
looking for them anyway. I love company you know. Mrs.
Hicks and family I guess are still in a notion of coming down
next week. We have plenty to do but you could entertain her
if it was a busy time.

The trouble is the vegetables are all gone most, even
pears are all blown away. We didn't have any this fall. The
storm did not hurt my chicks though. Don't get many eggs,
but have forty little young chicks and four are hens setting.
The little biddies are doing well so far. I wish I had lots big
enough to fly.

Last time we met the train. Will wait till you tell us next
time to meet it. The children want Aunt Lou and Golda to be
here so bad. I feel the little Shults children and these will
have a racket over Golda when she comes. Wish Silas would
be along.

Silas, make your papa write if he will, and you write too.
Tell your mama to please be good and not want Golda to
come back too quick, for no telling when she will ever get
away again. You and your mama will never come but never

mind. I don't expect to come see you until after you all come here. I would like for you to hurry and do so.

My time won't be so many years away. Poor Aunt Lou. Hasn't got anyone to stay with her now. I know she will miss poor Papa of course. Clark and Lou if we would have known dear papa would have left us so soon, most sure we would have told you, but did not know it ourselves in time to get Jim and the children here. I had written Survella that note to come already. So I am writing you this morning.

Yes we understand about the railroad passes business, but we just did not know in time ourselves. I have never had an idea that he would have gone so quickly, always have just thought he would all have plenty of time to get to him. Of course as I have told you, we knew he would not get well again. Well Lou when you come we can talk it over. Decide on what and how to do when, if we want to take him to George's Creek. You must see John and Maggie when you go back and tell them all for I know there isn't time for them to get here.

How is it dear little brother will not write me one scratch. How will I get him to write or let the children write. If anything ever happened to me, just keep it all to yourselves for if he won't write now he wouldn't care to say a word then.

Lou, what would you think if I was to let Jewel go home with you? If you had a good school, Henry has just now surprised me with such an idea. Now you and Clark just say what you think of such an awful thing to let my big girl go away from home that far, but rather she was there with you than as close as Houston, say among strangers.

You know Jewel is having trouble in her books now and Henry says she is bound to make something, if nothing only the looks of her by going. He doesn't want her not to look her best either, so he thinks by letting her go with you it would do her so much good. And there she would study harder than she has been used to and you would have more time to be with her and help her than I do.

Now here is someone to stay with you. What do you think? I know of course I would take many a cry, for you girls don't know how much I depend on her as she is so understanding. And as she gets larger I can tell her lots of my troubles but would truly like to see Jewel make a nice neat woman. Henry says he knows Lou can dress her as inexpensive as anyone and make her look nice too. I will not mention this to her. Drewy has asked three times to go and Mavyce says she is going.

Wish everyone could come down. Just seems I would give anything to see you all right now. By by. A kiss to all. Lou this is an oddly written letter, but excuse. I don't know what nor how I wrote it until I read it over. Seems like it is to everyone. I sent for the morning paper but Jim has not come with it yet.

Love to all,
Lizzie

~~~

From Cora and George:

Snyder, Oklahoma
August 8, 1909

Dear Lou and Clark,

Oh my I know we were expecting to lose papa but refused to think on it. He and Mama are together now. Of course we would rather have him at George's Creek but understand they couldn't get him to the undertaker's on account of the storm. I know Lizzie will look after his grave. We can be sure.

And now Uncle Jerry is going to Delta County. At least Clarence and Laura will stay though. Ban and Russ are going to operate the gin and Clarence still wants to stay a teacher.

George is working in the field right now. It is so hot—nights too. I keep a wet sheet on the head of the bed and at least it seems cooler when we go to sleep and if we sleep hard we don't know the sheet is dried out.

I guess you figured it wouldn't work for Jewel to live with you and Clark. Maybe she does need to stay with her family but I understand Lizzie's feeling in the matter.

Well I must close. I've talked again with John Robert. Love to all.

Cora and George

~~~

Ban and Russ Hawkins stayed in George's Creek to work the gins. Their brother Walter Scott moved to Oklahoma in December of 1909. Walter and Lillie's baby Leland was only six weeks old when they began their long wagon journey. He became ill on the way, giving his parents much cause for worry.

Walter rented a 160-acre farm near George and Cora in Snyder. The Shults were gratified to have other family members nearby.

Millicent Gilkison Hawkins Megason moved to Oklahoma with her two daughters. She remarried, to a Mr. Freeman. At the time of Millicent's death, they lived in Oklahoma where she was buried in Norman.

CHAPTER 18

Survella's school – Her chums write – A new house in Oklahoma – A broken leg – Deputy Shults and his prisoner – Jim never even read it – A letter edged in black.

~~~

Before Christmas of 1910, Jim discussed with Lou the possibility of Survella finishing out the school year in Wichita Falls. He felt the education there would be better and that Lou might offer Survella more than he could. Lizzie taught "Little Sis" to sew and she would have no problems having enough clothes to wear.

The thought of such a change did not appeal to Survella because she saw it as leaving all her school chums in Arcadia. But she also had acquired friends during visits to her Aunt Lou's. She decided a trial period would not be too long and after all, it was not as if she would be there forever. With a railroad pass provided by Clark, Survella moved to Wichita Falls to begin the last year in school.

During these years, letters were not saved as much as in the past; however, those saved linked the family together. Survella saved her correspondence and Louisa kept all the rest together after Anna Kate died.

~~~

From Doris, a friend of Survella's:

Arcadia, Texas
January 3, 1911

My dearest chum Survella,

I received your most welcome letter a few days ago and you don't know how glad I was to hear from you. Oh how we all miss you down here.

What did you get for Christmas? I got lots of things. mama gave me a blue pongee silk dress and a pair of kid gloves, and I got a silver belt buckle, a silver jewelry box, a pair of light cornet braid pins and a barrette and a gold scarf pin. Didn't I fare well? Got a lot more than I expected.

You had a sad time and a good time too on Christmas. I expect you were glad to see that chap once more? What does your aunt think about him? I never had so much fun on Christmas as I did on New year's. Last Saturday Mr. White, Theo, Arthur, and myself all went to a play at the opera in Galveston and I just wish you could have seen it. It was certainly fine.

So Maude and Clifford got married at last on Christmas Day. The big event finally came off. Christmas Eve when we were dressing the tree, after we all got the candy in the bags and the buckets empty, we put one big candy bucket and filled it full of paper and put it on the tree for them. We wrote "For a nice young couple, with the compliments of the church." You ought to have seen them open their eyes. When he went after the license he got drunk to celebrate (wasn't that a shame?)

John has him a girl, Adele. They are like two sick kittens. He walks home from school with her and they stand out on the ditch until five-thirty. She even goes out hunting with him.

No, Ivan and I are not that bad off yet. We are pretty good friends—rather thick. Millie and Bob have got it bad I believe. He gave her a gold necklace for Christmas. It had five chip diamonds with one red set. It is certainly pretty. You know my pearl ring? I broke one of the pearls and Ivan took it down and had that one taken out and a new one put in (wasn't he good?) Ha, ha.

I am going to visit the dentist again. My front teeth have got the fillings out again. He is going to put some gold in them this time to see if it won't stay in longer than the white. Wont' I look swell with gold in my teeth. I have got to go back on Saturday.

Say, can't I claim one of those pictures? It is darling, but why not, as you are so pretty. It looks like you would share up. I will exchange with you. I had some taken last Saturday. Now don't forget me.

I have me a new hat. It is a very very light gray. It looks like beaver with a big long scarf and a bow on one side. I am going to get me a coat soon.

Last Monday they gave Mandy and Cliff a party, and on Tuesday night the Woodmen gave a supper. Friday night there was another party at Charles' for Gracie's cousin. Oh my, have we been busy socially.

Effie and Halley went to Galveston last Saturday to the play we all went to. They missed the night train and had to stay all night. And people got it out two or three times that Ivan and I were going to get married but we haven't yet. Paul gave Flossy a diamond ring for Christmas.

They are getting rather thick all of a sudden. Effie told me to tell you she is still looking for a letter.

Now honey, I have been friends with you all this time. We miss you more than anything. I know you will have as many friends up there, or maybe even more than you have down here. I am glad you are enjoying yourself so much, but am sorry your Aunt Lou won't let you continue with your piano. Did she sell her piano? Now that is a real shame. I know you want to play so much.

I expect you are tired of reading all this nonsense and it is way past my bed time. You know how early to bed I am. Please don't wait so long next time before you write, as I am always glad to get a big letter from you. Well good night honey. Answer soon.

Lovingly,
Doris

~~~

From Jim Shults:

Arcadia, Texas
January 16, 1911

Dear Vella,

Well Sis, I will try to write you a few lines. We are well and this will find you all the same I hope. I haven't got much to write and not much time.

Sis, do something for me please. You write to Lizzy Bishop and see if you can find out from her where Davis is. You know who I mean. But don't let on to her that you know anything. Write to her on paper. Don't write a card. Put a cross mark on the right hand corner of the envelope on the back, with an X in ink. Let me know as soon as you hear from her. This is very important so do what you can. I want the money he owes me.

Henry went to Walnut Springs last night. Don't know when he will be back. Well, Sis, I'm going to quit for this time. You be a good girl and enjoy yourself up there. I am tired and sleepy. Write soon. I miss you.

A kiss,
Papa J.W.S.

~~~

From Cora and George:

Snyder, Oklahoma
March 20, 1911

Dear Lou, Clark, and Survella,

We hope you are all well, as we are. I suspect school is out any time now and we are all planning for Vella to come up for the summer.

The cows, horses, barn kittens and even the haystacks are waiting for you children to play so come as soon as you can. And Vella, we have a kitten that looks just like your mama's did. You may call it yours if you like. We are very satisfied with the country here. The land is rich.

Clark, I hope you are feeling all well now. My but I was sorry to hear you were ailing.

George is adding another smaller barn, well it's a big shed really. Anyway, it is to keep the donkey on. Somehow it needs a place of its own to keep the peace.

Well I started this letter at a bad time since I must get dinner ready for the hands. I promised Milton that I would bake a lemon cake, and I am way late gathering the eggs. He's a young man George hired—still only about seventeen, but one of the hardest workers there is. I must get on with it. Would so love to see you.

Our love to you all.
Cora and George

~~~

From Survella:

Wichita Falls, Texas
April 15, 1911

Dear Golda,

Well, it is almost the end of the school year. It has been a lot of work in school, and study, study, study. My marks are very good. Of course there was a small fuss about them earlier in the year, but I took care of that.

I started a diary on my birthday and planned to keep it until school was out. That's almost it for my diary. On my birthday, Ruby Theatt had a party at her house. It was fun. We have band concerts once a week and I almost always go, as long as I have my homework done for Monday.

You know Kate Ricks is one of my best friends and she doesn't live too far from us. We spend the night occasionally and often go down town after school. One of our school friends, Willie, stopped school for Business College. Anyway, back to Kate. She and I got mad and did not speak for a day and a half. We went to church and that afternoon, Mrs. Ricks came over and fussed about our fussing, so we made up. I don't remember why we got mad now.

Mrs. Irvin had a lovely musical entertainment in her home and we stayed until 12:20 that night. Mrs. Ash and Mrs. Wilson, Aunt Lou, and I went. After Sunday School the next morning, Mary Stirman came home with me and we went to Parkers to see Fern and Wanda Obelander. Ruth came down and we went to the band concert on the Court House lawn. We went to church at night.

One special evening this spring was a Ball I went to. I am not used to dancing that much. Aunt Lou and many of her friends went, but she says she doesn't believe in dancing. It was beautiful, with lovely food too. I have been sewing quite a bit and can even make a dress without any kind of pattern. I will teach you how to sew when I come up there this summer, unless Aunt Cora has taught you already.

Well, I've cleaned up everything, ironed, and have studied for my last test. Ruth and I went to the Lodge the other day and drilled in Royal Neighbors drills. Today we went downtown to the show and now and I am really sleepy.

Write when you get this. Love to all.

Survella

P.S. - I have to tell you Aunt Lou sent me for a block of ice and on the way back, some horses got scared by this automobile. The horses ran right into the auto and they hung up the street for the longest. By the time I walked home with the ice, it had melted off some. Aunt Lou was fit to be tied. I nearly had to get proof there was an accident before she would believe I didn't diddle daddle along with the ice melting.

~ ~ ~

From Survella:

Snyder, Oklahoma
May 30, 1911

Dear Papa and Loyd,

How are you getting along? I am fine and I enjoyed my train ride by myself. Uncle George came to get me and everything worked out fine.

I must tell you about Golda. It's terrible. She fell and broke her leg before I got here. The doctor came out and he had to set her leg immediately. Aunt Cora said the doctor set it with shingles, and she has to stay flat on her back for six weeks. He says that's the only way to heal it. She has about two more weeks to go before they take the shingles off.

Well since she can't go out and play, I go out to the pond here and it's real shady. I can read and just enjoy the smell of the countryside. The grass smells sweet. I do chores to help Aunt Cora, and you can be sure they bring in that old tub for a soapy bath and not just on Saturdays.

I will tell you we had a storm the other night and it was the most lightning and thunder I ever saw. Golda and I were asleep upstairs when it started and we heard a loud noise and looked out the window and lightning had struck the big barn. It was going up in flames and Uncle George was trying to put it out but it had gotten too good a start. We just had to watch it burn. There was a lot of hay stored in the barn and a plow and things, but no cows were in there. Oh, Jack the donkey, didn't stop with his noise making. We were all so sorry but Uncle George reminded us the lightning could have struck the house, so everybody felt better.

I have to tell you Aunt Cora surely can make good cakes. She puts an icing that has nuts and raisins in it. She starts out with a little flour and water to thicken it up and uses fresh cream and butter and mostly sugar powder. I could eat it without the cake.

Well I guess I better stop now. We have not heard from Aunt Lizzie in quite a while. She was always so good about writing. Lots of love.

Survella

~~~

From Jim Shults:

Arcadia, Texas
June 10, 1911

Dear Vella,

Thanks for the letter Sis. I'm glad you are doing okay. Hope it is a good day for you, and I will be thinking of you all day.

Well it looks like my boss thought I could handle prisoners and such without getting myself killed as he came in the jail office the other morning and sat down across the desk and says he is giving me a job to do. Said I had to be careful every minute. The judge gave this guy a long sentence and it's our job to see he gets to prison.

He said his deputy takes our guests on the train to their new home. So in the morning I take this guy the distance up to Huntsville. I went by to pick up papers I would need to hand him over. The sheriff kind a smiled and said he didn't reckon he was too eager to get behind those walls. Last time he was in those guards beat on him because he was always giving them a lot of sass. They don't take too much of that from anybody.

I walked on back to the cage and told him he better be woke up when I came for him cause we had some place to go. Your papa sounds tough doesn't he? Well we both know that's not so.

Henry and Lizzie and the children are well, except Lizzie has felt better. This is enough for now. I miss my girl. Excuse the hurried writing. I will have this mailed before I leave.

> A kiss,
> Papa

~~~

From Golda:

> Snyder, Okla.
> June 10, 1911

Hello Uncle Jim and Loyd,

How are you all getting along? I am fine. I can walk now as my leg is well. I thought as Survella was writing to you I would write a little too.

Loyd I wish I was down there so I could get some ice cream. Does Uncle Jim still work for the dairy while he's a deputy? Send me some up here. Ha ha. Did you get the card I sent you for your birthday? I wrote to Aunt Lou and Lizzie this morning.

I have got to help churn pretty soon so I will close for now. Write to me some time.

Survella and I sure do have a good time. So by by.

> Love and kisses to you all from
> Golda

~~~

From Survella:

Snyder, Okla.
June 10, 1911

Dear Papa and Loyd,

We got a good old letter from Aunt Lou and Aunt Lizzie's folks, so as I was intending to write them, and will just take this morning off and write to you. We were sorry to hear Aunt Lizzie is not feeling well. I need to write to her.

Aunt Lou certainly is proud I think, that she is going to get to keep me a while. I am glad in some things for I think it will be better for me than to be down there, but I certainly hate to leave you all. Aunt Lou says that she will take me down there this summer if you will promise to let me come back.

I am still at Aunt Cora's. I have been from Aunt Lou's some time now. I don't know just when I will go back, but I bet soon for Aunt Lou has the sewing stacked up in the corner for me. Ha ha. I have finished embroidering me a dresser scarf and am working Aunt Cora one now.

They are going to South Cold Springs this afternoon. Will be gone until Sunday night. I don't want to go so I intend to stay at cousins Walter Scott and Lilly's until they come back. Just Aunt Cora and Golda are going. Say Loyd, Silas is oh so bad. He is forever pinching me to see me jump.

There was a big day Monday. "First Monday" in town and we all went. And oh yes, Papa, you remember when we lived out in the country from West? Do you remember the Jones out there? They were kin to Mrs. Fullerton. Well one of the Jones boys, "Blanton," saw me Monday in town. He knew me. He is chopping cotton for Uncle George this week. I wanted to chop, but after he came I wouldn't go out there. They all will finish chopping this morning.

Golda has an organ and she can play one piece and I can play one piece from memory, so we have some music. I would like to learn how to play real good as it seems easy.

How are you all? How are you getting along with the store? Do you sell for cash or credit people? Do you get your money for your cows regular? I guess you are busy with being a deputy too. Always be careful with that.

And have they ever found Mark Davis yet? Be sure and let me know. When you write I want all the news.

We all spent the day at Uncle Allie's.[1] He is as mean as ever. He was lighting his pipe Sunday and threw the old match on my neck and burnt it, so Loyd you know I am ruined, or my beauty is for life. Ha ha. Oh it didn't burn much. Is all well now.

It is so warm I just know I will melt. Everything nearly is burnt up. People here have to haul water. I made some fudge the other day and it all went to sugar. Aunt Cora told me how to keep it from doing that. Mainly I boiled it too long.

Did you all keep one cow for your own use? We have all the sweet milk and light bread we can eat. Well I am going to stop writing for a while and write Aunt Lou and Aunt Lizzie. And then maybe I will have more time to write to you by then.

Aunt Lou says that she has something for me that she would have given anything for when she was about my age, but didn't get until she was twenty or twenty-one, and then paid her hard old money for, but she didn't tell what is was. We have guessed everything from a straw to a fortune, and still can't think what it could be.

It is looking a little cloudy. Rain would certainly be fine but I am not afraid of it raining much. Well I have now finished a letter to Aunt Lou and will write Jewel a few lines. So I will close this letter now.

Love and kisses to all. Answer soon. I suppose you had better send it to Wichita Falls. I guess I will be there by then. Love to all. Answer soon.

Sis

~~~

From Lizzie:

Alta Loma, Tex.
June 12, 1911

Dear Clark,

For fear you yourself will not come I will write you although we do not know for the particulars yet nor ever will. Jim has been to Galveston and there was a big excursion train loaded, steps and all. Whether he was knocked off or fell off a half mile this side of Arcadia I don't know. Anyway the 800A through-train knocked him off the track. They said he is bruised up but they will not tell me how bad. Henry is with him at Arcadia. Loyd is here. Has not seen him either.

The section men found him this a.m. about seven. We will write you more when Lou, Survella, and George get here. I hope they are well on their way. We notified you immediately. Hope you are well. I have been in bed all day from the shock. Be a good boy. Excuse scribbling.

Then some say Jim was transferring a prisoner from one car to the next and he knocked him off. Was trying to escape. They said he was supposed to be taking a prisoner up to prison. Oh maybe we won't ever know. I fear the worst and they won't tell me.

Your Sister Lizzie

~~~

The circumstances of Jim Shults' death were never verified—either by accident or intentionally. Jim Shults never got to read his daughter's last letter. When Survella got to Arcadia, either the railroad men or sheriff's department knocked on the door at Lizzie and Henry's. They asked for Jim Shults' daughter to identify her "papa's remains," which were in a thirty-nine cent wash tub. After her identification, they presented her with the bill for the tub.[2] Lizzie was distressed to think they asked such a thing of Jim's child, rather than herself or Henry.

After the funeral, Survella continued to live with Lou and Clark. She had preferred to live with Cora but since Lou had no children, her aunts made the decision. Loyd was only thirteen. He was welcome to stay with Lizzie or Cora, so for the time being, he remained with the Romines.

~ ~ ~

From John and Irene, family friends:

Arcadia, Texas
June 16, 1911

Dear Little Survella,

I am just broken to think I won't get to see you. Dear little Loyd is here now. I would give anything to see you but if I don't get to, I want to tell you that you all have our deepest sympathy and our prayers. I pray that God's richest blessings may be with you dear children.

I know it must be hard to have a dear father snatched away so quick without any warning. But God knows best and I am so thankful to think your dear aunt can take a mother's place. I do wish I could see you but I guess I can't, so by-by dear little girl.

With lots of love from your best friends,
John and Irene.

~~~

From Maud, Jim Shults' half-sister:

Sullivan, Missouri
June 17, 1911

Dear Cora, George and all,

How are all of you? Papa is improving. The rest are all well. We received your letters. But oh the sad news they brought us seems more than I can stand. To think of my darling brother taken away without a bit of warning. If we only knew he was prepared to die, how much better contented we could be but grieving doesn't help it. Do any of you have any idea for sure how it happened? It is awful to think how he was so torn up. I just grieve over that. Was Loyd with Mrs. Romine at the time?

I guess the children took it awfully hard didn't they? How sorry I am for them, with neither papa or mama. But if I can help them any time I will. If Jim had only written to us more, but I loved him just the same. And don't see why we all have to be separated from each other.

Yes we appreciate the kindness of the people down there. To think they were so good to help. But oh I am sure the children will have good homes. Tell them to write and I will write them when I know where to write. Now hope all are well. And we may all meet some day.

I will close. Do hope to hear from all soon and no more news like that. Give our love to brother Charles Allen, Clara and Babe. Tell them I will write soon. Answer soon. Love and many kisses.

I am your loving Sister and Aunt
Maud Shults

~~~

From Ida, a friend of Louisa's:

June 19, 1911

Dear Page,

Sorry indeed to hear of the children's papa's death. I felt so sorry for poor little Survella and Loyd, but then both will have good homes I'm sure. And that you know is something that lots of children don't have. I know it did hurt you all to give him up and the way it was—having to die away from home too. I think we ought not grieve so much for our loved ones. But it seems like we can't help it. "God doeth all things well," and of course we all have to die sometime.

I hated so much to hear of Sister Lizzie being in such bad health. Certainly hope your visit will help her, and you are keeping her baby awhile for her. Now isn't that fine—that she has a "dear old Sister Lou."

Sorry to hear that Mr. Page is not well. Maybe he needs to get out and visit around a while. Thought sure you all would visit us this summer. I know when we get back to Greenville you will come. We are kindly thinking about going back, but you know we are always talking. I'll let you know when we go.

Well, we are not feeling well this hot weather. Joe Frank has an awful cold cough and little old Bessie works herself nearly to death cleaning up and sweeping the yard. Mr. H. has a puppy that keeps things scattered in the yard. Bessie doesn't like it a bit, so she gets her broom and goes to work.

Well we had another right nice rain Saturday so everything is looking lots better. Guess I'll quit for this time as I want to go to town. Want to get me a new dress but don't know just what kind I'll get. Answer.

Your friend,
Ida

~~~

In June of 1911, George and Cora arranged for a family reunion in honor of the Romines and their baby Eva. Clark and Lou, John Robert and Maggie, were all present at this gathering, which Jim had mentioned earlier. According to a Snyder, Oklahoma newspaper report, the reunion was the first time the siblings had spent a day together in twelve years. The special time gave everyone reason to be grateful, for they would see one member of the family for the last time. Survella remained in Wichita Falls with her good friend, Kate Ricks.

~~~

From Lizzie:

                    Snyder, Oklahoma
                    Friday 14th, Uncle Henry's birthday

Dear Vella,
    Did anyone catch you last night, dear little Sis? It was Valentine's Eve you know.[3]
    Hello to Katie Ricks and her sister and family. Lou and Clark got here at 8 a.m. Henry and George went over to the railroad to meet them yesterday with the surrey and they were not there. So this a.m. they did not have the team up, and just walked over to meet them. It is not too far.
    Cora has breakfast for them now. Lou wanted to eat so I am writing. Hope you will not get lonesome and will have a good time. Be a good little guest. Loyd is still sweet as ever but teases all of them so much. We are going to have a birthday cake today I think.

                    Your Aunt Lizzie

~~~

From Cora:

Snyder, Oklahoma
October 18, 1911

Dear Lou and Clark,

I am sick with grief over Lizzie. I knew she didn't feel well when we were all here. Even John Robert commented on it, but he mentioned it to her and she had only a small complaint and then dropped the subject.

When the letter edged in black came I could hardly bring myself to open it. Of course you got one too. The note sent by Henry said that they thought it was appendicitis and the doctors entered her in the hospital. Their diagnosis was incorrect. It was cancer and it was too far gone to operate. She died October 14. Will you be getting railway passes? Surely under the circumstances, they will grant you the passes.

I am grateful that Henry has a successful business and I suppose he can take care of the children too. He will have to have some help for the younger ones though. And there's little Loyd. How hard it will be for him. Am I right that you won't consider taking him? He could stay here some too.

Oh my. We must make preparations for going down there. I must close now. How glad I am you all were up here just a while ago.

Love to all
Cora

~~~

Henry Romine mailed copies of this letter edged in black to family members.

From Henry Romine:

Alta Loma, Texas
October 14, 1911

Dear Cora and George,

Our dear wife, mother, sister and aunt, Lizzie Frances Romine passed away this afternoon, October 14, 1911, at twelve-twenty. She has gone to a far better place than this earth. Leaving six dear children and husband which we hope and trust will follow her.

R. H. Romine, children and relatives.

Lizzie dictated the following to a friend as she was too weak to write.

— from Henry Romine
October, 1911

To my dear ones,

My request to you all.

Raise my children right.

Teach them to be members of the Church of Christ.

If you can't keep the precious babe I am willing to let Lou keep it a while anyhow, but keep the rest together.

Bury me in white by the side of my dear little girl, Junnie.

And keep our graves clean and nice, with flowers on all four of them. Put tombs on them as soon as you can.

I want the songs in Gospel Gleaners sung, Numbers 209, 139, 113, 40, 208. If they can't sing these, others will do.

Children, all be good to each other. Do all you can, each of you do your part to get along nicely.

Be good to Ma and papa, and papa good to you.

Treat everyone nice and good, especially old people so you will have lots of good friends.

Jewell can wear my clothes after awhile, wear some now, no use to keep them.

Just give all some little keepsake.

Let my sisters and brother know of my death at once.
Don't buy an expensive coffin or clothes for me.
Save all you can to take care of these precious children.

Your wife and Mother,
Lizzie Romine

~ ~ ~

From Aunt Maud Shults:

Thursday 10:15 A.M.

My Dear Niece,

I will try to answer your welcome letter I received a few days ago. Was glad to hear from you, but I am so saddened to hear of your Aunt Lizzie. I will try to write Lou, but in the meantime, give her my feelings.

We are all well as usual. Your Grandpapa seems to be improving some. Can walk by holding to a chair. Maybe he will be better so he can walk by Spring. Hope so as it seems so long. Has been over a year he has been this way. Now do hope you and the rest are well. I got a letter from Charles Allen's wife, Clara, the other day and they are well.

A snow fifteen inches deep or more fell here the last of February. Roads were so bad and snow drifted up so high the carrier on this route didn't even come on Wednesday. The next day was Washington's birthday so of course he didn't come and on Friday the men dragged the road so he could get here. He couldn't get all the way around so went part of the way and then back to Sullivan. And has snowed twice since and has been trying to rain all morning.

I am so lonesome. My fellow has bought him 160 acres of land in Maries County about thirty-five miles from here and he went up there two weeks ago last Monday. Only intended to be gone a few days and the weather has been so bad he can't get back. He says seems like he has been gone a month. When he's at home we can talk any time as they and us are on the same telephone line. People have got us married already. But I expect we would be the first ones to know it don't you think so? Have you a fellow? I expect you could have any young man you set your mind on.

I know your dress must be pretty. I haven't worn any kind of a dress but black since your papa died, except a gingham dress I have worn two or three times. Wear black for every day with my sleeve aprons over them. Would seem so odd to wear anything else. I got so tired of black for a while so one day I got one of my white waists. Thought I would iron it to wear and Mama asked me why I was going to wear that. So I felt then that I didn't want to wear it so put it away.

What to do these days? Go to school I guess. We have only got two more weeks besides this one. Seems like spring never will come. How is Loyd? I haven't had a scratch from him but once and he sent a card then. Guess he just doesn't get at writing. I worry so for him not having a real home. Cora says he visits them some. Don't guess you can read my writing as I get in such a hurry when I go to write. Yes, you owed me that letter.

I don't believe I know anything else to write. Guess you will get tired of reading this, so I will close hoping to hear from you soon and to see you sometime. By by. Answer soon. Tell Aunt Lou hello for me. What does she do these days? Let me know what you hear from the Romines. I hear from Cora and George every now and then. Love and many kisses to all.

I remain your loving Aunt Maud Shults
to Survella Shults

CHAPTER 19

The Lusitania – Louisa's letter from a preacher's wife –
A rain of flesh – 1917 – A perilous trip to Arkansas –
College plans for Golda – An extraordinarily
handsome fellow.

~~~

From Cora:

Snyder, Oklahoma
May 8, 1915

Dear Clark and Lou,

We hope you all are well as we are. But can't think of anything but this dreadful news. I just think of what Clark went through before and now it will start all over again. We have all just heard the news that the Germans sank the Lusitania. Just think, hundreds of people drowned. All of Europe will keep tearing at each other til there won't be anyone left when it's all over. My, such a frightful thing. I wonder why we should be a part of it. Why can't we just stay at home and let them fight out their own problems.

George told me how the Germans were called packs. Wolf packs I think he said. They sank big ships and passenger liners could be mistook for carriers. I guess that happened to the Lusitania. Now we all know that President Wilson vowed there would not be a war but George wonders how we can stay out of it. Most people think we won't have a war. Oh how I have fretted over it.

George is adding on to the barn. I declare he is always building on something. Any time family or friend wants to build a house he volunteers. My, I don't think he could build a house without puffing on his pipe. It's a wonder he stops to take it out of his mouth to eat. Here he comes up to the house now. Pie's about done.

Write when you get this. Clark, what do you think of the news of war?

> Love from your sister and George,
> Cora

~~~

From Rose, a friend of Louisa's:

> Floresville, Texas
> July 15, 1915

To Mrs. Louisa Page
My Dear Lady,

It makes us sad to know Mr. Page is not rapidly improving. We did so hope his operation would be the turning point to the path of perfect health. Now that the warm sun shiny days are coming, I hope he will begin to mend rapidly.

What are you doing these days? I haven't felt well for the past week. Had a chiropractic adjust my back last Monday and I'm just now getting over it. Wish you could come see my boys. Little Charles is whistling a march and popping his hands, and the baby has on a little red cap and his show outfit, marching around the table that I'm writing on. They are having lots of fun.

Last Tuesday was "Loyalty Day" here so he caught the idea from that.

Oh, don't things look more serious? If we have a war I don't suppose my husband will have to go but think of the young men and maybe someone else's husbands that will have to go. I don't think any of them will ever come back that have to go to the trenches. And your husband has already been in one war. There is apt to be plenty of war grooms everywhere. Maybe I'm just too pessimistic and there won't be a war.

So Jordan got married. I wonder if he will buy any ice-cream for her this summer. He could be called stingy, don't you think? Hope he treats his wife better than he did his sweetheart.

You and yours always had something to say that would drive away the blues. I've had them all day today. I just feel that I'd like to say goodbye to this old world and go tonight. Enough.

Does that young man still call on Survella? Can't remember his name—was it Briggs? Candidly, I did like him. What cute little dresses does that pretty girl wear these days?

It rained all day yesterday and it was such a gloomy day, but that dear Jimmy Hill had sent two "Judges" magazines so I didn't care if it did rain. And Thurman has certainly been a dear about writing to me but it seems I just can't get around to answering. You know how sorry I am about doing things.

Have nine chickens that I'm fattening for the meeting in June. One has taken limber neck. If he lives I intend to feed him to the preacher. His wife and two children are coming and it's real funny. Some of the ladies want her to come and some don't.

Sure am glad I don't have to go with my husband all the time, but I'm going to Charco to his first meeting this year. Shall visit my roommate of school days. Can hardly wait to go, but oh my clothes! Guess they will do for war times. I shall go get me a new skirt to wear with my waist Mrs. Sparks gave me, and the skirt you gave me, and a middy (everybody wears them here to everything. I never saw the like.) Will make one dimity and a white voile made with those pretty coat-waists, and with a plaited green messaline belt.

I'll tell you something when I see you that will tickle you good. I guess you will have a postscript to add to that tale you told Brother Wills about me now, for being so naughty and not writing to you sooner. But I told you long ago that the folks I really loved I treated awful bad. Don't ever write to me if you don't want to, but I shall write you again anyway.

We haven't decided what to do next year. They want my husband to come back here but I want to hike to the farm where we can grow a little of this high priced produce. What will we do if things go higher. The merchants here are paying fifteen dollars a barrel for flour. The baker here uses Wichita Flour.

It is so cool tonight that we have a fire in the fireplace. Seems so cozy. Logan fell on his tongue today and cut a great hole in it. Don't think it will be serious though.

These folks here are afraid to do anything to make us have a good Sunday School because the presiding Elder doesn't exactly favor it. Haven't any young folks here just like in Wichita Falls. One boy and about a half dozen girls.

And do tell me what Kate Ricks is doing these days? How is Mother Ricks? My husband hasn't married but one couple since we came. Preached three funerals, and do you know we haven't but two babies at church and one of those had a mother that was a staunch Baptist, but was baptized fifth Sunday. The whole town is talking about it. Her father is one of the deacons in the Baptist Church so you may guess what she's done, but she came and had my husband answer her questions and explain things until she was prepared to answer all arguments before she changed over. Two babies are all we have and no prospects of any more.

If we move to the farm we will tell this place good-bye. I sure hate to ship this furniture again, but if we do I hope it doesn't get torn up like it did coming down.

It's bedtime honey and tomorrow is wash day, so I must quit. I have a girl to help me wash and she does all of my ironing for fifty cents. Do hope Mr. Page is improving and please don't forget that I often think of how good you all have been to me and that I love you whole heaps.

Survella, there's a girl here that is a little like you, but she's not smart nor as sweet.

Rose

~~~

From Survella:

Wichita Falls, Texas
May 20, 1916

Dear Golda and all,

Last night we had so much rain and thunder, the noise scared us all. We were on the porch and Aunt Lou had us hold feather pillows to keep lightning from striking us. She said she expected any minute to see it rain bits of flesh all over the place like in Bath County Kentucky before she was born.

Aunt Lou said pieces of real flesh fell from the red colored sky, and not just a little bit. I didn't believe such a tale but she said Grandmother Permelia bowed it to be true (Aunt Lou always says bow, but I think she means vow.) It was written up all over the country and some of grandmother's relatives even saw it. Well, with all the lightning and thunder, nothing but rain water fell here. Good.

We saw Opal last week but she is the only cousin I get to see very often, and cousin Clarence and Laura came up once. Aunt Lou sees cousin Ban every once in a while. I think he and Russell operate the gin down in George's Creek. I guess they still have enough cotton down there to crop. Aunt Lou knows so many people who live there, and we've been to the graveyard working day the last two years. We missed this May on account of Uncle Clark was sick. He's feeling better now. I think his sickness started with that war in the Philippines. Aunt Lou said he stayed in the hospital there quite a while.

I made me a dress and thought it would never get finished. Usually it doesn't take me long. But I couldn't find enough time all at once to get this one sewn. It's a new pattern and has about twenty pleats on each pocket. Now I think it won't be much fun to iron. Aside from that, Kate Ricks is out of town with her parents for another week.

> Write when you get this.
> Survella

~~~

The strange rain Survella referred to occurred in Bath County on March 3, 1876. This "shower of flesh" fell from a clear sky, covering an area approximately one hundred yards long and fifty yards wide. Several newspapers and books documented the occasion. This was not the first time a similar phenomenon had been reported in the nineteenth century.[1]

The first graveyard working day at George's Creek was held in May 1892.[2] It has been observed the first Saturday in May since that date. Descendants and friends of the citizens of George's Creek gather at the tabernacle and bring lavish layouts of food. The people arrive in the morning and enjoy talking over old times, sometimes not leaving until sundown.

~~~

May 10, 1917

Louisa joined Cora in her concerns over the war. They were worried that Silas would be called. Loyd worked in the cotton gin in George's Creek. He caught his hand in some equipment and as a result, lost a finger. He could have lost his arm had it not been for some quick acting on the part of two men at the gin.

That might not have kept him out of the war, but injuring his back in the oil field surely would. Loyd did so while taking the place of an oil field worker in Burk Burnett, Texas. Loyd made extra money by working for the man for one day. He was not experienced enough to be climbing over the derrick and fell to the ground. His injury plagued him the remainder of his life.

Cora and Lou were sure that when "our boys" got overseas, they would end this horrible war, but so far it looked bad. Two of George's hired hands went into the army.

~~~

From Louisa and Clark:

Wichita Falls, Texas
August 2, 1917

Dear Cora and George and children:

How are you by this time? I would like so well to see you all but it looks like we won't get up there any time soon. We are planning a trip to Arkansas to Mountain Home. Clark is right proud of his Maxwell and he will hitch a trailer to it.

I had a letter from John Robert and he is right concerned over the war. He said that men between the ages of twenty and thirty were conscripted as soldiers. They have probably never shot more than a squirrel or a rabbit. Oh, the casualties we will have and some dear ones being disabled for life. And the terrible gas weapons they talk about. I read it in the paper myself. Clark knows if anyone does what a war is like.

Do take care of yourselves and write soon or you best wait as we will be gone soon. Oh yes John Robert and Maggie tell us they are fine.

Love from your sister,
Lou and Clark.

~~~

From Survella:

Wichita Falls, Texas
October 2, 1917

Dear Golda, (This is for Aunt Cora and Uncle George too.)

I will have to write and tell you about our trip to Arkansas. What a time we did have. And maybe I will never want to go back! My friend Brownie didn't particularly want me to go at all. He said he would miss me too much. Well, he had to do a lot of missing because we were gone longer than we meant to be! Brownie had expected to go to the war before now.

We left on August the sixth in Uncle Clark's faithful Maxwell. We were going to Mountain Home and had a trailer hitched to the automobile. Soon after we got to Arkansas we were arrested for not having a license tag. Can you imagine! Uncle Clark told them that Texas law just began on June the first for tags and there wasn't enough steel to make all the tags they needed. Uncle Clark couldn't prove he had made an application. The man finally charged an eight dollar fine and said we could go on. Aunt Lou called him a gink but not to his face.

Then we couldn't get up a big hill and had to be towed separate from the trailer. It got dark before they could get the car and the trailer both up the hill so we had to divide.

The auto was at the top and the trailer was at the bottom and we pitched a tent. Then it started to rain! It rained pitch forks and shovels the next day and it was so muddy. We finally got started but hit another hill and backwards we went. Aunt Lou said we could have landed in eternity, and we had a smashed wheel on the trailer because it turned sideways. Uncle Clark fixed it.

We were finally in Madison County and had a blowout of the deferential (I didn't know what a deferential was.) We couldn't get the car out of the road and had to clear up around it, but couldn't find any level ground for our tent. Uncle Clark went to Pettigrew and took a train to Fayetteville for repair parts. That took five days and Aunt Lou and I camped until he got back. It was a good thing we packed enough food.

We finally got on our way and in just a little while the deferential broke again. We got a man to tow us on to Harrison and got coupled to a lumber wagon. We made the forty miles in two days! The roads were horrible. We made a funny sight with the mules pulling the lumber wagon that pulled the Maxwell that pulled the trailer. There were so many curves. And we had to pay for the man's trip back and we were with him only one way.

You'd think we were finished. But we got to Harrison on September ninth and Uncle Clark ordered the parts. They came on the twenty-second but a piece was missing. They had to order again, and I went back to Wichita, for I had already been away from the Western Union office too long. Uncle Clark wasn't feeling well when we left home in the first place, so all this didn't help him.

Aunt Lou said we had enough hardship experience so we ought to get rich in a hurry when things started going our way. One thing good came out of it though. We never thought it would be cold and I didn't take a warm coat. So I had to buy one in Arkansas. It's a real pretty one with a fur collar. I had to get one so it was a good thing I liked it.

Well that is about all there is to say on that story, but what more could have happened? Faithful Maxwell. Ha! But I had to come back to work and Uncle Clark and Aunt Lou came home later without ever getting to Mountain Home.

I guess if good or bad fortune is looking for you, consider yourself found. Tell me all the news. Hello to Silas.

Love and kisses to everyone,
Survella

<div align="center">~~~</div>

From Cousin Golda:

Snyder, Oklahoma
October 9, 1917

Dear Survella,

I will try to answer your nice long letter. Your experience was something to remember all right. I don't know if I would want to go to Arkansas or not. What made Aunt Lou and Uncle Clark want to go there instead of down to see Uncle Henry? At least they could have taken the train and not had all those problems. But then it was probably going to be fun to go.

Jewel wrote me a letter the other day and I answered it. Drewy would be the next to get married, but they've never mentioned a thing about having a fellow right now.

I know it isn't funny but your description of everything that happened on your trip—I couldn't help it, but when I read it again, I laughed and laughed. Don't get mad at me. I think of you probably getting your skirts muddy and how disgusted you must have been.

My parents have been talking of me going to college. They think a girl should have all the education she can have. I would like to be a teacher I think. They want me to go to a school in Texas, in Abilene. It's pretty far from home and about a hundred and fifty miles from Wichita Falls. What do you think of such an idea as me going to college?

Excuse such a short letter but wanted to answer yours in a hurry. There are some chores waiting for me and studies to catch up on, so my time has gone.

Love to all,
Your cousin Golda

~~~

Survella liked working at the Western Union Office, especially since this was the first time she had ever earned money to call her own. Actually, it wasn't all her own since her Aunt Lou expected her to use her wages as payment on their house. Survella got to keep very little for herself, but managed to save some.

~~~

From Survella:

Wichita Falls, Texas
October 17, 1917

Dear Golda,

Thank you for your letter which was received about two weeks ago. Excuse the delay. You know that I mostly answer as soon as I get your letters.

Thanksgiving isn't even here yet and people are talking of Christmas. Wouldn't it be nice if it snows?

I never mind work at the Western Union Office. It is downtown of course and I can look around the shops when lunch time comes. However, I've thought working in one of the stores might be fun, to work with clothes. Our little sewing machine just stays busy all the time. Aunt Lou likes how I sew for her.

You know Aunt Lou has said she will pay me back the money I have given her out of my wages to buy her house. She has always said it was just a loan. I hope she hasn't forgotten because I haven't. Ha!

What a wonderful thing for you to think of going to college. How nice to plan such a thing. You have a lot of time yet but tell me how did you know to come to a school in Texas and what all do you have to do to get ready. There are some people who would rather finish just high school and not go to college, but still I think it might be nice to go. However, Aunt Lou would not consider it anyway. I would know that without asking.

I entered a contest at one of our shops in town. It was to see who could decorate a shop window the best. Could you guess I won and got $5. I talked Aunt Lou into letting me keep it.

Tell Silas hello for me when you see him. How are they doing? Love to Aunt Cora and Uncle George. I love them both and Uncle George is like a papa to me. You are very lucky to have them. But you have always let me share.

Write soon and don't wait as long as I did.

Survella

<div align="center">~~~</div>

From Survella:

Wichita Falls, Texas
October 25, 1917

Dear Golda,

Do answer as soon as you get this. What I am writing for is to tell you about an extraordinarily handsome fellow I have just met. He is unlike any of my previous friends, both in ways and looks. His name is Hamilton Hallmark and is the dearest person I have ever met. We must look strange together as he is six feet three inches tall and I can easily stand under his arm. He is from Haskell and has four sisters and one brother.

Anyway, I have known him for a short while, but my heart fairly flutters. It seems he thinks the same of me. How does he sound so far? He will come to call again Friday evening. We went to a concert and will go again to the next one too.

But what do you think of the war? It is frightening. The newspapers make it sound very bad, not that it could be any other way. I know some young men in church who have gone, and I wonder about Silas. I have to tell you that Hamilton has been called up. Already he knows I will be waiting for him. I pray he will return safely.

Answer as soon as you get this. Love to all.

Your cousin,
Survella

EPILOGUE

Many more letters followed your grandmother Survella's correspondence of 1917. Her "extraordinary fellow," Hamilton, returned to her after the war. They married June 30, 1921.

When I was very young, I remember Aunt Cora as kind and loving. She baked delicious pastries. Perhaps country cream and butter from their Oklahoma farm added to their goodness. Your Aunt B remembered her better, as she was my older sister. I especially liked being around Uncle George, because he was my grandfather Jim Shults' brother. I asked to call him "granddaddy," since I never knew my own.

Anna Page, in California, married James Lewis. Her sister, Ella, married William MacReynolds Vanzandt in Somervell County, Texas. After his death, she remarried in 1906.

Permelia's son John Robert retired, leaving his successful freight business for his son Aubrey to run. John converted a school bus into a traveling home, complete with kerosene stove. He tried retiring to West Texas, but he and Maggie eventually returned to Frederick, Oklahoma, settling down in a house my great-uncle George might have helped him build.

Lizzie was buried in Arcadia Evergreen Cemetery. Arcadia and Alta Loma incorporated into the town of Santa Fe.

Newton was a deputy sheriff before he and Pearl married, although he was a farmer first. After their divorce, he became a motorman in San Francisco. He suffered a fatal heart attack and died in 1911. Pearl remarried and died in 1949.

As for Robert Isaac, Aunt Lou saved a 1914 telephone bill from Morehead. The only name on it was "Nickell."

Later, the family assumed the call concerned Robert Isaac's death, because there were no more letters from him. Just as Permelia predicted, he never left his Kentucky.

By 1915, Henry's milking cows increased to one hundred and fifty. Since he found help to be scarce, he sold the dairy farm and decided his remaining children could have a more quality education in Alvin.

With the passing of time, gravestones were broken or fell into Dickerson Bayou by the cemetery. Permelia's letters and your grandmother Survella provided proof of Jim Shults' and Andrew's gravesites. In 1994, the cemetery received a Historical Marker of the State of Texas, through the work of many, including our cousins Lois Brumley and Linda Gayle White Cheek. Jim Shults' and Andrew's names, along with many others, are engraved on a granite slab in the cemetery. Their original headstones are missing.

Permelia's brother Jerry and his wife, Belle, moved to the Texas Panhandle where Jerry succumbed to heart failure in 1927. Their brother Greenup died in 1929 in Oakwood, Illinois.

Remember Jefferson Bolling, who stabbed Jim Nickell? He served seven years before parole for killing his wife's father. He never received punishment for the attempted murder of Jim. I guess you could say he left the noose swinging in the wind.

Cora and George's daughter Golda married Ross Givens and had three children, Eva Jane, Duane, and Gale. Survella and Golda were close, as I have always felt close to Eva Jane.

Aunt Lou (Louisa) married Oliver Blanton after Clark died in 1917. Lou and Oliver were in a car accident in which Lou suffered broken legs. They were not set properly, and she had trouble walking. She passed away many years later in 1955. The beautiful crocheted coverlet in our old-fashioned guestroom was her gift to me. The China doll Permelia gave Louisa in 1886 sleeps amid the pillows.

Permelia would have loved seeing all her grandchildren and great-grandchildren. The twenty-first century brought Permelia's descendants a new frontier with their own bridges to cross. Some may crumble in the changing world of the future. But we have the inspiration of pioneer women like Permelia Hawkins to guide us.

I believe the leaves of spring can grow larger.

From your mother,
with love

END NOTES

CHAPTER 1

1. Ewell, T. T. *Hood County History in Pictures and Story: Covers Hood and Somervell Counties.* Fort Worth, Texas: Historical Publishers, 1978, H-93.
2. Elliott, Raymond and Mildred Padon. *Of a People and a Creek*, Cleburne, Texas: Bennett Printing Company, 1997, p. 22-24.
3. Block, Viola. *History of Johnson County and Surrounding Areas.* Waco, Texas: Texian Press, 1970.
4. Rowan County, Kentucky Court Records. A bench warrant was issued for the arrest of Jefferson Bolling for "cutting and wounding another with the intent to kill."
5. Brown, Fred Jr. and Juanita Blair. *Days of Anger, Days of Tears.* Morehead, Ky: Pioneer Printing Company, 1987, p. 5.
6. Brown, Fred Jr. *Smoke in the Woods, Vol. 1.* Morehead, Ky. A Crow's Nest Production, 1987. 74. "William C. Nickell, aged 55 years, lies dangerously ill at the house of his brother, Andrew Nickell, jailer of the county."
7. Sonnichsen, C. L. *I'll Die Before I'll Run.* New York: Harper and Brothers Publishers, 1851, p. 94.
8. Graves, John. *Goodbye to a River.* New York: Alfred A. Knopf, 1983, p. 234.
9. *Fort Worth Star Telegram.* Fort Worth, Texas: 4-6 March 1997, Section B, p. 2.
10. Correspondence with Maurine Hawkins Reynolds, Millicent's granddaughter.
11. Brown and Blair, *Days of Anger,* p. 6.

12. Daniel Nickell, eldest brother of Permelia's father, William C. Nickell.

13. Brown, Fred, Jr. *Days of Anger,* p. 11.

14. Leckie, Shirley A. *The Colonel's Lady on the Western Frontier: The Correspondence of Alice Kirk Grierson,* Lincoln and London: University of Nebraska Press, 1989, p. 180.

15. The Commonwealth of Kentucky issued a subpoena to Jim Nickell, to testlfy against Jefferson Bolling, 1 January 1885.

16. *The Glen Rose Citizen,* June 1885.

17. A term for leaving children with someone else.

CHAPTER 2

1. Brown and Blair, *Days of Anger,* p. 17-18

2. *Real Pen-Work.* Pittfield, Mass.: Hudson Maxim Publishers, 1882. Anna Kate's penmanship book is in the author's collection.

3. Elliott and Padon. *Of a People,* p. 45. The Rev. Lewis Elliott was an ordained minister at twenty-four, a teacher, and photographer.

4. Luchetti, Cathy in collaboration with Carol Olwell. *Women of the West.* St. George, Utah: Antelope Press, 1982.

5. 120-year-old school papers of Louisa Hawkins.

6. Elliott and Padon, *Of a People,* p. 39.

7. A teacher not having extensive education, "I'm well as common," referred to a person's general state of health.

8. Barker, W. F. *Personal Memoirs.* Barker was born in Princeton, Indiana, 19 February 1891.

9. Verification of this original family legend is included in private records formerly housed in the basement of the Fleming County Ky. Courthouse. Arthur Hawes–Ledger packet no. 9068.

10. *The Glen Rose Citizen,* 2 July 1886.

11. Receipts for Permelia's sewing machine in the author's collection. The machine burned in 1966, leaving three drawers intact.
12. The cream cake referred to a recipe including a cup of pure butter and rich cream "off the top."
13. *Fleming True Blue Democrat.* Flemingsburg, Fleming County, Ky., 22 September 1887, p. 4.
14. "Will of Jesse Atchison." 4 Oct 1887, Bath County Courthouse, Owingsville, Ky. Will Bk F, p.354.
15. "Estate Settlement of Charlotte Atchison." 23 August 1890, Bath County Courthouse, Owingsville, Ky., p. 488.
16. Nunn, W. C. *Somervell: Story of a Texas County.* Fort Worth: Texas Christian University Press, 1975, p. 64
17. Sprague, Stuart Seely. *Eastern Kentucky: A Pictorial History.* Norfolk, Va.: The Donning Company Publishers, 1986, p. 59.

CHAPTER 3

1. Elliott and Padon. *Of a People*, p. 45. The Cumberland Presbyterian Church was located on the east side of the George's Creek Cemetery.
2. Ibid., p. 45. Thomas and Fannie Gordon donated the land for the Methodist Church.
3. Several copies of the 1890s' *Cleburne Enterprise* are in Permelia's memorabilia, with her comments next to various paragraphs.
4. Swango, William and Maxine May. *Phelps Family.* South Charleston, W. Va.: Jalamap Publications, Inc. 1986, p. 35.
5. Ross, Nancy Wilson. *Westward the Women.* San Francisco: North Point Press, 1986, p. 72.
6. Ibid., p. 174.
7. Roberts, McCreary. "When A Man Rose From The Dead." *The Kentucky Explorer: Vol. II, No. 2.* Jackson, Ky. Charles Hayes Jr., June 1996, p. 49.

8. Ap (Absalom) Perry, an "amiable" man, survived the Tolliver-Martin Feud of the 1880s; shot and killed in ambush in 1936.

9. Schlissel, Lillian, Byrd Gibbens, and Elizabeth Hampsten. *Far From Home: Families of the Westward Journey.* New York: Schocken Books, 1989, 163. In 1890, citizens of New Mexico referred to a "new" disease called "La Grippa" or "Russian Influenza."

10. Sprague, Stuart Seely. "The Rowan County Trouble: Anatomy of Mountain Feud." *Mountain Review,* Vol. II, No. 4. Whitesburg, Ky.: Appalshap, July 1976.

11. Schaefer, F. W. "A Short Glimpse of the Deadly Rowan County War." *The Kentucky Explorer.* Jackson, Ky.: Charles Hayes Jr., November 1995, p. 58.

12. "Sore eyes" of the nineteenth-century and before, may have referred to present day "pink eye." Treated with rose water, this was "equally successful for common eye sores, or for granulated lids."

13. Circuit Court of the Commonwealth of Kentucky issued indictment no. 195 against Jefferson Bolling on the 3rd day of October 1882. According to Rowan County court records, Bolling's trial was put off from months to years. He had earlier been scheduled to hang for the murder of his wife's father in Ohio, with his Rowan County trial still on the dockets.

14. Schlissel, Lillian. *Women's Diaries of the Westward Journey.* New York: Schocken Books, 1982, 178.

15. *The Glen Rose Citizen.* Glen Rose, Texas: 2 May 1886. "Dr. Williamson seems perfectly at home in his new quarters in George's Creek."

CHAPTER 4

1. Stewart, Elmore Pruitt. *Letters of a Woman Homesteader.* Boston, Mass.: Houghton Mifflin Company, 1982.

2. Block. *History of Johnson County.*
3. Baxter, Annette K. with Constance Jacobs. *To Be a Woman in America 1850-1930.* New York: Times Books, 1978, 46. A minister is guest at a family's supper table. He is dressed in his Sunday suit, with black top hat, white gloves, and Bible on the floor next to his chair.
4. Elliott and Padon, *Of a People*, p. 54
5. McCutcheon, Marc. *Everyday Life in the 1800s.* Cincinnati, Ohio: Writer's Digest Books, 1993.
6. Elliott and Padon, *Of a People*, p. 46.
7. Nunn, *Somervell*, p. 168.
8. Elliott and Padon, *Of a People*, p. 46.

CHAPTER 5

1. James Joshua Nickell's first wife was Elizabeth Christy whom he married in Fleming County, Kentucky.
2. "J. J. Nickell." *A Memorial and Biographical History of Northern California.* Chicago: The Lewis Publishing Company, 1891, p. 375.
3. Schlissel, *Women's Diaries*, p. 60.
4. Ibid., p. 71.
5. Ibid., p. 113-114.
6. Block. *History of Johnson County.*
7. Ibid., p. 150.

CHAPTER 6

1. Will of Charlotte Atchison. 11 August 1890. Signed, W. W. Perry, Clerk of Bath County, Ky.
2. Elliott and Padon. *Of a People*, p. 47.

CHAPTER 7

1. Swango and Swango. *Phelps*, p. 33.
2. "Centennial Edition" of *The Rowan County News.* Morehead, Ky.: 10 May 1956.
3. Cousin of Andrew Hawkins

4. Permelia kept her tax receipts of Somervell County. They are in the family scrapbook.
5. Andrew's receipt shows he paid for the plow in full, signed H. S. Wilson.
6. Wooden frame, similar to a sawhorse.
7. Two of Anna Kate's quilts were handed down in the family.
8. *Rowan County News*, 10 May 1956.

CHAPTER 8

1. Young, William Henry. *Buy a Broom Besom: The Story of a Broom.* Germantown, Ohio, 1988, 21.
2. Apparently Joanne did not go to the asylum. No other reference was ever made.
3. *Ashland Independent,* Ashland, Ky.: Thursday, 5 January 1882.
4. Son of Dim Nickell
5. Husband of Ella Page
6. Photographers were often referred to as "artists."

CHAPTER 9

1. Alderson, Nannie T. and Helena Huntington Smith. *A Bride Goes West.* Lincoln, Nebraska: University of Nebraska Press, 1942, p. 252.
2. Block. *History of Johnson County.*
3. Young. *Buy a Broom,* p. 26.
4. Wilson, Gordon, Dr. "Pictures and Brooms." *The Kentucky Explorer.* Vol. 10, No. 4. Jackson, Ky.: Charles Hayes Jr., September 1995, p. 21.
5. Baxter and Jacobs. *To Be a Woman.*

CHAPTER 10

1. Elliott and Padon. Of a People, p. 45
2. Cleburne, Texas: *The Johnson County Review.* 9 August 1894. The reporters often used nicknames for bylines. The report including this quote was signed

by "Youngster," who for many years reported the local news of George's Creek.

3. "Centennial Edition." *The Rowan County News.* 16 June 1863, Colonel Courcey's 8th Michigan Cavalry Regiment engaged the Southerners. The fabled Kentuckian outwitted them by burning the bridge after crossing the Bluestone.

4. In 1935, Everett George, grandson of Moses R. Hawkins, wrote this account concerning Moses, Morgan Raiders, and William George. The original version belonged to Willard and Joan George who graciously allowed its use in this book.

CHAPTER 11

1. Black Draught—a laxative
2. A full dress, similar to a muu-muu

CHAPTER 12

1. Permelia's father, William C. Nickell, living with Robert Isaac in Morehead.
2. Baxter and Jacobs. *To Be a Woman*, p. 163.
3. "At the Queen City"—This could be Mt. Sterling, Ky., sometimes referred to by that name—more likely than Cincinnatti, Ohio. Also, in 1875, J. W. Sewell, a con artist from Covington, Ky., brought about a land scam under the name of the Queen City Land Association, in which 368 bogus lots near Farmers were offered for sale, including cemetery land.
4. "Centenniel Edition" of *The Rowan County News*, 10 May 1956.
5. Brown and Blair. *Days of Anger*, p. 70.

CHAPTER 13

1. Foster, A. P. *Valuable Prescriptions*. Dallas, Texas. The American Formulary Company, 1891.
2. Nunn. *Somervell*, p. 71.

CHAPTER 14

1. *The Weekly Enterprise*. Cleburne, Texas. 18 May 1899.

CHAPTER 16

1. The term "Dugout" referred to a place to live as well as to a storm cellar.
2. McCutcheon, Marc. *Everyday Life in the 1800s.* 101.
3. "Woodmen of the World," a fraternal beneficiary association.
4. *The Glen Rose Herald*. Glen Rose, Texas: 19 October 1905.

CHAPTER 17

1. Correspondence of Fern Hawkins Meriwether, granddaughter of John Robert Hawkins.

CHAPTER 18

1. Charles Allen Shults, Jim and George's half-brother.
2. The bill for the thirty-nine cent tub was presented to Survella. Jim Shults' red bandana, pocketknife, and sheriff's deputy badge were also given to her.
3. Referring to an old custom, the game in which a young man chases a girl, then tags her on the shoulder as his Valentine.

CHAPTER 19

1. Calvert, Stephen N. "Bath County's Famous Shower of Flesh." *Kentucky Explorer,* Vol. 9, No. 3. Jackson, Ky.: Charles Hayes Jr., July-August, 1994, 13-15. In addition, more information is in the book, *Charles Berlitz's World of Strange Phenomena,* published in 1990.
2. Elliott and Padon. *Of a People, p.* 54.

SELECTED BIBLIOGRAPHY

Alderson, Nannie T. and Helena Huntington Smith. *A Bride Goes West*. Lincoln, Nebr.: University of Nebraska Press, 1942.

Baxter, Annette K. with Constance Jacobs. *To Be a Woman in America 1850-1930*. New York: Times Books, 1978.

Block, Viola. *History of Johnson County and Surrounding Areas*. Waco, Texas: Texian Press, 1970.

Brown, Fred, Jr. *Smoke in the Woods, Vol. I*. Morehead, Ky.: A Crow's Nest Production, 1987.

Elliott, Raymond and Mildred Padon. *Of a People and a Creek*. Cleburne, Texas: Bennett Printing Company, 1979.

Ewell, T. T. *Hood County History in Pictures and Story: Hood and Somervell Counties*. Fort Worth, Texas: Historical Publishers, 1978.

Foster, A. P. *Valuable Prescriptions*, Dallas, Texas: The American Formulary Company, 1891.

Graves, John. *Goodbye to a River*. New York: Alfred A. Knopf, 1983.

Leckie, Shirley A. *The Colonel's Lady on the Western Frontier*. Lincoln, Nebr.: University of Nebraska Press, 1989.

Luchetti, Cathy, in collaboration with Carol Olwell. *Women of the West*. St. George, Utah: Antelope Island Press, 1982.

McCutcheon, Marc. *Everyday Life in the 1800s*. Cincinnati: Writer's Digest Books, 1993.

Memorial and Biographical History of Northern California. Chicago: The Lewis Publishing Company, 1891.

Nunn, W. C., *Somervell: Story of a Texas County*. Fort Worth: Texas Christian University, 1975.

Ross, Nancy Wilson. *Westward the Women*. San Francisco: North Point Press, 1986.

Schissel, Lillian. *Women's Diaries of the Westward Journey*. New York: Schocken Books, 1982.

Schissel, Lillian, Byrd Gibbens, and Elizabeth Hampsten. *Far From Home: Families of the Westward Journey*. New York: Schocken Books, 1989.

Sonnichsen, C. L. *I'll Die Before I Run*. New York: Harper and Brothers Publishers, 1951.

Sprague, Stuart Seely. *Eastern Kentucky: A Pictorial History*. Norfolk, Va.: The Donning Company Publishers, 1986.

Stewart, Elenore Pruitt. *Letters of a Woman Homesteader*. Boston: Houghton Mifflin Company. 1982.

Swango, William and Maxine May Swango. *Phelps Family*. South Charleston, W. Va.: Jalamap Printers, Inc., 1986.

Young, William Henry. *Buy a Broom Besom: The Story of a Broom*. Germantown, Ohio: 1988.

Court Records

Atchison, Charlotte Pearce. "Estate Settlement of –" 23 August 1890. Bath County Courthouse, Owingsville, Ky.

Atchison, Charlotte Pearce, "Will of –" 11 August 1890. Signed, W. W. Perry, Clerk of Bath County, Owingsville, Ky.

Atchison, Jesse. "Will of –" Will Book F., Bath County Owingsville, Ky.

Bolling, Jefferson. "Indictment of –" Indictment No. 195, 3 October 1882. Rowan County Courthouse, Morehead, Ky.

Hawes, Arthur. Family Packets, Fleming County Courthouse, Flemingsburg, Ky.

Nickell, Newton K. and Pearl Goodnow, "Divorce of –" Book G., Yolo County Courthouse, Woodland, Calif.

Manuscript

Barker, W. FD. Personal Memoirs. Glen Rose, Texas Historical Society Library.

Magazines

Calvert, Stephen N. "Bath County's Famous Shower of Flesh." *The Kentucky Explorer*. Vol. 9, No. 3. Jackson, Ky.: Charles Hayes Jr., July-August 1994.

Roberts, McCreary. "When A Man Rose From the Dead." *The Kentucky Explorer*. Vol. II, No. 2. Jackson, Ky.: Charles Hayes Jr., June 1996.

Sprague, Stuart Seely, "The Rowan County Trouble: Anatomy of a Mountain Feud." *Mountain Review*. Vol. II, No. 4, July 1976.

Schaefer, F. W. "A Short Glimpse of the Deadly Rowan County War." *The Kentucky Explorer*. Jackson, Ky.: Charles Hayes Jr., November 1995.

Wilson, Gordon, Dr. "Pictures and Brooms." *The Kentucky Explorer*. Vol. 10, No. 4. Jackson, Ky.: Charles Hayes Jr., September 1995.

Newspapers

Ashland Independent. Ashland, Ky.: 5 July 1882.

Fleming True Blue Democrat. Flemingsburg, Ky.: 22 September 1887.

Glen Rose Citizen. Glen Rose, Texas: 19 February 1885.

Glen Rose Citizen. Glen Rose, Texas: June 1885.

Glen Rose Citizen. Glen Rose, Texas: 2 July 1885.

Glen Rose Citizen. Glen Rose, Texas: 2 May 1886.

Johnson County Review. Cleburne, Texas: 9 August 1894.

Rowan County News. "Centennial Edition." Morehead, Ky.: 10 May 1956.

Primary Interviews

Blanton, Louisa Hawkins Page—Daughter of Andrew Jackson Hawkins and Permelia Nickell. Conversations on numerous occasions. Aunt Lou related the Hawkins' journey in 1880 from Kentucky to Texas as well as many other "I remember" incidents. She also clarified questions the letters brought about.

Givens, Golda Shults—Daughter of George and Cora Hawkins Shults.

Hallmark, Survella Irene Shults—Daughter of Jim and Anna Kate Hawkins Shults.

Mills, Billie Hallmark—Daughter of Hamilton and Survella Shults Hallmark.

Conversations and Correspondence

Ayer, A. L., Jr.—Grandson of John Robert and Maggie Scarbro Hawkins, and son of Al and Opal Hawkins Ayer.

Brumley, Lois—Great-granddaughter of Henry and Lizzie Hawkins Romine and granddaughter of Drewy Romine White.

Hawkins, Fern Meriwether—Granddaughter of John Robert and Maggie Scarbro Hawkins.

Hawkins, Walter Leland—Grandson of Daniel Boone and Millicent Gilkison Hawkins, and son of Walter Scott and Lillie Goodspeed Hawkins.

Nickell, Charlton—Grandson of James Joshua and Mary Ann Taylor Nickell.

Shults, Troy—Grandson of George and Cora Hawkins Shults and son of Silas and Tinnie Thorpe Shults.

Linda Gayle White Cheek—Granddaughter of Lizzie Frances Hawkins Romine and daughter of Fielden and Drewy Romine White.

www.ingramcontent.com/pod-product-compliance
Lightning Source LLC
Chambersburg PA
CBHW052030090426
42739CB00010B/1847